SOCIAL PSYCHOLOGY AND MANAGEMENT

SOCIAL PSYCHOLOGY AND MANAGEMENT

Issues for a changing society

Chris Brotherton

Open University Press
Buckingham · Philadelphia

Open University Press
Celtic Court
22 Ballmoor
Buckingham
MK18 1XW

email: enquiries@openup.co.uk
world wide web:http://www.openup.co.uk

and
325 Chestnut Street
Philadelphia, PA19106, USA

First Published 1999

ISBN   0 335 19800 7 (hb)   0 335 19799 X (pb)

A catalogue record of this book is available from the British Library

Library of Congress Cataloging-in-Publication Data
Brotherton, Christopher J.
   Social psychology and management: issues for a changing society /
Chris Brotherton
      p.   cm.
   Includes bibliographical references and index.
   ISBN 0-335-19800-7 (hb). — ISBN 0-335-19799-X (pb)
   1. Social psychology.   2. Management.   I. Title.
HM251.B667   1999
   302—dc21   98-22226
                                                          CIP

Typeset by Type Study, Scarborough
Printed in Great Britain by Biddles Ltd, Guildford and King's Lynn

To my family and to my friends

Contents

Preface

This book is about social change. It is also about management and about social psychology. Social change provides the topics for the agenda, motivation, groups and teams, gender and diversity, groups and technology, networks and careers. The attempt is to set a dialectic debate between social psychology on the one hand and management on the other. At first sight this is an unlikely pairing: the one based on experimental procedures and scholarship; the other based on decision and action. I want, unapologetically, to point out that much of what management actually does, or at least others say that it does, has a basis in psychology in general and social psychology in particular. This is generally unrecognized by both social psychology and management. Management is taking action that is fundamentally social psychological in its nature. Social psychology is often concerned with the issues of management. As with all dialectic debates, the aim is to achieve a little change in the perspectives of both elements. The agenda for social change is developing at a pace that could not have been conceived of even ten years ago. The implications of social change are generally more profound than ever they have been. Psychology needs to recognize the importance of social change and to take on board its implications. Managers need to feel that they are not the passive victims of change and to realize that they need science to help in the realization of the objectives of change.

The premise of the book is that the two disciplines are working together very much more than seems to be generally recognized by either of them. There has been a long history of social psychology providing the basis for organizational theory. In 1947, Renis Likert launched a programme of research at the University of Michigan. The programme was concerned with issues of morale and motivation, productivity, power and control, leadership and change processes in large-scale organizations. The research culminated in the publication of *New Patterns of Management* (Likert 1961). Daniel Katz and Robert Kahn followed this research tradition and in 1966 published *The Social Psychology of Organizations*. They took up many of Likert's points and developed a general theoretical position within the framework of open-systems theory. In Britain, J.A.C Brown's (1954) *The Social Psychology of Industry* and Michael Argyle's (1972) *The Social Psychology of Work* did much to popularize psychological research in its application to issues of concern to managers. The present book takes a broader view than its predecessors in both its approach to social psychology and its view of work. I have attempted to review work and organizations in the networked society that is emerging in the last decade of the twentieth century. This form of organization is producing changes in society at a level of intensification that has never before been experienced. Analysis of the networked society has been undertaken by Manuel Castells. Two of the three volumes of Castells's work appeared as the final chapter of this book was being written. Its findings are so immense in their implications that I found it necessary to revisit some of my points before releasing my manuscript. Castells's thesis has not been fully exploited in this book but it has had a profound influence on a direction that had already been embarked upon when I first proposed the book. In social psychology too, I have taken a broader view than that adopted by predecessors. I have self-consciously taken findings from the breadth of social psychology rather than from the one area of work to which it is usually confined in discussions on the topics raised here. Social psychology has much more to offer than is immediately apparent when we consider what is often called organizational psychology. This is because the framework of the broader discipline is being driven towards social movements and social processes that are society-wide – just as now the organizational world is being moved from bounded bureaucratic structures to networked arrangements that are producing large-scale social changes for both work and society.

The scientific perspective

In our early days at school we will all have taken part in an experiment in which a light source, a shutter and a prism were used to demonstrate the visual spectrum. The light source appeared to consist of white light, yet when passed through the shutter and on to the prism, what emerged was a rainbow of light in which suddenly we could see each of the colours from violet across to red. The shutter straightened the light beams and held them in parallel. We moved the prism across an angle so that the refracted light split the waves of different frequencies, which we saw as colours. Imagine our disbelief in having come to terms with this wonderful way of capturing a natural phenomena and then being told by our teacher that the visual spectrum was just one fraction of all of the energy waves in the physical universe, and that much existed, and could be demonstrated, but could not be seen.

Here I want to argue that work is rather like the prism if we take social change as being the light waves. We can see work in very different ways according to where we stand to look at it. What appears to be a single white light can also appear to be a range of different colours, according to the angle at which the separate beams are refracted by the prism. Work takes place in organizations yet can be seen and be affected by so many things that we are often not aware of them. Social change is a little like the energy waves in our school experiment – some can be seen, much cannot without the special help that apparatus can give us. Science is a matter of the attitude we take to our subject matter. In science we seek an objective detachment, a suspension of belief, an honesty, a critical scrutiny. We have, in psychological science in particular, to treat familiar phenomena as if they were unfamiliar. Only in that way can we test hypotheses, make intellectual progress and advance socially.

Personal reflections

In social psychology, scientific methodology provides us with the necessary apparatus to view work, management and organizations. All these processes are involved in change. I remember my father discussing with me an experience that passed for careers guidance in the 1950s, in which a mysterious person had turned up in the classroom and had shown us two films and said that we were to think about them because he would be coming back to talk to us about what we would do when we left school. One of the films was about coal mining and the other was about farming. We lived in Birmingham, which had no coal mines let alone any farms. My father agreed with me that neither was a real possibility, but that I would be all right if I learned a trade and he would do what he could to get me in to printing.

Printing, he said, was always going to be needed and had not changed for a very long time, so what I would learn would do me all of my life. I read a couple of books that told me that, indeed, printing had come to us from the Chinese, who had invented it 2,000 years ago, and that Caxton had made some small improvements when he brought it to England about 300 years ago. Printing looked like a safe bet. With a bit of help from Dad, I skilfully avoided both mine and farm and learned a trade 'for life'. Good paternal advice was the shutter straightening the light beams here, but the prismatic rainbow did not last long. Within six years, just as an apprenticeship that should have taught me all that I ever needed to know was coming to an end, the shadow of a technological revolution in the shape of computer-based typesetting loomed up as if from nowhere. The job that looked as though it could have been for life was threatened unless a whole new set of skills was learned. Printing had provided me with lots of time to read and to debate with friends and colleagues, and quite by chance I had picked up a considerable amount of social science reading. I escaped, with concerned encouragement from friends, to Ruskin College and thence eventually into higher education as a career. The light beams were kindly, though not always clear. Now the technological revolution is impacting on learning and instructional delivery. The World Wide Web and the file-served network provide a resource that outstrips my personal library and develops at a pace beyond that at which any individual can possibly cope.

Understanding change

The directionality of social change has always been difficult to establish, whether at an individual, an organizational or a societal level. Toffler's futurological text (Toffler 1970) tells us that we see social change as culture shock and that most of us respond with a feeling of being overwhelmed by the rapidity of accelerating change. He writes of the impact on our lives of the outputs of work: technological change in the goods and services that we purchase, rather than work itself. The futures he describes have been created by the work of people.

Historians and philosophers have written of the golden ages that tend to create the impression that the current state of advance marks the epitome of cultural and technological attainment. When the historical contexts of golden age claims are scrutinized, as they were by Pollard (1971), it is possible to demonstrate that the age is about to pass rather than to advance further. Some authors become overwhelmed by their social determinism and see current changes as a state of terminal ontological decline (Gortz 1980, 1985, 1988). Here the future without work is portrayed as a political nightmare slowly being played out before our eyes yet evoking little conscious awareness.

Even when social change is modelled with a modest attempt at mathematical precision (Kondriev 1925), it is difficult to know where the current reality resides in relation to it. Kondriev writes of social change moving in economic cycles fluctuating over long periods of time, but at any one point we probably cannot know whether the cycle is likely to swing up or down. Here the impact on work, mediated by the effects of economic investment patterns, is critical. Investment has maximum impact on employment at the bottom of a cycle, but there uncertainty is at its greatest. At the top of the cycle, markets are flooded with goods and profits for investments are narrowed by competition.

Charles Handy sees that the future has to be worked for now (Handy 1984), but his agenda is set at a level at which most folk who do not have the opportunity to enter high political office will find it difficult to place their weight on the levers of change, while those folk who do enter high political office seem not only to have pulled those levers but to have emptied every possible tank in the process. In this, managers have a special place because it is they who are the most influential conscious actors in the processes of change. Change is not due to blind and unthinking forces. It can be seen; it can be predicted; it can be acted with and upon.

We need theories to guide our approach to change, whether we are workers, managers, politicians or citizens asked to note with concern the impact of change in a world that seems not to be able to transform concern into responsibility. Theories are of different kinds and they have different utilities. With theories we are able to develop decision strategies that focus on issues that concern us most. Theories are a little like the shutter in our experiment with light. Without theories we are left simply with facts. The trouble with facts on their own is that there are a lot of them. They are rather like the white light that we see when the energy beams within the visual spectrum are not separated according to their different wavelengths. In other words, they are virtually indistinguishable one from another. Theories are usually developed around particular values. They enable us not just to look at some things rather than others – the things, we hope, that it is most useful to see – but also to make some judgements, based on our values, about what can be done. Positioning ourselves so as to understand social change in general, and its impact on work in particular, is what this book is about. The book chooses social psychology to advance the argument for science and for understanding. It could have taken other psychological perspectives and there may be other books to be written that do just this, but social psychology comes closest to meeting the challenges set by an agenda for change. The book also attempts to address management, by offering a more scientific and reflective mode than often seems to be on offer. Management would be better, in my view, if it were more scientific and more reflective; better able to consider the processes of change and its part in them; better able to predict the effects of particular actions or, indeed, the effects of not acting. The arena in which management operates is important. It is perhaps the most important of all social contexts. Social psychology will be enhanced by considering contexts not as abstract entities that provide political credibility in rather larger doses than scientific respectability, but as specifiable entities amenable to enquiry.

Work as a printer has changed out of all recognition in the years in which I have considered it from the relative security of a job in higher education. The changes have been organizational, managerial and social psychological. The small printers for which I worked were swept away as the new technologies ate away the opportunities for profit from customized work. The organization of the work was taken away from its craft base inherited from Caxton's days in the Guilds and put in the hands of corporations. The work groups of compositors, who controlled the basic production of typesetting almost in its totality, were phased out as computing and photographic work replaced those hard won skills of manipulating metal type. All of this happened against a chorus of voices that said 'it will never happen' and 'there will always be jobs in printing'. As I write, some of the energy waves that affected the light in printing are now being straightened to refract in the prism of higher education. Even the future of books as we have come to know them is under debate as electronic publications offer possibilities that paperbound productions cannot. Social, economic and technological change all race on apace and impact on our work and the way it is organized. Few would disagree with this very general sketch, but how is it to be understood and interpreted? More books at a cheaper price? Greater numbers benefiting from higher education at a lower standard? Efficiency? Effectiveness? Quality? Quantity? Rapid response? Market led? Teamwork? Performance? Responsibility? Accountability? We have to see all of this as progress, because, as Pollard (1971) tells us, the alternative is despair.

The buzzwords of social change are refracted through our work without much light being shed on meaning, process or cost. Some processes seem to be well managed, but most do not. Perhaps managers are not accustomed to moving light through a prism to obtain colour, so that social change appears always to be a question of white compared with black. It is worse still, perhaps, if the colour remains grey and the structure of light remains fuzzy. In the course of coping with the changes that have affected me, I have learned something of science. Science, rather than printing, now pays my rent. I want to develop a way of looking at some of the issues of change from a scientific perspective and to set these against issues of management. I am not interested in pursuing science for its own sake in a world that seems to value information but not knowledge. Nor am I interested in setting application against fundamental understanding in a world that cannot appreciate true cost. Science has always had to exist in the market place, but it is uncomfortable with its status as a commodity, which can only be exchanged with pain and difficulty. Rather, I wish to explore a dialectic between science and application – between social psychology and management – with a view to developing a synthesis in the understanding of change. Understanding is the only tool available to us in the toil involved in reducing our uncertainty.

To what extent can social psychology expand our understanding and offer insights into processes at work? How can these insights be understood by managers? Can the science of social psychology become more accessible to managers at the level of understanding social processes? Can it affect the way in which we, and the processes of change, are managed? Can change be managed with less pain and distress by utilizing scientific techniques such as the testing of hypotheses and the limits of prediction, as well as some of the accumulated knowledge derived from several generations of lifetimes' work in these areas? Can social psychologists come to know more of the world they seek to understand by knowing more of the tasks and the dilemmas facing managers? Work, and its performance, is usually conducted at an individual level. Even in creative work we suffer the pain of Goya's grotesque fates rather than the joyous reflections of the Muses who were the daughters of Zeus and Mnemosyne. We need our environment to be supportive and clear. Yet, particularly at times of change, when uncertainty provides the paramount pressure, clarity of purpose is elusive. Management in organizations is usually accomplished through groups. Groups are of central interest in social psychology, although they have gone in and out of favour as a central focus of research. Teams and leadership have emanated as topics of interest from our social psychological understanding as well as our management of groups. Groups take expression in particular forms, such as gender and race. The management of diversity now forms a positive expression of the contribution of difference. Conflict arises in part from the differences in fundamental interest of groups in organizations. How this is managed has become a central issue in social and organizational change. Technology has usually been the means by which groups are dispersed within an organization and is often the focus that brings their interests together or separates them in conflict. The printing industry has provided some apocryphal examples of both aspects of these processes. Economic change is accelerating to the point where work itself appears to some writers to be under threat of total extinction. Careers both as a way of life and as a scientific concept come under increasing scrutiny as organizations delayer, down-size, right-size or simply go out of existence. The progression of careers has traditionally depended on hierarchical advancement. Organizations are increasingly less hierarchical in their arrangements and the emphasis in the careers literature is now on personal, rather than organizational, responsibility. Some organizations are adopting the characteristics of virtuality, with offices disappearing as both physical and social realities. Meanwhile, social psychology's agenda now incorporates the concepts of discourse and the everyday in its attempts at moving out of the crisis of relevance. In considering this agenda we will examine many theories that are familiar. The book seeks to examine findings in the light of the new circumstances that are becoming clear. We need to ask new questions. How is the discipline to cope in a millennium that will throw into even sharper relief everything that cannot be immediately justified? To what extent do we need to reconceptualize our own discipline? How will the light that we generate be refracted through prisms fashioned in the new materials of a fresh era?

Acknowledgements

I knew that I had to write a book on social psychology and management when, at another university, I inherited a lecture series at very short notice and scanned the reading list that had been given to the students. Despite the class being devoted to social psychology and to organization, my predecessor took organizational behaviour texts as his framework. He referenced little that I recognized scientifically and less that I wished to espouse. I thank my former colleague for the opportunity of enabling me, by his absence, to take over his class – which I then would not return. I thank him, too, that in his absence I obtained the stimulation of being faced with the challenge of preparing my own reading list, lecture series and ultimately my own position in respect to these issues.

In dedicating this book to my family and to my friends I acknowledge them all. They are my way-markers on routes of social change. Adrian and Claire Brotherton have provided a constant source of quiet motivation to a father who has been distracted for just the past 18 months, although they might be forgiven for thinking it longer. Sheila Brotherton too has contributed in her own way. Sylvia Brotherton has provided motherly enquiries that have always reminded this author that there is life outside the study and much else that should be done.

I have gained much from the experience of discussing the ideas that appear in this book with my students, first at the University of Nottingham, then at Derry's Magee College in the University of Ulster and now at Heriot-Watt University in Edinburgh. It has been a privilege to have shared with so many enquiring minds my passion for psychology and my enthusiasm for the best ideas and practices in management. The communities of scholars in these universities have all been particularly supportive. Many have been encouraging. Special thanks have to go to Professor Celia Davies, who, as a distinguished sociologist, has always asked the most pertinent questions and kept me focused. Dr Aine Downey has willed me on with many a Gaelic grace. James Doherty, Dr David James, Dr Marie McHugh and Dr Rob Miller have provided many warm discussions, albeit in an often cold intellectual climate. Dr Philip Leather has provided many intellectual challenges in seasons that sometimes seem more clement.

Professor John Arnold, of Loughborough University, Dr Jean Hartley of Birkbeck College and now of Warwick University and Dr Cathy Cassells of Sheffield University made generous comments when I was planning this book, and my initial ideas were much influenced by them. The staff and students at Manchester Business School have kept me well informed on many of the debates in the literatures in which we share an interest. I am grateful to the Psychology Society at Magee and to the Department of Psychology at Goldsmith's College, University of London, for inviting me to talk to them at what, for me, were important times in the development of ideas.

A great many friends and colleagues in the British Psychological Society have expressed good wishes and provided opportunities for discussion. In particular, those with whom I have served on the Committee of the Division of Occupational Psychology, on the Professional Affairs Board and on the Council of the Society have done everything that committee friends might have been expected to and much more. They, particularly those with whom I have grown up in psychology, deserve special thanks for their tolerance and for demonstrating that cognition is really socially distributed and that management is a skill that is hard won.

The staff at the Open University Press have been patient and helpful throughout the process of producing a manuscript, particularly in the months following a move in employment that proved more disruptive to reflective processes than even a seasoned traveller across the Irish Sea anticipated. In particular, Justin Vaughan and Gaynor Clements have maintained the right balance between diplomacy, sensitivity and motivation to enable a moment to be reached that sometimes seemed like slipping.

June Lodder has done more than a secretary should be expected to do. She has protected my time. She has soothed my nerves when disks and source materials have been put in the wrong place by an author who is trying to manage at the same time as be a social psychologist. Most of all, June has rescued my word processing from the potential disasters that threaten me when I demonstrate that I learned the technologies of the keyboard in an era when the worry was that of keeping my tie out of the mechanisms.

It is not sufficient simply to thank Professor Geoffrey Stephenson. He has guided me through much of my life in social psychology, first of all, while we were together at Nottingham. Later, while he was at Kent and I was elsewhere, he proved a continuing source of good ideas. He has devoted a considerable amount of time to reading through the first draft of this book. He provided much needed support when it came to implementing the very necessary changes in the manuscript. Thanks also go to Dr Jenny Williams for her contribution. Jenny and Geoffrey have been unstinting in their generosity in this and in much else besides.

Despite the fact that authorship is a dreadfully lonely business, producing a book is a team effort. There must be many who deserve acknowledgement but who have been omitted on this occasion. They are valued nevertheless. It is the way of the world that many who might be acknowledged are protected, in the end, from public scrutiny. This is not the fate of the author who, after all this help, guidance and assistance, has to acknowledge the frailty of the human state and acknowledge the responsibility for all that follows.

Introduction

Chapter 2 of this book reviews the broad issues of social change and work. It begins by examining the central tenets of human resource management and asking whether there are indeed general principles of management. Human resource management has developed from its beginnings in personnel management to occupy a strategic role within organizations and as a more unified professional activity concerned with the management of people at work. The research base of human resource management as an academic discipline is methodologically restricted to surveys and case studies in the main. However, human resource management is seen by Karen Legge as lending itself to a critique based on identifying the rhetoric and the realities of the area. The chapter suggests that there is potential for a strong contribution to human resource management from social psychology, in the form of discourse analysis. Discourse analysis would examine the constructive and flexible ways in which language is used and evaluative expressions are used. Public pronouncements by human resource specialists are changing the ways in which the management of people is being regarded, and generally raising awareness of how people in work are regarded by managers.

Chapter 2 reviews some of the reasons for psychology's present status in management theories, and concludes that psychology deserves much more credit than has been afforded the discipline directly. Psychology has had, and continues to have, a much stronger role than is recognized in critiques of management theory. Chapter 2 looks at the interplay between theory and practice in management and at management's development as a profession. Social and technical change emerges as demanding greater consideration from a scientific position, within the more general context of management as activity, if only because that puts management in the driving seat of the prime processes of social and technical change. Management in its turn needs to be informed by a relevant science so as to understand and to predict.

Chapter 2 concludes with a manifesto for change in which the work of Manuel Castells's analysis of the networked society is the inspiration. The networked society is generating change at a pace that seems not to have been experienced in any former period of history. These changes make it urgent that the common territory between social psychology and management is explored and developed. The Castells analysis leads us to examine afresh the issues of motivation of individuals at work, diversity, teams, careers, our forms of communication interpersonally and technologically. The book presents chapters on each of these topics. It explores what some readers will find to be standard contributions in the literatures of social psychology at work, as well as their counterparts in aspects of related management texts. The presentations seek out common ground by attempting to identify the salient individual, interpersonal, group processes in organizational contexts old and new.

Motivation is traditionally seen in psychology and in management as being an inherently individual process. Chapter 3 argues that motivation needs to be seen in more social terms, partly because many of its core elements operate by our making comparisons with others and partly because the context of work is becoming more social. Work is becoming more distributed in economic, geographic and social senses. The Castells analysis demands that social psychology re-examines traditional approaches to motivation and examines some criteria by which future studies can become more closely focused on the needs of workers and managers in the networked society.

Chapter 4 examines groups, leadership and teams. Here there is a long and relatively fruitful history of social psychology and management working closely together, although the coexistence is not readily observed in many of the texts coming from many non-psychologist origins. Teams are likely to be the dominant form of work organization in the networked society.

Chapter 5 contrasts the problems presented by conformity within bureaucratic organizations with the benefits of diversity celebrated in gender, race and age. In the knowledge-based industries that will dominate the networked society, diversity is seen to have positive benefits in terms of the quality of decision-making and ultimately the quality of the product itself. Castells draws attention to the fact that cultural diversity is engaged in a struggle at the same time as the networked society is increasing its pace of change. This creates a fierce cauldron in which social psychology and management have to work increasingly together.

Castells draws attention to the way in which the networked society can exclude groups from participation in work as well as provide opportunities for inclusion. Gender and ethnicity become important features for consideration here. Diversity is raised to prominence in the agenda because without enhanced saliency it may polarize and struggle. Diversity is often expressed through community, which itself becomes an important focus for inclusion in the networked society. So, new forms have to be considered by management and by social psychologists.

In Chapter 6, the review demonstrates how technology both enables and transforms our interpersonal and group levels of relationship and communication. Technology is often seen by managers as being the solution to problems. The chapter sets out an argument for taking adequate account of social organization in equal part to technology in the decision equations. The chapter illustrates that social psychology has important findings that management texts as well as managers themselves are not translating into action. Joseph McGrath has completed the most detailed experimental social psychological research on technologically based forms of communication. His research demonstrates how, in time, information and process terms, electronically mediated communication distorts what he regards to be the prime features of unmediated social interaction. Managers need to know that electronic communication has this distorting effect so that they make allowances and provide opportunities for compensation in the arrangements that they make in organizations. This process raises important issues for the way in which we identify with our work when it is mediated by technology.

The final chapter considers the processes by which careers in the network society become focused on the development of an individual's portfolio of skills. Unless managers take on board the implications of this change, the social contract between employers and employed becomes one which is based solely on short-term gain and on payment. Psychology has long since demonstrated that these form the weakest bonds between the worker and the work. The alternative is that career development becomes a shared responsibility in which workers select those arenas in which their skills and chances can be enhanced and managers provide those opportunities.

The opportunities exist if managers can position their organizational operations so as to compete effectively in the global networked society with all of the challenges that it presents. Participative styles that involve the maximum number of people may be the only way to ensure survival. People themselves, as well as the institutions that support them, also have to be working on focused knowledge and products that can compete in the rapidly changing context within which technologically networked organizations operate.

These are new agenda issues for social psychology and for management. Science and precision find their place on the agenda when professional concern about processes and outcomes plays its full part. On the one hand, Castells's analysis indicates that the race goes to the swiftest, and perhaps to the most fortunate. On the other hand, simply to enter the race demands a high level of what, in psychology, Albert Bandura calls self-efficacy. By self-efficacy Bandura means believing in one's own ability. Self-efficacy is vitally important in career development terms, particularly in science and engineering. Gender is seen by Bandura as being an important moderator of self-efficacy. Maintaining self-efficacy in a rapidly changing global society is perhaps the key to the identity issues that Castells draws attention to. The chapter on careers and the networked society seeks to explore some of these connections.

Social psychology and management in a changing society

In this book, motivation, teamwork and leadership, gender and diversity, groups and technology, and the networked organization are the themes within which management and social psychology will be explored against the background of change. These are all issues raised by Castells's analysis of the information society. Each topic is contested in its way – within both the management and the human resource literature. This chapter will set the scene for later exploration in the book of the messages generated by Castells. Here, I want to set management and psychology in dialogue. The themes of the book probably fall more squarely into the realm of management concerned with what has become known as human resources than any other single realm of management. However, depending on our definition of management, the themes have much broader implications. Human resource management (HRM) was not an issue in the Barings Bank collapse or the *Challenger* disaster, which we shall examine in later chapters. Yet both cases had immense consequences for the people involved, and require social psychological analyses if the implications are to be fully appreciated. However, it is appropriate to start with a discussion of the development of HRM and the lessons to be learned from an appreciation of social psychology if the purported changes are, in reality, apparent in its changing emphasis.

Human resource management

Kast and Rosenweig's textbook sees management as involving 'the co-ordination of human and material resources towards objective accomplishment

1 towards objectives
2 through people
3 via techniques
4 in an organization' (Kast and Rosenweig 1985: 12).

Each management activity involves people – usually working in collectivities such as groups. Let us examine the HRM perspective first of all.

The intensive pace of social and economic change has been the fulcrum in moving personnel functions towards the potentially more strategic position occupied by HRM. The seminal work in HRM tells us that:

> in the last several years American business has begun to place more emphasis on the management of human resources. Buffeted by recession, deregulation in some industries, and international competition in others, business executives have been looking for ways to improve productivity and quality. They began to realize that these goals could not be achieved without a dramatic change in the relationship between management and workers and between union and management. Simultaneously, improvements in the development of managers would be needed. When they looked to Japan, our chief competitor, they saw a different yet successful model. Within the context of their own society and culture, the Japanese had developed a collaborative relationship between management and labour and between unions and management. Improved productivity and quality were the results.
>
> It became quite clear to many large American enterprises such as General Motors, Cummins Engine, Ford Motor, Bethelem Steel, Honeywell Corporation, People Express, and Goodyear Tyre and Rubber, to name a few, that they must manage their human resources quite differently if they are to compete successfully. American corporations have learned to manage their financial and other resources effectively. Enormous time, care and effort goes into ensuring that money is employed most effectively; the most current ideas and methods are applied to obtain the greatest return on invested capital; strategic alternatives are carefully developed and weighed using strategic planning models and processes. Yet implementation of any of these plans requires committed, concerned, and competent employees.
>
> The evidence seems to indicate, however, that in many corporations, human resources are under-utilised and underemployed. Adversarial union–management relations, low employee motivation and trust of management, excessive layers of management, restrictive work practices, and employee resistance to changes required by competitive forces are examples of the problems. Just as instructive in assessing the extent to which human resources are under-utilised are the human commitment, productivity, and quality, that are obtained not only by Japanese companies but by American companies that have invested in developing more

effective human resource management policies and practices. When such significant improvements in productivity, quality, and union–management relations are demonstrated with a relatively low financial investment, the potential for effective human resource management becomes quite clear. Given the relative sophistication in the management of financial and other resources, human resources may offer the best opportunity for management to improve competitiveness.

(Beer *et al.* 1984: vii–viii)

Beer and his colleagues present a programme which explores a wide range of organizational factors. In drawing specific attention to the consideration of whether an HRM policy enhances the performance of the organization, the well-being of employees or the well-being of society, Beer and his colleagues set four particular questions. First, they ask to what extent HRM policies enhance the commitment of people to work and their organization. Second, they ask to what extent HRM policies attract, keep and/or develop people with skills and knowledge available at the right time. Third, they ask what is the cost-effectiveness of a given policy in terms of wages, benefits, turnover, absenteeism, strikes and so on. Fourth, they ask what levels of congruence HRM policies and practices generate or sustain between management and employees and their families, and within the individual. In their discussion of how the answers to these questions are to be assessed, the indications are that psychologists are well placed to develop measures. The discussion makes it clear that the measurement and assessment issues are not easy because the issues themselves do not present themselves as discrete variables but are embedded within the processes of managing and organizing. The Beer *et al.* text marks a major shift in the literature on the management of people, away from a personnel approach, based on a mix of welfare at work activities as well as on recruitment and sometimes on training, towards a more thoroughgoing approach based on the implementation of broad policies at a strategic level. The shift was not simply one of emphasis, it moved the level of analysis from an individual level and towards the organization. It provided an opportunity for a paradigm shift within the psychology of work as well as for more work by psychologists. Personnel management could no longer be equated, as Drucker had been able to do, with 'a collection of incidental techniques without much internal cohesion . . . a hodge podge' (Drucker 1961: 243).

In Britain, David Guest has been vigorous in the encouragement of psychologists into human resource areas. He saw the emergence of HRM as an opportunity for psychology to become involved in important issues in work organizations. He saw the main thrust of development in the area as requiring that policies had a focus at the strategic level; otherwise, what he saw to be the jaded view of personnel would not be overcome by the new movement (Guest 1987). He noted, in later papers, that the emergence of the

HRM perspective had provided opportunities for the development of a great many new psychologically based techniques as a specific organization became the focus for study (Guest 1991). It is interesting to note that the enthusiasm for the shift in paradigm within the personnel community itself was initially more tentative and orthodox. For example, Torrington and Hall (1987: 14) contrast personnel management with the HRM approach as follows. 'There has been some tendency for the term "human resources" to be adopted as an alternative to "personnel" simply for a change, or to move away from an image that has been associated with previous eras. It has also been used to avoid the word "manpower", seen as sexist in phrases like "manpower planning" and "manpower administration". There is a more substantive difference that needs to be made clear.' The distinction Torrington and Hall make is between personnel management, seen as directed mainly at the organization's employees – finding and training them, arranging for them to be paid, explaining management's expectations to them and seeking to modify management actions that could produce unwelcome employee response – and HRM, which is directed mainly at management needs for human resources (not necessarily employees) to be provided and deployed. There is greater emphasis on planning, monitoring and control, rather than on problem-solving and mediation.

Significantly, Torrington and Hall (1987: 14) write of HRM that 'it is totally identified with management interests, being a general management activity, and is relatively distant from the workforce as a whole'. In this first edition, *Personnel Management* carries a total of four pages under the index heading of human resource management. By 1995, the third edition of their textbook had become entitled *Personnel Management – HRM in Action*. 'The title remains as *Personnel Management*, first to maintain the continuity and secondly because it describes the content. The specialist people in the field still retain the badges of "Personnel Director", "Personnel Manager" and so forth and the "Personnel Standards Lead Body" appear to affirm that "Personnel" is the appropriate label for those specializing in aspects of human resource management. The subtitle *HRM in Action* acknowledges the main current influence on personnel practice' (Torrington and Hall 1995: xv).

In the British literature, the debate over the identity crisis created for personnel management by the HRM approach began at least as early as 1989, with the publication of Storey's edited book, *New Perspectives on Human Resource Management*. In that book, Karen Legge considered the question and the possible implications of whether the shift had been one of substance or one of emphasis. In doing so she explored the potential contradictions and paradoxes that might be embedded in both approaches. Legge notes that while most HRM models have taken on board the personnel management ethos that employees have a right to dignity and are to be valued assets with an emphasis on commitment, adaptability and employees as a source of competitive advantage, the image might as well be presented as 'resourceful' humans. She agrees with others who are more critical of the HRM approach, who point out that the term 'human resource' might be understood in the completely different sense of being a factor of production, along with the land and capital, and an 'expense of doing business' rather than 'the only resource capable of turning inanimate factors of production into wealth'. This perception of 'resource', says Legge, appears to underlie Torrington and Hall's model of HRM, with its emphasis on appropriate factors of production ('numbers' and 'skills') at the 'right' (implicitly the 'lowest possible') price. In their model, says Legge, the human resource appears passive – 'to be provided and deployed' – rather than as the source of creative energy in any direction the organization dictates and fosters. This leads Legge to a distinction between 'hard' and 'soft' models of HRM. The former represents the management aspect, and emphasizes the quantitative, calculative and business strategic aspects of managing the headcount in as rational a way as for any other economic factor; the latter represents the human resource aspect. Underlying the whole debate is the issue of whether the HRM approach leads to a unitarist view of the management process, in which only the management will prevails, or whether there is scope for a plurality of views. Legge also points out that HRM does not represent one single unvarying approach but a wide range of different approaches to philosophy and technique. This means that it is difficult to compare like with like when seeking to analyse conceptually or empirically the difference between the approaches. In 1995, Karen Legge produced a text entitled *Human Resource Management – Rhetorics and Realities*. The book is a penetrating analysis of the contradictions that run through organizations, no matter which philosophy they espouse towards those who work within them. She agrees with those who see both continuity and change in all periods of history. Legge sees continuity in the aspects of the approach of personnel management, no matter whether in the 'hard' or in the 'soft' models, that leads it to mediate the harsher effects of capitalist society. She also sees continuity in the opportunistic and pragmatic employee relations style adopted in some companies, particularly in firms that are non-unionized. Legge notes the general emphasis on individualism in the HRM approach despite the fact that there is an underlying need to draw on collective resources in many companies and with many techniques. HRM, for Legge, is both a rhetoric and a series of initiatives which is very much part of the enterprise culture.

In the late 1980s, before the descent into recession, it appeared part of the 'feel good' scenario that embraced rampant consumerism and the so-called 'Thatcher economic miracle'. In the cold light of the 1990s, HRM and the enterprise culture both appeared tarnished – not least in the eyes of those managers simultaneously suffering the twin shocks of the 1990s, negative equity in property combining with job insecurity consequent on the delayering and downsizing. 'Soft' model HRM

appears a shallow rooted plant, save in the most exceptional fertile soil
. . . (viewed against the background of then current political developments) the widespread implementation of the 'soft' . . . model of HRM
appears as a mirage, retreating into a receding horizon.

(Legge 1995: 338–9)

Legge's analysis makes it clear that there are difficulties, at least in Britain,
not only with the location of HRM within the system but, as a result of the
unevenness with which the approach is developing, that researching the area
so as to make recommendations on improving practice is difficult. Legge's
1995 book raises sufficient concern about the state of HRM practice, but
there is little sign of concerted testing of the model developed by Beer and
his colleagues.

The *Handbook of Human Resource Management*, edited by Brian Towers
(1996), presents a thorough survey of British HRM. There is a sizable and
comprehensive review of European HRM by Sparrow and Hiltrop (1994).
Both present surveys, case studies and critical conceptual analyses, but little
by way of empirical testing of the elements of the model itself. HRM techniques are reviewed in both, and many telling points are made. The work is
multidisciplinary and it is not easy to spot the particular contribution made
by psychologists, except where the techniques are almost totally derived
from psychology, as is the case with psychometric testing. Paul Sparrow has
written extensively on business psychology. Christopher Mabey and Graeme
Salaman's (1995) *Strategic Human Resource Management* marks the collaboration between a psychologist and a sociologist who produce an eminent and scholarly text which is seamless in its description of HRM.

None of this is by way of complaint or criticism. The HRM literature is
developing a multidisciplinary framework and psychologists are involved,
but their contribution is not sufficiently distinctive to enable a work such as
this present one to carry through an argument, perhaps because in part it has
already been won. But there is more to be uncovered. It ought not to be
impossible to design investigatory studies which systematically test the four-
part model that Beer developed within organizations compared for effectiveness at the same point in time. Storey's (1995) critical text provides
chapters that address the four components, but the methodology involved in
each chapter varies across the expected possibilities. The model goes largely
untested. Sheila Rothwell's contribution to Storey's text investigates strategic planning activities in HRM and finds a gap between theory and practice. She explains this under several headings.

Firstly, the extent of change impinging on organizations externally, or
generated by them in terms of changing patterns of world trade and
increasing competition, new forms of foreign or domestic government
policies or regulations, or through new technologies, may mean that
planning becomes so problematic as to be useless, despite the growing
need for it. The need for planning may be in inverse proportion to its

feasibility. This could be one explanation of why, even if planning takes place, it is rarely implemented.

Second, and related to it, are the 'realities' of organizations and the shifting kaleidoscope of policy priorities and strategies which depend on the policies of the powerful interest groups involved . . . Thus, planning will need to take account of these, but by virtue of doing so may become overtaken in turn, or become merely a presentational 'gloss' on a rather different reality. Human resource planning may be particularly prone to these pressures, especially at a time of economic recession, by virtue of the weak power base of the human resource function, which either precludes the allocation of adequate resources to planning, or, more often, detracts from the ability to ensure implementation (Legge 1978; Collinson *et al.* 1990).

A third and similar group of factors relates to the nature of management and the skills and abilities of managers, who, in the UK particularly, have a preference for pragmatic adaptation over conceptualization, and a distrust of theory or planning.

Fourth, explanations must therefore also be sought in the way research is done on HRP. Have some approaches to 'successful' human resource management been over-prescriptive and idealistic? On the other hand, have some academic approaches to testing been over-theoretical, taking insufficient account of the realities of organizations and the way in which managers operate in response to specific problems, so that the form and extent of planning used in practice has not been adequately explored?

(Rothwell 1995: 178–9)

Rothwell cites Storey's (1992) selection of fifteen case studies to illustrate her point. She then goes on to suggest that it is possible that there are difficulties of interpretation because the research categories have been too aggregated to be able to explore the differences, so that case study and survey research methodologies become mixed together in an unhelpful way. Rothwell's observations on planning have implications for the very notion of HRM. If planning is not engaged in, then strategy can be only weakly formulated at best. If planning in the sense of regular monitoring and feedback on the operation of policy is not possible then alternative means of testing the effectiveness and coherence of HRM operations have to be found. In my own view, it is possible that a socially based psychology could test central assumptions, providing the method is robustly grounded in the particular context of the organization in question.

Social psychology and HRM research

The search for best practice in HRM itself is probably a mistaken research strategy. If social change is so dominant a concern in practice, as Rothwell indicates, then best practice can never really be identified – it is a search for a grail (holy or otherwise). If best practice were consistently found there would be little or no variance to be explained, and hence understanding would be difficult to advance. Research requires contrasts between its variables so that processes can be articulated. Social psychological research does this all the time. It is the strength of the experimental method. But the lessons of social psychological research seem by and large not to carry over to the HRM field, except where psychologists themselves have self-consciously used the lessons learned in more systematic research and tested some aspect of the HRM model. Hartley and Lord (1997) examined attitudes towards change in a public service organization employing some 600 staff, and in doing so provide a clear example of a stronger methodology being employed to good effect.

They began the study by conducting some initial interviews which revealed that there was a great deal of anxiety about change, as well as lack of trust between different grades of employee. They took a range of questionnaire-based measures consisting of several specifically developed change items, including 'need for change', 'involvement in change', 'belief in equity', 'global insecurity' and 'belief in permanence of change'. They factor analysed the questionnaire and amended it accordingly to combine two similarly factored scales. They used standard measures to assess attitudes towards 'them and us', 'organizational commitment', 'job security' and 'job satisfaction', all of which were rated on a five-point scale ranging from 'strongly agree' to 'strongly disagree'. The most striking finding was that employees with particular high or low commitment felt the greatest need for change. Tracing the findings back to the initial interviews, Hartley and Lord found that highly committed staff saw the need for continuous change and for a clear vision of how things could be improved in the particular area of public service. Hartley and Lord then found that those who are most critical of the organization are also those who are most committed. What at first sight appears as a paradox becomes comprehensible when a methodology that enables inferences to be made about process is employed. The Hartley and Lord study exemplifies precisely what can be done in the HRM area, and meets the concerns that I have about HRM methodology in general.

A research agenda for HRM

Hartley and Lord employed a standard methodology derived from social psychology. The present book has identified a range of topics that fall within the HRM remit – motivation, teamwork, diversity, groups and technology – where social psychology has a great deal to say. There are other possibilities that have yet to be employed. Discourse analysis is one possibility that needs to be employed in the HRM arena. Discourse is, of course, multidisciplinary as well. We can find those working in linguistics, philosophy, semiotics and ethnomethodology all using discourse as the foundation for their research. In social psychology, discourse analysts see language as being used for a variety of functions and having a variety of consequences. They see that language is both constructed and constructive, that the same phenomena can be used in a number of different ways and so that there will be several different accounts. They note that there is no foolproof way to shift those accounts that are 'literal' or 'accurate' from those which are rhetorical or misguided. So, noting that there are constructive and flexible ways in which language is used, they make this the first stage of their study. Issues such as how discourse is put together, how samples of discourse are selected, how records and documents are collected are added to the methodology. In doing this, 'the discourse approach shifts the focus from a search for underlying entities – attitudes – which generate talk and behaviour to a detailed examination of how evaluative expressions are produced in discourse. Two central and novel questions become dramatized. How is participants' language constructed, and what are the consequences of different types of construction?' (Potter and Weatherall 1987: 55).

I can find no examples of discourse analysis actually being applied to HRM, nor, for that matter, to management discourse in general. There is a potentially rich source of data here for discourse analysis.

As just one example, I recall being invited to a conference on management held in Prague in 1990. Among a distinguished list of keynote speakers was Rosabeth Moss Kanter. Her address, largely devoted to employee empowerment, had the majority of the 2,000 or so strong audience of managers and academics from across the world, but mainly from Central and Eastern Europe, applauding with more enthusiasm than I have seen on sporting occasions. On returning to my hotel, I shared a taxi with a member of staff from the International Labour Office with whom I had already enjoyed many lively discussions. I asked him whether he had enjoyed the address as much as the Russian delegate sitting next to me had done. He replied that he found the address lacking in analysis and in evidence, but enjoyed the performance. I said I agreed, but added that the rhetoric was perhaps the most important aspect in Prague in the period immediately following the fall of communism and at the commencement of the rebuilding of the economy along much more open principles. The rhetoric was likely to produce change far greater than could be envisaged on the basis of evidence alone. Rosabeth Moss Kanter had captured the mode of the moment – Prague was still celebrating its six-month old liberation and determined to release all its pent-up energies in securing its political and economic freedom. An audience of managers and academics was examining every possible means of securing the most profound change for half a century and mixing freely with the politicians who had brought the change into being. Seven months prior to Moss Kanter's address, empowerment was being rung from a regime that expressed its opposite by force majeure. A discourse analysis of Moss Kanter's address would have revealed far more than could be realized on the basis of those studies she recalled to her audience – hers was more than a critique of bureaucracy, more than an offering of a hypothetical alternative. It was offered as a significant contribution to the rebuilding of the country in which she had a family roots. She was returning to those roots in her address, feeding them so that they would flourish after years of undernourishment. Kanter demonstrates the power of discourse – should science now make so bold as to test the impact of this power?

Management in general

In a measured analysis, Guest (1992) examines the effects that Peters and Waterman's *In Search of Excellence* (1982) has had on American management. He shows, despite the criticisms that can be made of the book from a social scientific viewpoint, the impact the book has had in establishing HRM practice in the USA. The title of Guest's paper is 'Right enough to be dangerously wrong: an analysis of the *In Search of Excellence* phenomenon'. The title itself provides a strong functional message.

The substance of the paper is that Peters and Waterman, in popularizing their social science in the way they have done, have created one of the few books that managers read. Despite a methodology that can be criticized in virtually every way, the overall results can be confirmed by other studies. As a result of the publication, other books have been written and read. Guest's view seems to be that the overall approach to excellence is being implemented by Peters and Waterman through their consultancy work.

Guest also applauds Rosabeth Moss Kanter's (1984) book *The Change Masters* as presenting easily read case studies and presenting a series of practical recommendations. He contrasts the success of these American books with the generally poorly received texts that are produced by British social scientists writing on management themes. Undoubtedly, Peters and Waterman and Rosabeth Moss Kanter have generated change beyond the publication of their books. A discourse analysis of how they accomplished this would be rewarding. Without a discourse analysis, the scientific and the management community has to rely on anecdote, on the sales figures of books or on other very indirect evidence as to the effects of publications. The world has seen other books that sell well but seem to be little read and still less practised. What is much more important is to know what is happening in our organizations. What are the processes that lead to high-quality experience for those who work in organizations, as well as those using their services and purchasing their goods?

Huczynski (1996) suggests that for a management idea to secure fame, fortune and immortality for its writer it has to meet five prerequisites. The idea has to be timely: that is, it should address itself to the problems of the age. The idea has to be brought to the attention of its potential audience. Here, all the media of communication that link the world of business with consultancies, training and publishing companies have to be aligned so as to play an impactful role in the dissemination of the idea. The idea has to address organizational requirements in a way that meets the individual needs and concerns of the managers to whom it is addressed. The idea has to possess the essential ingredients which allow potential users to perceive it as relevant to meeting their needs. Finally, the idea has to be verbally presentable in an engaging way – not because the majority of managers will learn about it at a public presentation session, but because video- and audio-based materials will be developed from the author's presentation of the idea itself. Huczynski uses the analogy of a filter funnel, and sets the prerequisites as labels on the filters, to help to explain why only a very small fraction of all the available management ideas ever achieve popular status. Because the majority of the management ideas fail to meet the requirements they get filtered out, and only a small number of them ever re-emerge as popular ideas. Huczynski (1996: 2) writes, 'This explains why there have only been six truly popular management idea families in the last hundred years.' In presenting the idea families, he includes few that we as psychologists would recognize, although most are mentioned in this book at different points.

Huczynski's fourth chapter is devoted to the historical context of management. He assigns the years spanning the 1950s to the 1980s to the psychological period.

It can be divided broadly into two phases. The high points of the psychological period were in the 1960s in the USA. The idealism of the 1960s was part and parcel of a time when affluence left room for more liberal methods of management. Among sections of the industrial community, the consensus model of society and organizations held sway. There was no difference between the interests of the individual and the employer provided that the interpersonal skills of managers could be improved.

(Huczynski 1996: 139)

In the first phase of the psychological period Huczynski places the work of Maslow (1943), Hertzberg *et al.* (1959), McGregor (1960) and Likert (1961).

The founding fathers of the first phase provided the theoretical and philosophical underpinning to a set of therapeutic ideas. Their writings stressed self-awareness, self-knowledge and self-understanding. They emphasized democracy and humanitarianism. The theme was developed by social psychologists, like Kurt Lewin, who had fled from European totalitarianism and authoritarianism. These refugees saw in

American society the potential for human fulfilment and democratic involvement of a type that they had previously never envisaged.

(Huczynski 1996: 139)

Huczynski places the second phase of the psychological period as being from 1965 until the late 1970s.

It emphasized empirical research and the application of results to the solution of individual and organizational problems. This later strand of the democratic-humanitarian movement held that scientific investigation should seek to realize the potential that people possessed. This thread in American thinking flourished in a variety of forms in the warmth and affluence of places such as middle-class California where it first appeared. It was strange that a creed coming from this particularly rarefied and often self-indulgent quarter of the intellectual world, should have been taken up so much in the traditionally hard-headed world of management thinking and organizational behaviour.

(Huczynski 1996: 140)

Huczynski does not present particular authors in this section of his analysis, but he notes recurring themes from the literature of this time. First, the reality that was experienced subjectively was real. Second, anything that might cause even the most minimal emotional discomfort was held to be illegitimate. Third, human personality was believed to be under constant attack by illegitimate, cruel and savage forces. Fourth, anyone could be as good as anyone else, providing he or she had the right training. Finally, in determining the truth or validity of anything, new ideas and techniques were held to be better than old ones: 'If it felt good to practically everybody involved and if nearly everybody endorsed it, it was good!' (Huczynski 1996: 140).

I understand that Andrew Huczynski is not a psychologist by training. He has nevertheless written texts which cover a considerable amount of recognizably psychological literature. He has also set a definitive criterion in classifying the specific historical periods. He refers to the eras in which particular ideas and approaches held guru status – largely defined in terms of the five criteria mentioned above.

It would be a mistake to assume that psychology had contributed nothing of significance outside the period he assigns as the psychological. Indeed, many to whom he assigns status in this period are still writing and touring on the conference circuit. Perhaps there is a salutary warning to those whose work becomes immersed in the multidisciplinary frameworks of management studies to the extent that psychology can become indistinguishable from other approaches under certain conditions. This can be seen as extending the boundaries of the discipline as well as infusing the discipline with new ideas. However, it can also be misleading in the circumstances that seek out historical significance for different sources of influence.

Some approaches that have begun in psychology have taken on an intellectual life that is almost of its own. Chris Argyris addressed the British Psychological Society's Annual Conference held at Heriot-Watt University in 1997 and told about his having been credited with having created the area of organizational behaviour. 'It was my PhD subject. My supervisor said well – you are studying behaviour – but not in an experimental way. And, you are studying organizations. Let's call it "Organizational Behaviour".' Argyris is mentioned frequently by Huczynski but either in terms of his contribution to management theory in general or as a member of the psychology period. But it is organizational development that Huczynski assigns to the psychological period. Organizational development is seen by him as being concerned with feelings and emotions rather than with behaviour and with learning – which are Argyris's central themes. So the history of psychology and management can be misleading and distorted, as can all other histories if the examination of evidence becomes unbalanced by the search for very particular phenomena. We also misunderstand the present status of psychology, particularly social psychology, if we see its methods as being solely confined to the experimental. Ours is a rich and diverse science capable of adopting a great many approaches.

Organizational behaviour and social psychology

Argyris and Schon (1974) distinguished between espoused theories of action and theories-in-use. Espoused theories of action are those that people report as theories that inform their actions. Theories-in-use are the theories of action inferred from how people actually behave. Theories-in-use are inferred after analysing empirical records, such as videos or audio-tapes of directly observable behaviour.

Theory-in-use often leads people to behave in ways that seem to be based on automatized, ill-considered premises, as though they are unable to make choices or exercise discretion. After long analysis of the social psychological literatures on groups, attitudes and so on, Argyris concludes that a considerable amount of laboratory-based experimental social psychology may support the proposition that people are acting in this ill-considered way. They seek to take control, they are defensive, they do not test hypotheses about others' behaviour and so on. The central problem seems to be that the experimental work does not readily translate into the organizational context. In organizational settings, people have very different knowledges of those with whom they interact as compared with the brief encounters that are possible in experimental situations. The demand characteristics of the studies vary dramatically in the respective contextual settings. It could be, says Argyris, that the form of behaviour that he describes is innate in the human condition, in which case there are formidable problems in seeking to encourage openness and creativity within organizations. Argyris wants social psychology to develop new espoused theories that enable us to test the more open and learning-based emphasis that he seeks to champion. One possibility, he notes, is for social psychology to concentrate more on process than on input–outcome designs. He cites researchers such as Hackman and Alderfer, who do this in their studies, and has to admit that the evidence supports the notion that the environment does have a part to play and that defensive behaviour may not after all be owing wholly to innate factors. The emphasis of the approach adopted by Argyris is 'on producing social science knowledge that practitioners can use in taking action, such as executing policies. The domain of focus is on human beings as they are interacting in order to achieve their intended goals' (Argyris 1992: 397). He goes on to suggest that what is needed is the development of 'maps for action' formulated by researchers in a form that can be utilized by practitioners. For example, Argyris produced a map for action for a group of top executives who set about providing the appropriate structural conditions in which policies could be developed and acted on in ways that were rewarded. They helped each other to develop the skills that they needed to tackle the issues facing them as a team. The sessions were recorded and the records passed to the research team, who examined the transcripts for indications of stresses and strains as well as opportunities for learning. The maps attempted to identify and to describe the interdependence of the variables that the actors defined as relevant. On the basis of the maps, Argyris and his team made loose assumptions about the nature of the interdependencies and he then interpreted them in terms of the overall story or drama that seemed to him to unfold. The aim was to have the participants identify the stories for themselves and thereby learn from them.

If Argyris is correct in identifying the role of social psychological experimentation, namely in identifying the elements of our behaviour that prevent learning, then he has indeed identified an unintended consequence of the research tradition. It could be that he is using the experimental approach as a rhetorical opponent. As yet, we have no overall independent evaluation of his approach. In more recently developed approaches, psychologists would have seen cognitive issues, rather than feelings, as being the most important focus for study. A cognitive approach could, for example, have unfolded the strategies involved in decision-making. Cognitive psychologists usually adopt very much more formalized methodologies than Argyris has done. Typically, cognitive psychologists adopt procedures such as causal mapping (Laukkanen 1994), reasoning in decision processes (Melone 1994) and formulation processes (Nutt 1993). The procedures of cognitive psychologists often enable propositions to be more rigorously based on experimental findings, as well as to be mathematically modelled. However, Argyris's work is useful in terms of the present argument because he draws attention to the need for social psychology to take account of context and situation.

Argyris also views management as being about action. His research is not intended to result in passivity. The sadness of the perspective that Argyris represents is that his view of organizational behaviour has created a division where one need not have existed. Probably without his wishing it, Argyris's position has moved field-based research into a different camp from laboratory work. Much else has followed to take that development further away. The argument in this book is that the separation is unnecessary. Social psychology is operating closely with managers in organizations. It needs no further defence.

Management as a profession

Management can be described as comprising three related phenomena: an activity, an occupational group and the values of that group. Mant (1976) argues that the term 'manage' derives from the Italian word *maneggiare*, which means to handle things (especially horses). This, he says, is a masculine concept that implies taking charge or directing, especially in the context of war. Grint (1995) points out that the Italian term is derived from the Latin root *manus*, meaning hand. Mant suggests that 'manage' also comes from the French word *menager*, which means using something carefully and has more gentle, almost feminine, connotations. Grint suggests that the term carries connotations of control of labour supply, wages, product prices, quality and quantity, which became deeply embedded into the fabric of the community at the time the medieval guilds came together. There is a sense in which the continuity of management, as a semantic definition, has a long history. In the sense of examining management as an activity, history is so short as to become momentary.

Johnson and Gill (1993) note that

> there is little consensus about what managers' everyday activities actually are. This uncertainty is made worse because management is not an undifferentiated, homogenous occupational group . . . writers at different times and for different audiences seem to agree that management's main purpose is the exercise of control over human and inanimate resources in various organizational contexts . . . So while it is important not to treat management as a monolithic whole, and while management's work requires a variety of skills . . . there appears to be a unity of purpose in managerial hierarchies and in different organizational contexts: that is, management's role is, to a large extent, that of controlling.
>
> (Johnson and Gill 1993)

The control to which Johnson and Gill refer primarily relates to labour and to materials. They place the ability to control close to the requirement to be able to predict the behaviour of people in organizations. Control is exercised through the utilization of a range of techniques such as management accountancy, as well as the system and social processes that are put in place and operated in organizations. Does this equate to management being a profession?

If we were to produce a composite definition of what constitutes a profession, it might look like the list of characteristics described by Millerson (1964). Millerson listed six defining features:

1 A profession involves a skill based on theoretical knowledge.
2 The skill requires training and education.
3 The professional must demonstrate competence by passing a test.
4 Integrity is maintained by adherence to a code of conduct.
5 The service is for the public good.
6 The profession is organized.

Developing these issues, Hales (1986: 160) points out that 'The essence of professional organization is the selective recruitment of employees with technical and moral rules "built in".' Hales adds that, through formalized training and experience, professionals are then left to themselves, subject to meeting professional and organizational performance criteria.

Torrington and Hall (1987) argue that while personnel management meets most of Millerson's criteria for being a profession, HRM cannot, as 'it is inevitably an integral part of general management and the job holder becomes a manager first and a personnel specialist second' (Torrington and Hall 1987: 17–18). They note, on the evidence of their own empirical research, that many managers had reached the highest level of attainment at the expense of disassociation from the personnel function. There will be other groups within management functions who meet all or most of Millerson's listed criteria for professional status. Legge (1995), taking the example of the National Health Service, presents illustrations of organizations using techniques to control the autonomy of particular professional groups. She reinforces the point that management is not a homogeneous block, and indicates that even within the same organizational setting management comprises a range of technically distinct groupings of activities. Project teams will usually coordinate the skills and knowledges of particular professional specialisms when working together, and performance control will add a further dimension to organization along professional lines. Within project teams, professional discretion will form an important element of self-motivation. Particularly in knowledge work, of the kind exercised in Microsoft or by specialist organizations such as law firms, professional contacts are especially important to the maintenance of functioning and flexibility within teams of managers. All these elements point to the requirement to regard management as a profession.

On the other hand, Pascale (1991) has argued that management in the post-1945 period was seen as being based on a set of generic concepts that underpinned management everywhere. Such presumed universal concepts reduced management reliance on information and activity at the lower levels of organizations and lent itself to mass marketing of standardized packages of 'managerial techniques'. These techniques consisted of devices, events, interventions and programmes. Huczynski (1996) seeks to locate what he calls the development of management fads in such processes as fear of competition, leading to the encouragement of an idea for innovation being adopted. A further motive for adopting a new idea might be that it is perceived as acting as a means of enhancing an individual's career. Huczynski's analysis demonstrates the relative lack of system-wide analysis leading to consistent management practice or to the management of change in the management literatures.

The adoption of fads reduces the opportunities for developing coherence in the theory and practices of management. The possibility is that a management driven by the adoption of fashion and fads assists small steps in personal advancement but does not help management as a professional activity. The world becomes one in which the quick fix rules all other considerations. In a world in which analysis and evaluation are marginalized, social change becomes an end in itself, rather than a process that has to be managed with skill and care. Management becomes reactive and concerned with dealing with here and now issues, rather than with broader priorities. Analysis and evaluation are central techniques in the social sciences, which to a large extent protect it from the whims of fashion. Could the same techniques have the same effect for management? The practising manager will be left with questions as to what is to be analysed.

Clear candidates for analysis and evaluation are social and technical contexts. The contexts in which management operates determine the way in which activities are imbued with power. Who managers are depends on who has the power to constitute certain forms of action as the actions of managers. This contextual delineation of power also translates the many and various separate activities that managers engage in from the activities that other people engage in. As Grint (1995: 47) puts it, 'If managers are engaged in conversation they are managing, they are not engaged in idle chatter; but if children are involved in conversation they are more likely to be deemed to be engaged in idle chatter rather than any form of management.' A further set of candidates for analysis and evaluation are the people with whom managers must work. What are their goals and motivations? How do they work as teams and in groups? What range of skills and knowledges do they bring to the work that is on the agenda of the organization? The organization itself sets the framework of power and the distribution of resources – it too requires analysis and evaluation. How does the organization operate? What is its operating culture? What is the espoused theory of the directorate and the top management?

As the book demonstrates, technology is significantly affected by the social context in which it has to operate – just as the context itself is dramatically changed by technological change. The alignment of organization and technology will make constant demands on managers, since these processes are not socially or organizationally neutral. Jobs, careers, service delivery and motivations are all affected, and their relationships change as technology impacts and develops. The decisions that have to be made about each element of the technology–organization relationship require analysis and evaluation on a frequent and iterative basis. Fads and fashions might have played a part in the initial introduction of information technology to organizational 'needs' such as accounting or word processing. In the networked society, the need to focus on strategic aims, and the sheer size of social and capital investment required when information and communication technologies are brought together, demand analysis.

If management as a profession is comprised of particular specialist groups, each contributing skills and knowledge to the overall activity of producing goods or services, a key issue for analysis and evaluation is the nature of interdependencies and their means of coordination within the organization.

The personnel specialist needs to work alongside the accountant. Both need to work closely with computer specialists and systems engineers. The specialists cannot work effectively if they attempt to work alone. In a networked information and careers situation, inter-dependency could require special realms of analysis. Suppose that our systems designer moves to another project as soon as the installation of a new IT system is complete and has been trialled. Does the accountant have sufficient knowledge of the IT system to be able to respond if user departments find access to the new system less than optimal once they begin to wish to work with their own accounts? Situated learning studies tell us that cognitions, knowledge and understanding are all socially distributed. Turbulent patterns of mobility for individuals could become a disaster for organizations if there is not some means of maintaining the basis for the distribution of cognition. If the people who constructed the system have moved on to the next project, it may not be possible to reconstruct the team that has the knowledge necessary for significant amendment. Manuals, training and telephone help lines may have a role to play, but they will soon be found to be inadequate if there is a need to do more than rectify a small fault. In these circumstances, the professional associations could be the only means of saving the situation. In the networked society, in which products seem to have a shortened life, there has to be some repository of stability. The professions seem likely to have the best prospect of managing the arena in which stability, continuity and change are played out. If organizations no longer provide the basis of career development then the professions could – providing they enable their knowledge and training to keep apace with the quantitative and qualitative changes that are unleashed within the particular contexts their specialisms address. In a world which seems no longer able to provide the fundamental sources of motivation, but in which people still look to work as a primary source of personal and social identity, the professions may come to have a special role.

> Most professions have evolved strong cultural attributes that provide a unity of identity for their members. Accountants, architects, doctors, engineers, solicitors, are just some of the professional groups that huddle under a strong cultural umbrella. Workers from within these groups may therefore prove to be most suited to the new free agent, portfolio style working arrangements of the future. Even if people from within such groups lose their organizational ties as long-term employees, they still maintain a strong sense of professional identity.
>
> (Barnatt 1997: 97)

The professions themselves need to maintain and develop further their training programmes into lifelong learning: continuous professional development that meets the needs of rapidly changing organizations and societies. Organizations need to help employees, particularly those who are close to the frontiers of change and who are forging new knowledge, to play a full role in their professional bodies. If projects are always to be short term, they have to carry the full costs of producing, advancing and retaining the knowledge won in that work. Analysis and evaluation are fundamental skills in the management of the networked society. The professions must be encouraged to remain the repositories, the reference sources and the schools for development of the output of the activities of analysis and evaluation. In the networked society, the professions have a pivotal role to play in maintaining the fundamental sources of identity in work and society.

Social psychology as a profession

In Larson's (1977) analysis, universities were crucial to the emergence of the modern professions, in that they served as institutional locations to which prestigious bodies of knowledge could be attached. Expanding on this theme, Abbot (1988) argued that the true use of knowledge is symbolic, serving to legitimize professional practice by giving it a rational base and connecting it to major cultural values.

The extreme proponent of this thesis is Collins (1979), for whom professional knowledges are functionally irrelevant to practice. On this view, formal knowledge is no more than the raw material for the social construction of status and barriers to entry. The implication is that the content of professional knowledge is disconnected from professional practice and is solely driven by the academic status scramble.

On the other hand, the idea that professional knowledges are essentially arbitrary significations of status is not shared by all. Friedson's sensitive analysis of the social processes played out on the basis of medical science never loses sight of the fact that some of these depend upon its practical efficacy (Friedson 1970). In Friedson's view, professional knowledges are subject to a complex of pressures. Practitioners accumulate rule of thumb procedures, while academics strive for theoretical systems and administrators issue codes of practice. There are more sophisticated pressures in operation. Because professional services are offered on competitive markets, a certain codification of professional knowledge is required in order to ensure that products are stable and identifiable. So the control of practice requires that there should be indeterminate elements within professional knowledges which can only be passed on by personal contact between senior and junior practitioners. How this process can be sustained in the face of all of the pressures of the networked society and of lifelong learning is an issue that faces all of psychology, whether university- or practitioner-based.

It is as difficult to locate the specific activities of social psychology within the professional framework as it is for management, but perhaps for the opposite reasons. Psychology as a whole certainly qualifies as a profession – or at least as a set of professions. The British Psychological Society, like the American Psychological Association, is organized so as to meet all the criteria set out by Millerson (1964) and cited earlier in this chapter. In Europe, psychology is organized in ways varying from the state recognized bodies that act almost as trade unions in Scandinavian countries to the loose affiliations based on activity and upon location in France, with Dutch and German psychology coming close to the British model. In Britain, social psychology forms one of the fundamental areas that have to be provided in first degree courses if recognition is to be afforded to graduates wishing to attain the Graduate Basis for Registration. Although, at the time of writing, the British Psychological Society does not have a legally protected procedure covering registration of practitioners, it has invoked the powers granted in its Royal Charter to require members to adhere to the provisions and statutes covered by the Charter. Additionally, it has a Code of Conduct governing the way in which members provide the public with services and securing members' agreement to work within their levels of competence. To progress to full chartered status, members must graduate in the discipline as defined by the coverage of a qualifying examination. There is then a postgraduate level of knowledge test within one of the areas of practice, such as clinical, educational or occupational psychology, and a period of supervised but independent work which has to be verified by members of the professional body's panels.

Social psychology is a significant part of the core curriculum and forms important parts of the postgraduate knowledge base in particular areas. There is not a distinct area of professional practice assigned to social psychology. Rather, as an occupational psychologist one might be engaged in practices such as organizational development, or interviewing for appraisal and counselling, which call on social psychological knowledge. As a clinical psychologist, one might use social skills training programmes to improve the quality of life of those suffering a specific mental illness such as schizophrenia, or work with groups providing social support for those suffering anxiety. As an educational psychologist, one might be engaged in work in classrooms that involved group-based teaching or set out to improve the styles of presentation of teachers. Of course, the professional groups call not just on social psychology but also on developmental, cognitive, biological and individual difference psychology, as well as a range of methodological techniques drawn from all of psychology and statistics. Ideally, these new contexts provide an opportunity for testing the ethological validity of social psychology as well as advancing the discipline itself.

As it happens, the areas known as applied psychology have developed somewhat independently from the areas known as fundamental psychology. In both Britain and the United States, the intellectual roots of much of applied or professional psychology have developed relatively independently and at different times from the core areas (e.g. Dunnette 1976; Gale 1994; Shimmin and Wallis 1994). We will touch on some of the issues that are raised by the origin of psychological studies of work in Chapter 3. None of this is to say that those working within the fundamental areas do not engage in work which can be of use beyond the laboratory – indeed, there is a sense in which no one in psychology does work that cannot be used in practice. There is also a real sense in which those of us engaged in applied work which specifically addresses issues raised in practice have to consider, and indeed, to invent areas of theory that assist the interpretation of findings and advance understanding. However, perhaps as a result of its separated intellectual origins, the entire range of psychology is wide, rich and diverse. Within the breadth and richness of psychology, the majority of those concerned with social psychology will see themselves as primarily concerned with scientific study, albeit that they are addressing issues that are important in our conduct within society. So the social psychology of attitudes is concerned not just with how our cognitive and emotional processes combine to operate in complex and conflictual social context, but also with the origins of prejudice and perhaps with the harm that is done to those receiving the hostility invoked. In all of this, the agenda of social psychology and the agenda of management have developed in ways that appear to be separate. Yet when we come to examine the texts of people such as those by Drucker or Rosabeth Moss Kanter, we find that there is much which has a close parallel with social psychology. I can imagine that some social psychologists will be puzzled as to why I have laboured to produce a book which seeks to link their interests with those of management. Some social psychologists will find the exercise entirely antipathetic. Some managers will find the issues raised by social psychology trivial, and others may find them tedious. Yet at many points both agendas coincide. One danger of management theory being developed beyond its scientific roots is that it becomes abstract and disembodied. It is no good those teachers of management drawing upon theories of organization that call on practitioners to behave in particular ways without also being able to illustrate some of the processes implied in doing so. Disembodied theories produce principles that cannot be acted upon. Disembodied theories provide no guidance. A great many management propositions at least imply that underlying social psychological processes are important, but either do not refer to them or do not acknowledge them. It is probably up to social psychologists to draw attention to these problems. The use to which knowledge is put is clearly a concern of the professional.

One of the underlying values of psychology has long been the tendency for us to give our knowledge away. George Millar's famous address to the American Psychological Association (1969), calling on the profession to enhance the good of people, proved a great inspiration to a great many psychologists in its day, and may well have done a great deal to enhance our credibility. At the same time, there have been costs to our professional claims to credibility, because many aspects of our knowledge base are claimed by others. There is a sense in which there is little to be lost by going a little further down the road of ultimate collaboration. Many social psychologists working in the area of occupational psychology have long since embarked on careers in management and business schools. There is much to gain, in the sense that Tajfel and others sought to gain, from investigating phenomena that are facing humankind squarely and are of profound psychological interest. The agenda facing management in the networked society is approaching gigantic proportions, and raises scientific and social issues that are crucially important. Moreover, managers are social actors with influence in the arena of change. If they are ignored by social scientists, especially those whose work many are most likely to recognize, they may come to see themselves as passive victims in situations that are beyond control.

Social psychology and science

Much of social psychology has been driven by an underlying motive to learn the lessons of history that civilization itself has not taught us. Adorno *et al.*'s (1950) work on the authoritarian personality was a direct response to the events in Germany during the late 1930s and early 1940s. Milgram's (1974) studies of obedience were heavily influenced by the responses given to the Israeli courts by Adolf Eichman, who claimed that he was not responsible for the massacre of thousands of Jewish people in the prison camp of which he had oversight because he was following orders from a higher command. Tajfel, as we will see later in this book, was concerned to discover whether the processes of categorization, which he held responsible for the loss of his kin and his people in Poland, were general properties of all populations.

Zimbardo (1970) constructed his study of imprisonment so as to investigate whether depersonalization resulted from pressures of situations rather than from people and the roles they adopt. Relevance has always been an item high on the scientific agenda of social psychology. Yet all of this was university- and laboratory-based research. However, in Tajfel's case the research was supported for relevance, as we will see in later chapters, by considerable social theorizing and wide dissemination so as to maximize influence.

Of course, only Plato and Pythagoras searched after knowledge for its own sake. As peer review has tightened its grip on the scientific community, the market has become the dominant place in which all action takes place. Science has been seen as a commodity since Francis Bacon wrote his seventeenth-century treatise *New Atlantis*, which extended the world of science to a position where all problems would be solved. Bacon also saw science as comprising an open but elite community in which responsibility for openness lay with the individual.

The organization of science has changed beyond all recognition since Bacon's day – so too has the role of the universities. Studies in the sociology of science have prided themselves on discovering 'life in the laboratory as the "factory in which order is produced" ' (Latour and Woolgar 1979). As in other factories in which capital investment is taking place, the operation is geared towards production – in this case of scientific facts which have to be stabilized, and to be invented with credibility in order to be traded, sold and appropriated. The scientists working in this factory are said to be obsessed to a certain degree with the economic categories of success; they speak of the costs they incur, they think of cost–benefit analyses, they bargain with each other in 'the manufacture of knowledge'. They behave like bankers who control budgets and balance accounts, pay-offs and trade-offs alike. The rules that dominate research are in turn dominated by the economic laws of investment and return, of profitability and success. Through information technology and the Internet, scientific openness has acquired a new meaning: openness is an external value that can be accessed by all. Universities are no longer the sole repositories of knowledge and research expertise. The Internet, as well as many aspects of the funding mechanisms for research, has also ensured that peer review now has less control over quality and relevance. So social psychology and management both face inescapable pressures from the market. There are so many parallels that there is almost a common fate between social psychology and management as the pace of change intensifies.

Social psychology and management: a manifesto for change

John Harvey-Jones asserts that 'Without question, the most desirable management skill for the nineties will be the ability to manage change. This is one of the rarest and most difficult skills to learn – for very good reasons. Management has always been about change, for it is uniquely, the task of making more, or better, from less' (Harvey-Jones 1993: 21). In the same vein, social psychology has always been about change, and there has been an accumulating literature specifically addressing social, and particularly organizational, change. I have self-consciously set out to do no more than acknowledge the existence of that literature, despite the title of this book. The literature that is more readily recognized as being about organizational change does not begin to provide comprehension of the scale and the depth of societal change exemplified in the networked society.

Instead, I have taken the topics of motivation, groups and teams, diversity, technology and the networked society as exemplars of the accelerating pace and process of change. I have addressed a selected range of social psychology positions almost in the tradition of exergisis – what do the teachers tell us about these selected matters? What has formed social psychology, particularly in Britain and in Europe, for it to have become the discipline that it now is? I have attempted to set the position of social psychology alongside positions drawn from what I have taken to be the management literatures. The attempt has been to establish a dialogue between the two subject areas with a view to exploring differences and communalities. The intention has been to address a separate but related problem within both literatures. I believe that social psychology has a considerable amount to offer to management in theory and in practice. However, social psychology, despite its espoused aims, does not deal with the issue of situational context with any precision. Rather, social psychology deals with context as a generality. There are some very good studies that deal with situations, particularly in the areas of distributed cognition. However, a strict definition of the boundaries of social psychology would place these studies in the disciplines of social anthropology or sociology, despite their origins in the work of Vygotsky, the founder of Soviet psychology. Social psychology itself is continually contested territory.

In Britain, it requires, in my view, a breath of fresh air that might well be offered if it were to take on board its scientific agenda some, if not all, of the issues raised by an important set of activities denoted by the term management. This is the more so if the topics taken for study are those addressed by the major forces of social change, some of which have been addressed in this book. So, item one on the agenda is that social psychology itself seeks to adopt a small change in its procedures by taking better, more precise, account of the properties of situations.

Item two on the agenda is addressed to management, as practitioners and as theorists. Despite drawing heavily on psychological literatures and principles, a great many management texts do not pay adequate attention to the science that underpins behavioural accounts. Much that is offered by the management gurus becomes assertion and generalization that is premised so broadly that almost any form of activity could be justified on its basis. There is a robust and dignified literature being developed in economic sociology and in the sociology of management that indicates that other possibilities for dialogue exist that could be more fruitful. At points in the book I have drawn on these. Many of these texts soften the distinction between social psychology and management literatures – a distinction which I had initially seen as being much sharper than perhaps the eventual dialogue will sustain. I leave the reader to decide. These most optimistic of sociological texts suggest that the entire dialogue of management is a dialogue with the social sciences (Thomas 1993). However, the same work casts psychology as an art form, and states that the dream of a science of man in society has largely lost credibility. What Thomas sees is the natural science model of experimentation and measurement that may have been a goal for a number of psychologists some years ago. What I have tried to demonstrate in this text is that social psychology in particular has never really been party to the model that Thomas rejects, and has much more to offer methodologically and epistemologically.

Item three is that social psychology and management need to explore, with some urgency, the common territory that lies within the arena of social change. The networked society is generating change at a pace that seems not to have been experienced in any former period of history. The implications of the changes rest with organizations, and the need to maintain a position within a market for goods and services, as well as with individuals, and the need to maintain knowledge and skills. Common territory for social psychology and for management resides with the need to facilitate personal career development opportunities by developing feasible strategies as well as time and support for knowledge advancement, for individuals, within organizations and with the professions and institutions of learning and education. The mastery control programmes reviewed in Chapter 7 provide strong examples of what can be done in instruction at an individual or a group level. I know of no such examples that meet larger-scale needs in organizations. Few British professional associations engage in professional development on a scale that meets likely demand in the coming years. The new communication technologies offer tremendous opportunities for high-quality and responsive training and have to be brought further in to play. The new communication technologies offer further developments in the way in which work is designed and distributed. Work organization is likely to be transformed dramatically in the near future.

Item four on the agenda for management and social psychology in a changing society is the broader social fabric within which the networked society is operating. Volume II of Castells's (1997b) work is devoted to the power of identity. He counterposes the twin forces of global networking and the crisis of collective identity that is following in its wake as people seek control over their own lives and environment.

For Castells, nation, ethnicity, gender, family and locality seek a highly diversified expression of their values and beliefs through means that interplay with technology-induced globalization. Castells's analysis is pitched at the general level of social movements, but it is also the very stuff of social psychology as well as the arena within which the management of people in organizations is played out. Castells locates the tension between the power of globalized technology and issues of identity in terms that social psychologists should find amenable. 'The new power lies in the codes of information and in the images of representation around which societies organize their institutions, and people build their lives, and decide their behaviour' Castells (1997b: 359). If the processes of power and of identification are not managed with care, they will remain oppositional. These are processes that demand the creative activities of both managers and social psychologists at present. Castells's description of the networked society offers the prospect of increased action and interaction.

The fifth point on the agenda for social psychology and management in a changing society is political. In his third volume, Castells holds out the promise of the Information Age, in which there is an

unleashing of unprecedented productive capacity by the power of the mind. I think therefore I produce. In doing so, we will have the leisure to experiment with spiritualism, and the opportunity of reconciliation with nature, without sacrificing the material well being of our children. The dream of the Enlightenment, that reason and science would solve the problems of mankind, is within reach. Yet there is an extraordinary gap between our technological overdevelopment and our social underdevelopment. Our economy, our society and culture are built on interests, values, institutions and systems of representation that, by and large, limit collective creativity, confiscate the harvest of information technology, and deviate our energy in self-destructive confrontation. This state of affairs must not be. There is no eternal evil in human nature. There is nothing that cannot be changed by conscious, purposive social action, provided with information, and supported by legitimacy. If people are informed, active, and communicate throughout the world; if business assumes its social responsibility; if the media become the messengers, rather than the message; if political actors react against cynicism, and restore belief in democracy; if culture is reconstructed from experience; if humankind feels the solidarity of the species throughout the globe; if we assert intergenerational solidarity by living in harmony with nature; if we depart for the exploration of our inner-self, having made peace with ourselves. If all this is made possible by our informed, conscious, shared decision, while there is still time, maybe then, we may, at last, be able to live and let live, love and be loved.

(Castells 1998: 359–60)

There is some hint that perhaps the current British government is in touch with the broad spectrum of possibilities that Castells outlines. It remains to be seen whether the spectrum can be translated into party political policies. But it is clear that to achieve these aims social psychologists and managers will have to work with families, community groups and work organizations to support and to maintain their place in the networked society. It would be very easy for whole societies to be excluded. It is already apparent, though, that the political agenda demanded by the conditions Castells describes must be contrasted sharply with the years of Reganism and Thatcherism. Now technology and inclusion must work together. The alternative is exclusion, inefficiency and conflict on a broad scale.

I can hear the followers of Thomas expressing their doubt that social psychology can even consider an agenda for change. Social psychology, above all the areas of discipline, has a very wide range of approaches to its subject matter. An important feature of this breadth is that social psychology has a number of levels of analysis and explanation that enables the focus to range between highly focused internal psychological processes and the broadly based ideological level (Doise 1982). The sixth item on the agenda is then that social psychology seeks to develop the reflective stance that has often been part of the general repertoire of analysis in each of the levels it has adopted in its various approaches.

Psychology needs all its many and varied approaches. Sometimes, those within the discipline seem not to recognize that each approach depends upon the other, if not for intellectual sustenance then for professional coherence. Tolerance of difference is perhaps the first value in a profession of the social. Honesty and objectivity are precious values in science as a profession. They have to be cherished and nurtured. In the new millennium these values will be tested to the full. It is vital that they survive, for they will be needed within the profession of psychology and in the arena of social change. The chapters that follow seek to elaborate a framework in which this notion of the professions of social psychology and of management can not only coexist but flourish.

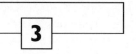

Individual performance at work: the problem of motivation

In one of the many spare moments that gave me opportunity to read during the days when I was paid to print, I came across an essay on work that drove me on to understand more of why things are as they are, as well as what might be done about them.

Factory life

I work in a factory. For eight hours a day, five days a week, I'm the exception to the rule that life can't exist in a vacuum. Work to me is a void, and I begrudge every precious minute of my time that it takes. When writing about work I become bitter, bloody-minded and self-pitying, and I find difficulty in being objective. I can't tell you much about my job because I think it would be misleading to try to make something out of nothing; but as I write I am acutely aware of the effect that my working environment has upon my attitude towards work and leisure and life in general.

My working day starts with that time-honoured ritual known as 'clocking-in'. In a job such as mine this is one of the more constructive acts of the day. For the uninitiated: a lever is pressed and, in blue ink, a time is recorded on one's card. It's so mechanical that one expects the time to be always the same. But it isn't. Just have the effrontery to be late: then you will find that your time has been stamped in R E D ink. The management may condone bad timekeeping, but that blasted clock seems to shed blood in anguish.

After clocking-in one starts work. Starts work, that is, if the lavatories are full. In an hourly paid job it pays to attend to the calls of nature in the firm's time. After the visit to the lavatory there is the tea break to look forward to; after the tea break the dinner-break, after the dinner-break the 'knocking-off' time. Work is done between the breaks, but it is done from habit and is hardly given a passing thought. Nothing is gained from the work itself – it has nothing to give. The criterion is not to do a job well, but to get it over with quickly. The trouble is, one never does get it over with. Either one job is followed by another, which is equally boring, or the same job goes on forever: particles of production that stretch into an age of inconsequence. There is never a sense of fulfilment.

(Johnson 1968: 11)

Dennis Johnson may have embellished his account a little, if only for literary effect. We cannot, though, doubt his sentiments or his values. He, like me, left his factory work to become a student of Ruskin College and eventually a teacher. The factory he describes was a cigarette manufacturer in Nottingham – a city that I came to know and love while I worked in its university. Using the essay in my own teaching, I frequently asked my students to consider why that work had become so lacking in everything human. Why was it so unsatisfying? What could be in the mind of the factory managers who organized work so as to have it become so denatured? This really is the starting point for social psychology in its organizational setting. What could be changed so as to make work at least tolerable?

The response of psychology

Supposing that managers were to look to psychology for assistance, what would they find the discipline telling them? The majority of standard texts on work psychology begin by tracing out theories such as those of Maslow (1943, 1970), who offered a general theory of human functioning rather than a specific approach to behaviour in the workplace. Maslow proposed five classes of needs.

- Physiological: the need for food, drink, sex and so on.
- Safety: the need for physical and psychological safety within a non-threatening environment.
- Belongingness: the need to feel a sense of attachment to another person or group of persons.
- Esteem: the need to feel valued and respected.
- Self-actualization: the need to fulfil one's potential by developing one's capacities and expressing them.

Evaluations of the theory revealed a range of problems. For example, Rauschenberger *et al.* (1980) pointed out that needs did not always group together in the ways predicted; the theory was unable to predict when particular needs would become important; there was no clear relationship between needs and behaviour, so that, for example, the same behaviour could reflect different needs, and different behaviours the same need; there was insufficient precision in the description of the needs; and, finally, the whole notion of need as a biological phenomenon is problematic. It ignores the capacity of people and those around them to construct their own perceptions of needs and how they can best be met.

Need theories, such as Maslow's, place heavy emphasis on the content of motivation. Most psychologists are more interested in process, so Vroom's (1964) theory has found more favour. The theory sets out to explain how people choose which of several courses of action they will pursue. According to Vroom, three factors are appraised for each of the actions being considered. First is expectancy: if I tried, would I be able to perform the action I am considering? Second is instrumentality: would performing the action lead to identifiable outcomes? Third is valence: how much do I value these outcomes? Vroom proposed that expectancy and instrumentality can be expressed as probabilities and valence as a subjective value. He also suggested that force to act is a function of the product of expectancy, instrumentality and valence. This would mean that if any one of the components was zero, overall motivation to pursue that course of action would also be zero. For Vroom's theory to operate in the workplace, managers would have to ensure that all conditions implied by the theory were satisfied. Employees must see that they possess the necessary skills to do their jobs at least adequately (expectancy), employees must see that if they performed their jobs well, or at least adequately, they would be rewarded (instrumentality) and employees must find the rewards offered for successful job performance attractive.

Again, research evaluation has not supported Vroom's theory sufficiently for psychological science to be completely satisfied. Most attempts to utilize Vroom's theory in the workplace have compared different people with each other, rather than comparing different outcomes for the same person. Research also suggests that the theory works best where the outcome measure is objective performance, or self-reported effort and performance, rather than effort or performance reported by another person. People also seem to add components, rather than multiply them (Schwab *et al.* 1979). A useful feature of Vroom's theory is that it draws attention to the role of expectations and to the attempts by employees to predict outcomes from their own behaviours at work. The theory pays little attention to why an individual values or does not value particular outcomes. No concepts of need are evoked by Vroom to handle this issue, as his theory might if it were to address issues of content as well as process. There are obvious difficulties for managers in establishing a system of motivation based on Vroom's theory. Taxation, inflation, social welfare inputs and the career development point attained by individuals will all impact on whether or not an outcome is seen as desirable or attainable. These are all factors that are embedded in systems that are outside the control of any employing organization.

However, managers might wish to consider the total framework of employment opportunities in the general light of Vroom's theory. How attainable is a given level of salary, the lifestyle that comes with it, a given level of promotion and so on? Should recruitment and training programmes reflect the realities of choice patterns that might flow from such considerations?

Fairness

Adams (1965) provided social psychology with the most frequently cited proposition on what came to be called equity theory. The theory focuses on the cognitive processes which govern a person's decision whether or not to expend effort. The theory proposes that individuals evaluate their relationships with others by assessing the ratio of their outcomes from and inputs to the relationship against the outcome/input ratio of a comparison other. If the outcome/input ratio of the individual and comparison other are perceived to be unequal, then inequity exists. The greater the inequity the individual perceives (in the form of either over-reward or under-reward), the more psychological distress the individual feels. The greater the distress an individual feels, the harder he or she will work to restore equity. People restore equity by altering or cognitively distorting inputs or outcomes, acting on or changing the comparison other or terminating the relationship. The aim is to maintain the same balance between their contributions and rewards as that experienced by a salient comparison person or group. The process involved is said by Adams to be motivating.

Laboratory experiments have generally provided support for equity theory. Because rewards and availability of comparison others are controlled by the experimenter, the only way in which people participating in the experiment can establish equity is to increase or decrease the quantity or quality of their work. In the world beyond the laboratory, the range of options and choices is much greater, so the processes involved are more complicated. This makes it difficult to make predictions and has led some psychologists to doubt whether people are attempting to establish equity at all or, if they are, whether they construe equity wholly in terms of outcome rather than as a ratio between input and output (Birnbaum 1983).

There are several variations on conceptions of fairness. Deutsch (1975), for example has suggested that the rules of equality (all individuals should receive equal rewards, regardless of inputs) and of need (rewards should be distributed on the basis of relative need) will influence perceptions of fairness. Research suggests that although rules of equity and need are used by people, the rules become more salient when they appear to be violated (Martin 1993). Thibaut and Walker (1975) found that procedures were perceived to be fairer when the individual had a say in the process. Leventhal (1980) identified a number of procedural rules that had to be satisfied for a procedure to be considered fair: decisions should be made consistently, ethically, without personal bias and using as much accurate information as possible.

Decisions should also have the capacity to be modified if they are to be perceived as fair. Similar rules have been found to be important in situations of performance and other appraisals. Greenberg (1986) focuses on the fairness of the behaviour of the decision-makers, which is termed interactional justice. Interactional justice has two components: first, the provision of an explanation for the decision, which has been shown to reduce the negative consequences of an unfavourable decision; second, the interpersonal treatment received by the individual during the process, which can include respect, rudeness and invasion of privacy. There are obvious lessons for the management of people in this study. If we run them past the description provided by Dennis Johnson of his factory work we can infer a profound sense of injustice. He provides us with no information on the management line on 'clocking-in' or on the management of the boredom of the work he has to undertake, and we can be fairly sure that he does not have his opinion on it sampled in any other way than by writing an essay. Could his work have been less soul-destroying had he been asked or had matters explained more frequently, or would that simply have been seen as being patronizing? The work had to be done, despite its managerial presentation, or despite the lack of presentation.

Goal setting

Ed Locke and co-workers (1981: 126) tell us that 'A goal is what an individual is trying to accomplish; it is the object or aim of an action. The concept is similar in meaning to the concepts of purpose and intent.' The characteristics of a goal and attitudes towards it are thought to be influenced by incentives, self-perceptions and the manner in which the goals are set. In turn, those goal characteristics and attitudes are thought to determine behavioural strategies, which lead to performance within the constraints of ability. Feedback is thought to be essential to the further refinement of behavioural strategies. Difficult goals lead to higher performance than easy goals, provided they have been accepted by the person trying to achieve them as being attainable. This follows from the proposition that people direct their behaviour towards goal achievement, so that difficult goals produce more effective behaviour than easy ones.

Specific goals lead to higher performance than general goals such as 'do your best'. Specific goals seem to create a precise intention, which in turn helps the person to shape his or her behaviour with precision. Feedback is essential if the full performance benefits of setting difficult and specific goals are to be achieved. Besides providing information on achievement, feedback is also seen by Locke to have motivating properties. Hollenbeck and Klein (1987) focus their attention on the concept of goal commitment, which they define as the determination to try for a goal, which implies unwillingness to reduce or to abandon it.

Participation

Hollenbeck and Klein distinguish between goal commitment and goal acceptance, the latter referring just to the use of a goal as a point of reference. This raises the issue as to whether participation in the setting of goals is important. Latham *et al.* (1988), working in the United States, consistently found no effect of participation on performance, but Erez, who worked mainly in Israel, consistently found that participation in goal setting enhanced greater goal commitment (and sometimes performance) than simply assigning goals. John Arnold *et al.* (1991), in reporting these findings, draws attention to a collaboration between the two research groups, as well as with Locke himself. The manner of participation seems to be the defining principle. If goals are 'sold' by way of encouraging people to believe that they are attainable rather than being simply assigned to them, commitment is much higher. Feedback and information exchange increases the accuracy with which information is transmitted. This accuracy can be directly transmitted into expectancy theory. Supposedly, through participation, the participant should come to know which behaviours are likely to be rewarded and which are not. The effort–performance relationship should be clearer and potentially higher in magnitude under a participative system. According to Mitchell (1979), a further way in which participation may directly influence the components of expectancy theory is through the values that workers have for organizational outcomes.

Through the process of participation, employees may be able to help to set work standards, negotiate on working conditions and influence the reward structure. They would therefore ascribe higher valences to the outcomes that are contingent on their efforts. Of course, most jobs have conflicting goals, particularly, it seems, with the increased emphasis being placed on performance monitoring and the various schemes intended to assign rights to particular sets of expectations on the part of the client, and this may undermine goal setting. The goals of individuals and of groups may result in there being different priorities. One task for managers is to attempt the alignment of goals at an individual and group level with those expected by the organization itself. If this was done with clarity and sensitivity, then the cognitive processes involved in aligning individual with organizational goals would probably be quite staggering in their motivational properties. However, we have yet to see an adequate evaluation of the entire process of goal setting across its full organizational range. This is bound to create problems for the manager who might wish to apply these findings if the belief is that there ought to be a direct relationship between findings and application.

Printing, at least in the days in which I had involvement, was never so impoverished a working environment. It had scope for creativity and for autonomy, for self-management, for the expression of tradition, for social support and for collegiality. In many ways, modern universities fare less favourably on many of these dimensions! So Dennis Johnson's trauma was not inevitable – both his cigarette manufacturing and my printing took place within the confines of a factory.

Motivational systems theory: an integrated approach

In opening an integrative approach to motivation Martin Ford tells us that 'A brief review of the history of scholarly work on motivation reveals numerous obstacles to the application of motivation theory and research to real world problems ... The most fundamental of these obstacles is an "identity crisis" centring on the problem of how to define and delimit the field of motivation' (Ford 1992: 5–6). Ford asserts that what is needed is a clear, coherent and comprehensive conceptualization of motivation that can retain the detail and precision of specialized theories and can also integrate a range of mini-theories into a broader theory focusing on the basic substance and overall organization of motivational patterns.

Such a theory also needs to be embedded within an even larger framework that can specify how motivational patterns operate as one of several kinds of factors influencing the whole-person-in-context. Ford offers motivational systems theory as being designed to meet these criteria. Summarizing such an all-encompassing approach is difficult, but fortunately Ford offers assistance. He takes the behaviour episode as the basic unit of functioning. A behaviour episode is a context-specific, goal-directed pattern of behaviour that unfolds over time until three conditions are met: (a) the goal is accomplished or accomplished 'well enough'; (b) the person's attention is pre-empted by some internal or external event, and another goal takes precedence (at least temporarily); or (c) the goal is evaluated as unattainable, at least for the time being. There are various forms of episode. The first is an instrumental episode. Here, people may be engaged in some motor or communicative activity ('output' designed to influence the environment in which they are active). They seek feedback information ('input') from that environment about the results of that activity. In an observational episode, the person is actively seeking relevant informational 'input' from the environment about someone else's instrumental activity. In a thinking episode, both the output and the input processes associated with instrumental activity are inhibited, and no effort is made either to influence or to watch others influence the environment. The purpose of the thinking episode is to experience, enjoy or try to improve the information in a person's repertoire or to construct a plan for future action from such information. People are said by Ford to guide their behaviour in new episodes using behaviour episode schemata. These are internal representations of sets of related experiences, including episodes that have been only imagined or observed.

In any behaviour episode, the person must have the motivation needed to initiate and maintain activity until the goal directing the episode is attained. The person must have the skill needed to construct and execute a pattern of activity that will produce the desired consequence. The person's biological structure and functioning must be able to support the operation of the motivation and skill components. The person must have the cooperation of a responsive environment that will facilitate, or at least not excessively impede, progress towards the goal. Effective functioning requires a motivated, skilful person whose biological and behavioural capabilities support relevant interactions with an environment that has the informational and material properties and resources needed to facilitate (or at least permit) goal attainment. If any of these components is missing or inadequate, achievements will be limited and competence development will be thwarted. Motivation is a psychological, future-oriented (anticipatory) and evaluative (rather than instrumental) phenomenon. Motivation is defined within Ford's systems theory as the organized patterning of an individual's personal goals, emotional arousal processes and personal agency beliefs. Personal goals are thoughts about desired (or undesired) states or outcomes that one would like to achieve (or avoid). Goal evaluation processes are cognitive evaluations of the goals being pursued or contemplated in terms of their continuing or potential relevance or priority. Goals play a leadership role in motivational patterns by defining their content and direction. When goals are conceived of in sufficiently concrete terms, they can define a precise 'target' that an individual or group can try to 'hit' or approach with goal seeking efforts. Moreover, if the target is set at an optimally challenging level of difficulty – that is, at a level that is 'hard' but attainable – progress and continuing motivation are likely to be maximized (assuming an adequate level of feedback). Goal orientations can have pervasive effects on motivation, achievement and competence development. The system specifies four criteria that may be used in the psychological evaluation process as a means of arriving at priorities in the context of a specific behaviour episode: first, goal relevance (what goals are meaningful or appropriate in a particular context); second, goal importance (to what extent are the relevant goals in a particular context personally significant to the individual; third, goal attainability, in other words the personal agency beliefs; fourth, the emotional salience of the actions and consequences associated with pursuing and achieving the goal. 'The motivational burden tends to shift from goals to personal agency beliefs and emotions once a commitment has been made to pursue a goal' (Ford 1992: 250). Personal agency beliefs are evaluative thoughts comparing a desired consequence, such as some goal, and an anticipated consequence, such as what the person expects to happen if he or she pursues that goal. Personal agency beliefs then have no meaning or functional significance if that goal is not active or is of no value to the individual. All the motivational system theory principles for motivating people are intended in terms of the general conception that facilitation, not control, should be the guiding idea.

Managers in motivational system theory

Even when the manager is in a position of power or authority, the strategy of trying to motivate people through direct control of a person's actions – as opposed to indirect facilitation of his or her goals, emotions and personal agency beliefs – should be reserved, according to Ford, for situations in which swift attainment of a goal is urgent and no other means are available. Because short-term motivational gains often come at the expense of longer-term motivational patterns, the manager should consider whether efforts to promote a particular achievement would also facilitate the development of an individual's competence to deal with similar situations in the future.

Rather than being seen as a problem, multiple goals are seen as a positive advantage in Ford's approach. He sees them as anchoring the strongest motivational patterns. So the manager should try to organize, design or modify tasks, activities and experiences so that they afford the attainment of as many different goals as possible.

Even in cases where this strategy fails to activate a strong motivational pattern directed by multiple goals, it may provide some motivational insurance against the possibility that no relevant goal will be activated. When multiple goals are aligned within and between people, motivation is strong and productivity is high. Motivation is facilitated by aligning proximal and distal goals in such a way that attention is focused on immediate subgoals that signify progress towards meaningful long-term goals. Motivation is maximized under conditions of 'optimal challenge' – conditions in which standards for goal attainment are difficult given the person's current level of expertise, but still attainable with vigorous or persistent effort. Under such circumstances, successes are unusually satisfying and exciting in terms of emotional arousal and highly empowering in terms of personal agency beliefs. Personal agency beliefs can help to compensate for weaknesses in the non-motivational parts of the system by facilitating efforts to increase skills or seek out responsive aspects of the environment. In the long run, though, positive capability and context beliefs are difficult to maintain in the absence of skills and a truly responsive environment. The emphasis then needs to be on the facilitation of motivational patterns characterized by 'flexible optim-ism', by which Ford – taking the point from Seligman – means optimism that is grounded in but not overly constrained by the current reality. To achieve qualitative changes in motivational patterns, a series of incremental change experiences has to be designed to produce significant additive effects.

Finally, the motivational system theory reminds us that people are think-ing, feeling, self-directed human beings with a very personal repertoire of goals, emotions and self-referent beliefs that must be treated with respect and care if efforts to facilitate desired motivational patterns and the develop-ment of competence are to succeed.

Evaluating motivational systems theory

Ford's theory takes us well beyond the rather narrow confines of those moti-vational theories currently on offer in standard textbooks. Ford's theory is very much more complex than the theories of Maslow, Vroom, Adams and Locke, although aspects of each of them are to greater or lesser extents incorporated within Ford's analysis. The evidence is carefully accumulated from a wide range of sources, the majority of them having their base in clini-cal and educational settings. Although Ford makes frequent reference to industrial and commercial studies of motivation, he makes no distinction between work derived from different contexts. This adds to the richness of the approach and provides a much fuller picture of motivational processes. Can managers in industrial, service and commercial contexts act as if they were clinicians or educationalists with respect to motivation? Can they develop the empathetic and listening skills of clinicians and the supportive skills of educationalists, in addition to those that they possess as managers of business? The dominant characteristic of management as an activity is control. Johnson and Gill (1993) quote Storey (1983), who argues that despite contrasting approaches, a manager's 'quintessential role', especially when dealing with labour, is that of control: 'the incessant though tactical rather than "strategic" day-to-day campaign to render labour tractable'. They write themselves:

> Control means making potential labour power real, and it also entails controlling and manipulating the non-human factors that make this power possible. If managerial work is concerned with controlling human resources, then all managers will have to cope with the vagaries of organizational behaviour and with their subordinates. Therefore, all managers must be able to understand and predict how humans behave in organizations.
>
> (Johnson and Gill 1993)

These tactics and strategies seem to run quite counter to the ethos of clinical values in developing motivational systems. Perhaps there needs to be a shift towards the clinical in management strategies. Otherwise, the tendency will be for all organizations to function in ways that are fundamentally unhealthy and stressful (McHugh 1996).

Learning, the business of education, perhaps runs closer to the managerial philosophy of some corporations. Learning so as to avoid error has for some time been a concern of organizational development practitioners (Argyris 1982, 1992). Knowledge enhances competitiveness when it becomes the keystone to transformations of structure and culture. (Wikstrom and Normann 1994). Knowledge and information are becoming the stuff of the new business, and in the context the role of management is to provide employees with a conceptual framework that helps them to make sense of such information (Starkey 1996). So the educative function may become increasingly important for managers. What is clear is that management as an activity might well be impelled to move towards a more person-centred dynamic than the literatures on management currently suggest it is.

Ford's motivational systems theory is very much more social in its theoretical focus than are many other motivational theories in psychology. Although we may see social factors imposing on Maslow's and Vroom's approaches, they do so almost in a metaphysical way. There is very little specificity in Maslow's notion of self-actualization, and in Vroom the social influences on valence have the apparent status of unexplained variance. Adams's theory could well qualify for the opprobrium of Henri Tajfel, who referred in a landmark essay to 'experiments in a vacuum' – experiments in which people were asked to respond to totally rigged situations (Tajfel 1981). This is despite the fact that equity theory has played a prominent part in social psychological theorizing.

Locke's theory is not fully supported by empirical work, and is unclear on crucial organizational points – perhaps because his fulcrums are the internally derived processes of cognition. Ford's theory takes multiple perspectives: cognitive and social, developmental and biological. His approach is usefully integrative as well as thoroughly supported empirically. The remaining difficulty is establishing whether the fact that it has taken support from studies conducted across a range of contexts impacts on the ultimate utility of the approach if it is to be acted upon by managers seeking to develop a motivational programme with their employees. What is clear is that Ford's motivational systems theory comes close to being adequate in terms of its explanatory power. None of the other theories of motivation reviewed here, with the possible exception of Locke's, comes remotely near to explaining satisfactorily why, still less how, we might be motivated by the factors they describe. Psychology makes a fundamental error if it adopts the position that managers need oversimple models of what are actually extremely complex processes. The usual proposition is that managers are busy and do not have time, but this ought not then to lead to the continual advancement of inadequate conceptualizations. There is too much pressure on managers already to have them accept the quick fix. Science has to be reflective, evaluative and continually adding to the sum of our knowledge. It does no one favours, least of all itself, if it avoids the difficulties involved in effectively delivering adequate understanding to managers and to the rest of us. Adequacy presents its own problems, largely those of complexity. For managers to begin to work with Ford's motivational systems theory there has to be not just a culture shift but also a shift in value and training. While the culture shift may already be under way, values and certainly training have not yet moved to adopt a more complex approach, such as that of Ford. Those of us concerned with work and organizational psychology who have extensive memories will recognize the similarity between Ford's motivational systems theory and a meta-analysis produced by Peter Warr in 1976. Most of the central tenets of Ford's thesis were anticipated by Warr's paper. While this is encouraging in terms of agreement on what constitute the most important points for motivation, it is discouraging to realize how long change can take to become evident in both theory and practice. One important point in Warr's paper that has not been taken up by organizational change theorists is that of different levels of action and explanation in both motivation and organizational action, this despite the fact that, as he points out, there can be no objection in principle to psychology attempting to relate specific actions of individuals to specific processes within organizational settings. Managers must wonder why this has not become the central preoccupation of behaviour in organizations' programmes.

The psychological contract

Makin *et al.* (1996) offer an approach to employer–employee relations based on the psychological contract. The orientation of the psychological contract is primarily motivational, in that it focuses on reward for extra effort. Makin *et al.* contrast the psychological contract with the economic, where the content focus is money, as well as the terms and conditions of work. They introduce the concept of the psychological contract as having been formulated by Argyris and refined by the work of Schein (1980).

Schein's definition of the psychological contract is 'an unwritten set of expectations operating at all times between every member of an organization and the various managers and others in that organization'. The expectations can, as these authors indicate, be concerned with economic issues such as the pay to be received in return for the work done. However, the essence of the psychological, as opposed to the economic, contract is that the expectations concern non-tangible, psychological issues such as the relations between individuals at work. As Makin *et al.* point out, Rousseau and her co-workers (Robinson and Rousseau 1994) have suggested that the psychological contract is characterized not only by expectations but also by 'promissory and reciprocal obligations'. Rousseau apparently sees these as being stronger than expectations, so that when the obligations are broken they produce more emotional and extreme reactions than when weaker expectations are broken. Broken expectation produces feelings of disappointment. Broken obligations lead to feelings of anger and a reassessment of the individual's relationship with the organization.

The psychological contract is far from being clear-cut, but might be concerned with 'organizational citizenship', which in turn could be construed by some as covering the expectation that there is a right to be consulted before there is any change in working practices, such as the restructuring of work or the implementation of a 'no smoking' policy. In return, workers might be willing to work extra hours if the load suddenly increases, or speak well of the organization in conversation with others, and support its aims and objectives. Although the psychological contract is often subjective and implicit, it can, Makin *et al.* point out, have elements that are explicit at some points. So it is not unusual for organizations to include promises such as tenure or progression and development to new recruits (from personal experience I would advise everyone to have such promises put in writing – using blood if this can be extracted!). 'Past behaviours of organizations are often used as a basis for expectation. Long-service awards are often used as a basis for expectations, whereas general expectations of "fair and equitable treatment" may be taken for granted, by one or both parties' (Makin *et al.* 1996: 7). Breaches of the psychological contract usually have serious consequences, since they lead to a reassessment of the broader contract of employment, particularly in transactional aspects such as pay and tangible conditions. In fact, there is evidence that violation is the norm rather than the exception, with 59 per cent of the respondents in a study reporting that their employer had violated the contract. There were individuals who also indicated that the employer had lived up to obligations. Likewise, there were individuals who indicated that the contract had not been violated even though they reported that the employer's obligations had not been fulfilled. It appears that there had been some attempt at resolving disputes, and this could account for the discrepancies (Robinson and Rousseau 1994). For these reasons, Makin *et al.* believe that the psychological contract should be made more open and more specific than is often the case. They outline Claude Steiner's requirements for an effective contract. Mutual consent is the first requirement. Both parties must agree. Terms must be negotiated, not imposed. There must be valid consideration, by which the legal sense of the term is implied, so as to include money and other forms of recompense. Competency means that the appropriate skills are employed, so that both sides of the contract may be delivered.

Finally, the contract must be legal and have an appropriate code of ethics. Thinking of these issues contractually is intended to provide a mechanism for the active involvement of the parties in the process. At best, though, the psychological contract is highly subjective and dynamic, and so not a good basis for legalistic transaction. The concept of the psychological contract has resonance with social change. During times of high unemployment, job insecurity, technical change and organizational restructuring, people's expectations of employment are certain to vary a great deal. The notion of the psychological contract has to be worked on by both individuals and by organizations. The notion will also benefit from further testing in research settings.

The social psychology of payment

It may surprise many readers that this far into a discussion of motivation no mention has been made of pay. That is usually the first factor the new recruit to a position seeks to settle – conditions follow later in the list of priorities. Pay and its means of determination carry the weight of the legal form of the employment contract. Payment has become embedded in administrative and organizational issues, away from the considerations of the psychological contract.

The earliest systematic effort to study the relation of pay and reward to productivity dates from the scientific management movement around the early years of the twentieth century. During this period, Frederick Taylor and his colleagues emphasized the use of piece-rate incentive systems for blue-collar workers, feeling that these systems provided the most efficient way to simultaneously maximize both productivity and worker income. Taylor saw such systems, when used in conjunction with his work design techniques, as being the fairest for both the organization and its employees.

Scientific management concepts had their origins in the 'economic man' assumption that people work only, or principally, for money. According to this line of reasoning, efforts to increase productivity meant using money as the basic incentive. It has been argued that the concentration on non-psychological aspects of motivation led to the demise of the scientific management approach (Lawler 1971; Schein 1972). Whether these approaches actually disappeared completely I personally doubt. What is clear is that human relations theorists, building on the work of the Hawthorne studies of the 1930s, were able to gain acceptance for their propositions of 'social man' because scientific management had focused on apparently antithetical assumptions. They contended that people in work settings were generally motivated by group forces, such as group pressures, social relations and organizational structure. Pay was seen as less important.

According to Opsahl and Dunnette (1966), there are at least five explanations of the role of money in motivation. Money acts as a generalized conditioned reinforcer, since it is repeatedly paired with primary reinforcers.

This view of the role of money is consistent with advocates of behaviour modification. Others suggest that money is a conditioned incentive. That is, it is felt by some that the repeated pairing of money with primary incentives helps to establish a new learned drive for money. A third explanation for the role of money in employee motivation focuses on anxiety. Specifically, it is suggested that people learn to become anxious in the presence of a variety of cues that signify an absence of money. Such cues include being told 'That it costs too much money' or 'We can't afford that'. Such cues lead to feelings of anxiety (and perhaps of insecurity) which money can satisfy. A fourth category of explanation for the role of money comes from Hertzberg's two-factor theory (Hertzberg 1966). In this model, it is suggested that the absence of money causes dissatisfaction, although the presence of money does not satisfy. It merely eliminates the source of dissatisfaction and brings people to a neutral state of satisfaction.

Finally, according to expectancy theory, money can serve as an instrument for gaining other desired outcomes (taking a holiday, for example). Money acquires value for an individual to the extent that it can help to fulfil these other desires and needs. Equity theory also provides relevant conceptualizations of the effects of payment on motivation in considering under- and over-reward as sources of input to the equity calculation. The threshold for inequity would, Adams (1965) writes, 'be higher presumably in cases of over-reward, for a certain amount of incongruity in these cases can be rationalized as "good fortune" without attendant discomfort'. In his work on pay differentials, Jacques (1961: 26) notes that in instances of undercompensation, British workers paid 10 per cent less than the equitable level show 'an active sense of grievance, complaints, or the desire to complain, and, if no redress is given, an active desire to change jobs, or to take action'. He states further, 'The results suggest that it is not necessarily the case that each one is simply out to get as much as he can for his work. There appear to be equally strong desires that each one should earn the right amount – a fair and reasonable amount relative to others.' Adams has no doubt that comparisons with other people in terms of the question 'Am I being paid fairly?' produce the same feelings of cognitive discomfort as comparisons on other social dimensions if the internal computation produces the answer 'no'. There is, as Edward Lawler tells us, considerable research evidence

> that under certain conditions pay can be used to motivate good performance. The required conditions are deceptively simple in the sense that establishing the conditions is easier said than done. Theory and research suggest that for a pay plan to motivate people it must (1) create a belief among employees that good performance will lead to high pay, (2) contribute to the importance of pay, (3) minimize the perceived negative consequences of performing well, and (4) create conditions

such that positive outcomes other than pay will be seen to be related to good performance.

(Lawler 1971)

Management and payment systems

Beer *et al.* (1984: 116), in their seminal text on HRM, write: 'Despite the enormous amount spent on wages, commission, cost of living increases, bonuses, and stock options, many studies have shown that in most organizations 50 per cent or more of employees are dissatisfied with pay, and that this percentage is increasing.' Beer and his colleagues see the source of the problem on pay as being

a contradiction between the theory of pay systems and the reality of pay practice. Research has shown that employees are more satisfied with pay when it is based on performance . . . The belief in pay for performance is undoubtedly rooted in national culture, which stresses individualism. Yet there is considerable evidence that in many organizations pay is not based on performance. For example, a survey of Fortune 500 companies showed that 42 percent used no formal system for assessing the performance of professional and technical personnel, while 41 percent used single rate compensation systems for blue-collar workers so that wage increases could not be based in individual performance but only on general increases, job promotions, or on subjective performance judgements. Without a formal appraisal system it is inevitable that employees would question the equity of pay decisions. The gap between espoused beliefs of managers and employees and actual practices undoubtedly causes some of the general dissatisfaction with pay.

(Beer *et al.* 1984: 116–17)

Rosbeth Moss Kanter holds strong views on pay, as she does on most things.

Old ideas about pay are bankrupt. The post-entrepreneurial agenda cannot be accomplished without rethinking matters of money. Innovations in compensation are necessary to succeed at the doing-morewith-less balancing act: simultaneously reducing capacities, lowering fixed costs and encouraging new ideas. In the post-entrepreneurial corporation, pay must more nearly match contribution. Status, not contribution, was the traditional basis for the numbers on people's paychecks. The paycheck was the critical element in reinforcing corporacy. Pay was cemented to hierarchical position, guaranteed regardless of performance. But this system does not square well with the new business realities. It burdens the company with weighty fixed obligations while failing to encourage or reward entrepreneurial behaviour. The importance of money is not absolute but relative; it often lies not in the amount but in how the amount was arrived at. Money represents both tangible value and a signal of importance.

(Kanter 1989: 230–2)

Once more, the sensitivity of administration seems to outweigh the objective outcome in terms of the salience of individual perceptions. In pay administration, sensitivity is clearly difficult to achieve. If pay is openly linked to performance through transparent and observable policy, then, as Beer *et al.* point out, companies are likely to attract those who have high expressed needs for money. The company then becomes locked into a vicious cycle that is somewhat of its own making. One alternative to hierarchically justified pay increases is skill-based pay.

Person- or skill-based evaluation systems base a person's salary on his or her abilities. Pay ranges are arranged in a hierarchy of steps from the least skilled to the most skilled. People come in at the entry grade and progress on the skill-base ladder after they have demonstrated competence at the next level. The system is designed to encourage the development of new skills and to allow for greater flexibility in moving people from one job to another and in introducing new technology. The challenge to management working with this system is to utilize the skills of people to the full rather than offer them limited projects. The scheme rests on the adequacy of skill-based job evaluation, which has to be capable of providing measurable and quantifiable comparisons for each and every level of skill, which, if used effectively, can communicate to employees a concern for their development (Beer *et al.* 1984). The approach is best used, according to Beer *et al.*, as a means of supporting training and development programmes rather than having the payment system lead the philosophy. Problems of equity are raised when people reach the top of the skills ladder and have no further progression available, as well as when comparisons are made between the skill-based systems and more traditional jobs. The systems are well suited for situations in which the organization has a high level of skill requirement and is undergoing constant change. According to research conducted by the American Compensation Association, it takes an average of three years for a worker to maximize his or her salary in a skill-based system. As Sparrow (1994) points out, the transition to a skill-based system is difficult, particularly when the traditional system maintains a small number of highly paid people with just a small range of important skills. The options for management are to reduce the level of pay, provide a period when others acquire new skills and catch up, or hold the base constant while offering a one-off payment for each new skill acquired until others catch up.

The issues for skill-based payment systems are political and administrative rather than fundamentally psychological, although managers must expect employees to make social comparisons and to feel inequity if the process of installation and maintenance of system is not managed adequately. The challenges are to managers, who are cautioned by advocates of skill-based systems not to see the approach as being a quick fix or a once and for all solution to the problem of pay. The maintenance of a skill-based system will also demand a considerable level of knowledge of the labour market and of the rates that particular skills are able to attract. In the world of payment systems, the search for external sources of similarity is as important as the process of internal comparison. Imbalance in either process may be expected to impact on employee behaviour in terms of motivation through to termination of employment. Payment systems will need constant monitoring and management. Kanter completes her review of payment systems, all of which she sees as having a downside as well as generally some benefits, by saying: 'the successful systems will be those that balance the drives for individual achievement with the co-operative effort of the whole corporate team' (Kanter 1989: 266). The balancing of individual motivation with the needs of the organization clearly requires a special kind of management.

Challenges for psychology and the management of motivation

As critical theorists point out (Hollway 1991; Townley 1994), psychology has been remarkably constant in its adherence to the paradigms set for it by the early theorists in motivation. I am concerned that the price for constancy is adequacy and relevance. However, there are new challenges on the horizon. The traditional motivational approaches of psychology and of management are presented in the texts as being little concerned with context. The contexts of the networked society demand careful consideration in terms of the factors that will motivate employees. Development takes on a new meaning. Diversity offers new challenges. Technology offers new opportunities. The networked society's new agenda presents the requirement for a re-examination of motivation in a wholly new context. Payment systems need to take account of the costs of social mobility and come to see compensation in broader terms. There is evidence that chief executive pay is seen in terms of compensation, but little evidence that other groups of employees are so recognized. Payment systems need to take on board the problems created by exclusion, with its implications for citizenship and for the economy. Motivation, as we will see, needs to extend towards lifelong learning and personal skill development. Research is urgently needed on these developments. The networked society will become a nightmare if instrumental approaches to work drive all considerations.

4

Groups, leadership and teams

Castells's thesis is that the rise of the informational economy is characterized by a new organizational logic which is related to the process of technological change – but is not dependent upon it. He argues that this organizational logic manifests itself in different forms in different cultural and institutional contexts. However, it is possible to examine some of the commonalities of organizational arrangements within the networked society (Castells 1997a: 162).

Groups

This chapter explores some of the points of tension between individual and social levels of interaction in groups and teams and sets these against some issues for management. Groups are ubiquitous within organizations. Schein writes, 'Groups of all kinds will always be found in organizations, some formal ones created by deliberate design to do specific jobs, some informal ones created by the needs of people to interact, and some which form simply because of the probability of interaction created by physical proximity, similarity of interests, or other fortuitous factors' (Schein 1980: 149). Not unexpectedly, managers spend a great deal of their time working with groups that have been formally constituted to perform a particular task. Handy (1985) tells us that, 'On average, managers spend 50 per cent of their working day in one sort of group or another. Senior managers can spend 80 per cent.' He continues: 'Organizations use groups, or teams and committees for the following major purposes:

1 For the distribution of work. To bring together a set of skills, talents, responsibilities, and allocate to them their particular duties.
2 For the management and control of work. To allow work to be

organised and controlled by appropriate individuals with responsibilities for a certain range of work.

3   For problem solving and decision-taking. To bring together a set of skills, talents and responsibilities so that the solution to any problem will have all available capacities applied to it.

4   For information processing. To pass on decisions or information to those who need to know.

5   For information and idea collection. To gather ideas, information or suggestions.

6   For testing and ratifying decisions. To test the validity of a decision taken outside the group, or to ratify such a decision.

7   For co-ordination and liaison. To co-ordinate problems and tasks between functions and divisions.

8   For increased commitment and involvement. To allow and encourage individuals to get involved in the plans and activities of the organisation.

9   For negotiation or conflict resolution. To resolve a dispute or argument between levels, divisions or functions.

10 For inquest or inquiry into the past' (Handy 1985: 155–6).

Handy points out that some of these functions may be combined or may overlap. Groups will need to behave differently and need to be managed differently according to each of these functions, so that committee work, for example, is quite different from negotiating in terms of the ways interaction proceeds. How do those writing for managers portray the importance of groups? Drucker writes:

The human being works in groups and he forms groups to work. And a group, no matter how formed or why soon focuses on a task. Group relations influence the task; the task in turn influences personal relations within the group. At the same time the human being remains an individual. Group and individual must therefore be brought into harmony in the organization of work. This means specifically that the work must always be organized in such a manner that whatever strength, initiative, responsibility and competence there is in individuals becomes a source of strength and performance for the entire group. This is the first principle of organization; indeed, it is practically a definition of the purpose of organization. Nothing is more contrary to the nature of human resource than the common attempt to find the 'average work load' for the 'average worker'. This whole idea is based on a disproven psychology that equated learning speed with learning ability.

It is also based on the belief that the individual worker is more productive the less control he has the less he participates – and that is a complete misunderstanding of the human resource. Above all, the concept of the average work to be performed is inevitably one that considers what any but a physically or mentally handicapped person could do. The man who is just barely normal but who has neither aptitude nor liking for the job becomes the measure of all things, his performance the norm. And human work becomes something that requires neither skill, effort, nor thought, presents no challenge, allows no differentiation between the highly skilled and highly motivated and the near-moron . . . The nature of man demands that the performance of the best, not of the poorest worker should become the goal for all.

(Drucker 1955: 260–1)

Managers and groups

The management writer, Rosemary Stewart, following Homans's (1961) social psychological analysis, makes the important point that, when people work together in organized contexts, they form social relationships within the group and develop their own distinctive ways of getting their work done. This may, as Homans indicates, work for or against management objectives. Stewart writes:

> People who work in close contact with each other for any length of time are likely to become a social group. They are then more than a collection of individuals who happen to be working together and they acquire a sense of identity as a group, in which some people are inside and others outside. There may be several social groups within one work group and some individuals who do not belong to a group. The social group is likely to have a sense of like-mindedness among its members and to agree on many subjects of immediate importance to them. This tendency for people who work together to develop social groups has important implications for management as it can materially assist or considerably handicap management objectives. A number of studies have shown that enthusiasm for work is much greater where group affiliations have been built up, provided the aims of the group do not run counter to those of management. People enjoy their work more, and are less likely to be absent from work, because they become part of a social group in which they are important as a person.
>
> Informal groups within the formal organization can also work against management aims. Numerous research projects have shown that, even with an incentive scheme, workers will not necessarily aim at the highest output they can achieve. Instead a group of workers may establish their own output norm which may well be considerably less than that which could be maintained by the fastest worker, and even less than that of the average worker. The group may establish quite elaborate procedures for ensuring that this norm is obtained but not

exceeded. As well, it may apply various forms of pressure to ensure that no individual exceeds the norm. Hence the informal group will have its own aims which may support or oppose management aims . . . But it may also be developed by people to adjust the formal organization to the needs of the situation. Then it can be most useful . . . Informal organization adjusts to the strengths and weaknesses of people; by so doing it can increase efficiency.

(Stewart 1967: 58–63)

Homans makes the important observation that as groups become more socially cohesive they develop norms that may restrict or enhance productivity. However, despite their importance to the understanding of organizations as well as to managers, the literature is not exactly overwhelmed with explorations of groups at work. The current literature is much more concerned with teams, although often the term is used in a way that does not distinguish it from groups, and with leadership, which clearly relates to group processes. When groups are written about in management literature, the substance of the message is little different from that which we might find in the social psychological literature, even though we might, as with the examples of Drucker and Stewart, find that the emphasis if not the structuring of the message varies somewhat. There are at least three reasons for this lack of discussion.

1 The effects of social change.
2 The synthesis of the professionalization of management as an activity and as a body of knowledge.
3 Movements within the discipline of social psychology.

I want to explore each of these reasons in turn.

Social change and the analysis of groups and organizations

Viewed against the long-term perspectives of history, social change has impacted on management very much more than can be appreciated from reading texts such as Stewart's or Roethlisberger and Dickson's (1939) seminal Hawthorne studies. Hill tells us that management as we know it is a comparatively recent phenomenon, and that workers in organizations previously controlled their own work. In the early days of industrialization, work seemed to be organized in a way that appears relatively seamless. Groups were not, at this point, directly a management problem:

industrialisation and factory production were well established in Great Britain and the United States long before the emergence of management as a distinct system of control and separate social stratum. Indeed, the seeds of modern management were established only in the last two decades of the nineteenth century, and came to fruition in the early twentieth, first in the US and more slowly in Britain.

The essential characteristic of work control systems and employment in many late-nineteenth century factories was the delegation of what are now regarded as managerial responsibilities to other groups. This created systems of indirect control and employment, and left factory owners or managers to concentrate on other aspects of running the enterprises, notably finance and marketing.

(Hill 1981: 17)

Hill quotes Hobsbawm, who tells us that 'Capitalism in its early stages expands, and to some extent operates, not so much by directly subordinating large bodies of workers to employers, but by subcontracting exploitation and management' (Hobsbawm 1964: 297). Hill continues, 'Subcontracting of management was the typical organizational form in British and American factories prior to 1900. In subcontracting, skilled men or foremen were responsible for the co-ordination of production activities and the direction of labour' (Hill 1981: 17).

The nature of the subcontracting system varied considerably. Sometimes owners sublet premises to others, who then employed others to do particular jobs at specified prices. These employees often took complete control of the work themselves. Sometimes skilled men hired their own helpers and paid them out of their own wages, or were themselves paid piece rates and supervised unskilled labour on time rates. Craftsmen had relatively fewer managerial functions in these circumstances: they worked under foremen, were given set amounts of raw materials, had a minor role in the cost-accounting system and organized a small number of helpers. Hill tells us that this form of work control was widely spread throughout British and American industry and continued into the early years of the twentieth century. Given that workers had very considerable discretion over wide ranges of their work at least up until the period immediately prior to that covered by the Roethlisberger and Dickson studies, it is not surprising that the Hawthorne workers maintained control over much of their work. Indeed, in many industries, as I experienced for myself in printing, workers maintained considerable control over large elements of their work until the late twentieth century, when computing techniques intruded deep into the decision processes and moved discretion away from the point of production. Judged in its historical context, the pressure towards groups' norms of production makes considerable sense. Viewed as context-free, the behaviour of work groups appears irrational and against management interests. Once established in the framework of explanation, the empirical sciences concerned to advance our understanding of work have built on the initial assumptions rather than strived to move the paradigm. Groups have been regarded as being oppositional, at least in part, or they have not been regarded at all in the management and social literature of work. Morgan (1986) draws attention to the term 'counterorganizations', which was used by John Kenneth Galbraith to refer to groups of people who respond to the building of a concentration of power in relatively few hands by coordinating their actions within a rival power block. This analysis puts trade unions in a situation in which they are able to act as a check on management in industries where there is a high degree of industrial concentration.

The fact that people may wish to join trade unions as a means of rationally expressing collective values seems to have escaped this form of analysis. Rather, it is proposed that trade unions are a means of influencing a structure where one is not part of the established power structure. Similarly, the notion that management itself is a collective activity seems not to occur to authors adopting this stance.

The professional development of management

The oppositional view of groups takes on greater salience when the social changes that have impacted on the organization of work over the past century are taken into account. Hill tells us that there were several forces of change in the late nineteenth and early twentieth centuries that led to the replacement of subcontracted and delegated management by the system of control as we broadly know it today. First, technological change outstripped the capacity of traditional craftsmen to organize production at the scale, and pace, that large-scale technologies demand. Second, Hill tells us that the size of the workforce itself increased dramatically at the end of the nineteenth century and into the early part of the twentieth century, and that in the USA the increase came from immigrants who had little or no prior experience of industry. The traditional control structures of the workforce could not cope with the change and with the resultant skill shortages that occurred at this time. Hill cites Gutman as saying that 'the continued infusion of prefactory people' (Gutman 1977: 69) into a mature workforce created its own pressures for new forms of work organization and control.

Finally, writes Hill, 'management changed their views about delegation and came to regard the organization of work processes and the direction of labour as functions which they had to control in the interests of maximum profitability. This change of philosophy was particularly associated with the rise of industrial engineers, who felt that the systematic application of engineering principles to factory organisation would create a more rational system' (Hill 1981: 24). Modern management techniques were developed primarily in the USA and were rapidly adopted there, and spread to Britain more slowly.

Scientific management provided the rationale for the integration of the production process.

The work of every workman is fully planned out by the management and each man receives written instructions, describing in detail the task which he is to accomplish, as well as the means to be used in doing the work.

This task specifies not only what is to be done, but how it is to be done and the exact time allowed for doing it . . . Scientific Management consists very largely in preparing for and carrying out these tasks.

(Taylor, quoted in Hill 1981: 26)

Scientific management became, through the political efforts of Taylor him-self, and the adoption of similar techniques by works study engineers such as the Gilbreths and later by Cooley, a 'systematic philosophy of work and the worker' (Drucker 1955: 274), which was disseminated across the Western world by management associations who found the techniques to be sim-plicity itself. It was not that Taylor himself was a social scientist (Rose 1975), simply that he claimed science as being the essence of his procedures. 'Under the new order management must assume heavy burdens. Systematic study of the production process would reveal its "laws": was this not "sci-ence"? Workmen would be selected, trained and paid strictly in line with their ability to perform the new task structure: was this not "science" too?' (Rose 1975: 50). Taylor's approach cried out for a psychological and socio-logical grounding and ultimately failed as a set of techniques for lack of these elements. As Rose tells us, the failure of Taylor's system did not stop it playing an essential and significant role in management philosophy.

Reading authors such as Drucker, it is hard to see what managers might have taken on board except Taylor. 'Although its conclusions have proved dubious, its basic insight is a necessary foundation for thought and work in the field' (Drucker 1955: 274). Hill notes that a recurrent theme in contem-porary British and American managerial thought since the 1920s has been the notion of professionalism.

This has involved the idea that management is a highly technical func-tion which requires appropriate levels of education, training and exper-tise, and that managers have earned their positions of authority and status because they have been recruited on the basis of widely accepted criteria of ability and then trained in a body of managerial knowledge. In addition professionalism has involved a second notion, derived from the advocates of the 'managerial revolution'. This is the idea that man-agers, because they are not the owners of capital, do not ruthlessly pursue profit like old-style owner-managers, but share the service and social responsibility ethics of the traditional professions.

(Hill 1981: 39–40)

Professionalism encourages a unitary view of the organization in which workers cannot be fully trusted and a particular style of intervention is called for by managers. The administration of companies is often then conducted on the basis of low trust and high technical control. Within this general process, it was assumed that management could and should assume the role of disseminators of social harmony in work organizations and this ensured the popularity of the human relations approaches of Mayo and of Roethlisberger and Dickson.

We find Kurt Lewin – regarded by many as being the founding father of group dynamics, and perhaps of social psychology – attempting to demonstrate

> that managers (leaders) through communications (social skills), could manipulate participation (informal organization) to produce a superior group climate (morale), thus enhancing satisfaction (integration) with the group life (social system) and improving performance (output). Applications of these notions in an industrial milieu were achieved first in a series of experiments carried out at the Harwood Manufacturing Company just after the Second World War. The findings supposedly established that if managers involved difficult employees in the planning and execution of technical changes the employees' antagonism to change would be overcome. The title of the best known report of the study, 'Overcoming Resistance to Change', suggests optimism and practicality – and management bias.
>
> (Rose 1975: 163–4)

Human relations and organizations

The human relations movement produced thousands of empirical studies about group motivation, morale and leadership that in turn influenced management practices, including work such as that by Coch and French (1948), which saw participation as being an important means of promoting a climate to stimulate motivation. Perhaps the best known human relations theory was developed by McGregor (1960). His work focused on managers in organizations and their subjective 'theories' or beliefs about motivation. McGregor described two belief systems and their effects on organizations and the people in them. The first theory, called theory X, is based on the belief that workers have an inherent dislike of work, and consequently a lack of concern for organizational objectives. The attainment of organizational goals therefore depends on the strict control of workers. Control, in turn, depends on the use of formal, hierarchical authority, and externally administered rewards and punishments. In McGregor's view, most of classic organization theory seems to have been based on theory X assumptions.

McGregor contrasted theory X beliefs with theory Y, in which the view is held that the limitations of workers are due not to shortcomings in human nature but to a lack of ingenuity on the part of managers, who are often unable to discover and utilize their employees' potential. He believed that the central principle of organization was integration, and could be derived from theory Y. That is, it is the duty of management to create conditions in which the personal goals of workers can be achieved by working towards organizational goals. McGregor set down his assumptions as follows:

Theory X
1 The average human being has an inherent dislike of work and will avoid it if he can.
2 Because of this characteristic of dislike of work, most people must be coerced, controlled, directed or threatened with punishment to get them to put forth adequate effort toward the achievement of organizational objectives.
3 The average human being prefers to be directed, wishes to avoid responsibility, has relatively little ambition, and wants security above all.

Theory Y
1 The expenditure of physical and mental effort in work is as natural as play or rest. The average human being does not inherently dislike work. Depending upon controllable conditions, work may be a source of satisfaction (and will be voluntarily performed) or a source of punishment (and will be avoided if possible).
2 External control and threat of punishment are not the only means for bringing about effort toward organizational objectives. A man will exercise self-direction and self-control in the service of objectives to which he is committed.
3 Commitment to objectives is a function of the rewards associated with their achievement. The most significant of such rewards, e.g., the satisfaction of ego and self-actualization needs, can be direct products of effort directed to organizational objectives.
4 The average human being learns, under proper conditions, not only to accept, but to seek responsibility. Avoidance of responsibility, lack of ambition, and emphasis on security are generally consequences of experience, not inherent human characteristics.
5 The capacity to exercise a relatively high degree of imagination, ingenuity, and creativity in the solution of organizational problems is widely, not narrowly, distributed in the population.
6 Under the conditions of modern industrial life, the intellectual potentialities of the average human being are only partially utilized.

(McGregor 1960: 33–48)

McGregor seems to wish to use his two theories as a means to argue against a particular form of bureaucratic organization and to develop a programme for the enlargement of jobs, participative leadership and decentralization (Rose 1975: 189). Although he suggested that there might be other forms of organization than the two he proposed, he did not ever make them explicit. The theories, though, may act as filtering and giving meaning by managers to employees' behaviour and so may give rise to particular courses of action being followed by managers. Theory X seems still to dominate: indeed, there is evidence that it has now spread deep into the public service sector in Britain, and, together with Taylorism, even as far as its universities (Kirkpatrick and Martinez Lucio 1995; Legge 1995). The development of professional management has progressed over a considerable period.

Henri Fayol, writing around 1916, certainly espoused views that supported the development of a profession of management in the sense that its activities were based on established knowledge that was capable of transmission through education and training and dedicated to general rather than sectional interests. There is always a problematic relationship between knowledge and action, theory and practice, the social sciences and management, and social scientists and managers (Thomas 1993), and this makes the setting of any particular scientific approach alongside the development of management activities within organizations very uncertain. However, many professional groups adopt the view that 'professional activity consists in instrumental problem-solving made rigorous by the application of scientific theory and technique' (Schon 1983), and it is not inconceivable that, given the importance of groups to management and organizations, social psychology might provide the necessary scientific theory and technique.

Unexploited developments in social psychology

Beyond the examples already given, together with many that are like them, social psychology as a scientific discipline has been far less successful than might be expected if this was the endeavour. It could be that, having taken note of McGregor's application of group dynamics, management theory then disregarded all else in social psychology. I wish to argue that there is a great deal of material that managers might find useful within formal social psychology if they were to wish to articulate and understand the processes of organization in which they find themselves. I also want to argue that social psychology has not developed in a way that makes its findings readily accessible to managers. Given the prominence of group approaches to organization and management practices, the careful student might have wished to find far more material. What follows is a summary of some of the more important findings of social psychology in terms of management issues.

Group productivity

Triplett (1898) became interested in the impact of the presence of others after noting that cycle racers always produced superior times if they had a competitor. He also found that children reeled in fishing line more quickly when there were others around than when they were alone. Social conditions were found to facilitate task performance. The results of these early studies were replicated in both animal studies and human studies across a great many tasks, although not in all tasks. Baron *et al.* (1992) report Allport (1924) as finding that social facilitation occurred on tasks such as simple multiplication problems, but that such tasks as writing refutations of Greek epigrams in the presence of others impaired performance. Zajonc (1965) attributed the social facilitation effect to an increase in excitation and arousal in the mere presence of others, which in turn led to the most dominant, well learned, response being likely to occur. So group productivity may vary according to the effect that group membership has upon the abilities of the members comprising it to perform a particular task. The presence of others can be a distraction in some circumstances and for certain tasks, particularly those that require considerable attention and where group members might wish to check their own performance with the performance of other people around them (Sanders *et al.* 1978; Baron *et al.* 1992).

Competition between individuals may be motivating, but it can also be distracting. Some researchers have argued that this distraction can give rise to conflict between the various demands upon our attention, although as Baron *et al.* say, there is not yet a very strong body of research evidence available to support this possibility fully. In many situations, particularly in organizations, people have a shared interest in working together towards some common goal. As Baron *et al.* note, in many ways the early research on group performance paralleled the early work on social facilitation. The simple question, 'which is more productive, groups or individuals?', was set.

A typical problem for experimentation was set by Shaw (1932), who asked both individuals and four-person groups to attempt a series of puzzles such as the one in which three married couples are trying to cross a river. The available boat can carry only three passengers. Only the husbands may row and no husband will allow his wife to be in the presence of any other husband unless he is also present. The solution involves nine moves and involves a sequence in which more than two husbands are taken across together so as to have one able to row back for the remaining wives. The problem turns out to be difficult for people working on their own, whereas most people working in groups were able to solve the problem. Several researchers point out that it is not just the fact that group members catch one another's errors and reject incorrect proposals; it depends on how capable members are of solving the task. Groups with incapable members may underperform a skilled individual.

The superiority of groups over individuals may again depend upon the nature of the task being performed. Tasks requiring considerable precision are likely to be better performed by individuals than by groups. Steiner (1972) reviewed much of the then available literature on group performance and proposed a model based on the central concept of the group's potential productivity, by which he meant the group's maximum possible level of productivity at a task. The model suggests that this depends on two factors: member resources and task demands. Member resources 'include all the relevant knowledge, abilities, skills, or tools possessed by the individual(s) who is attempting to perform the task' (Steiner 1972: 7). What makes a particular resource relevant is the nature of the task – physical strength in a tug of war but not an anagram task (Baron *et al.* 1992). A task's demands encompass several task features, the most fundamental of these being the task performance criterion, or what aspect of performance is being measured – reading for comprehension is quite different from reading for maximum comprehension. Steiner suggests that if the resources of the group and demands of the task are known, the group's potential productivity can be estimated. Continuing with the tug of war example, if the amount of effort each member could put into pulling on the rope was known, the estimate might be the sum of the pulls. However, Steiner points out that it would be rare for the group to achieve 100 per cent efficiency. He called the loss 'process loss', and proposed that actual productivity equals potential productivity minus process loss. Process loss reflects a group's failure to act in the most productive way possible. Steiner suggests that there are two general sources of process loss. Coordination losses occur when group members do not organize their efforts optimally. For example, each member of the tug of war team pulls at different times, so that the force on the rope is diminished. When group members fail to be optimally motivated, motivation losses result. So, if members of the tug-of-war team did not try as hard when working together as when working alone, motivation losses would contribute to process loss. Steiner produced a classificatory system for tasks in group performance situations. Can the task be subdivided into subtasks, each of which can be performed by different individuals?

Tasks which can be, he called divisible; those which cannot, he called unitary. The nature of the performance criteria offers a second classificatory feature. Maximizing tasks make success a function of how much or how rapidly something is done. Optimizing tasks make success a function of achieving some correct or optimal solution, such as in Shaw's experimental tasks. The final task feature in Steiner's classification was how task demands link individual resources to potential group productivity. He identifies four types of unitary task. In a disjunctive task, the group must select the answer or contributions of a single member (that of the most proficient member, it is hoped!). Shaw's experimental problems were of this type. The second category of task is the conjunctive task, in which the group's level of productivity is necessarily that of the least capable member. A group of mountain climbers roped together may progress only at the pace of the slowest member. Additive tasks are those in which the group product is the sum of group member contributions. The tug-of-war task is a good example here. Steiner's fourth category is discretionary tasks, in which group members can combine the individual inputs in any manner they choose.

A jazz band is perhaps the most clear-cut example of a group which has considerable discretion as to how to perform the particular task that is set. The extent to which tasks generated within organizations match the specifications identified by Steiner has yet to be explored systematically. It is likely that different processes throw up different possibilities, so that creative problem-solving in the early phases of design might resemble the discretionary task. Purchasing strategies might be examples of additive tasks. University departments sometimes operate a little like the disjunctive approach when settling curriculum issues that are particularly contentious. A considerable amount of assembly line production would resemble the additive category if production management techniques were not employed to smooth production problems. The issue is that real groups may not fully follow the dynamics of statistically aggregated groups.

However, Steiner's model makes many issues in group productivity amenable to investigation, and lays many processes open to scrutiny where, before his propositions, the properties of groups remained somewhat vague and mysterious. His model clearly does not exhaust all possibilities in task demands – instead, he categorizes those features of groups that he finds in the laboratory-based social psychological literature produced up to the date of his review. In many contemporary organizations, tasks are likely to be both more collective and more accountable at an individual level: collective, in the sense that many production tasks involve entire enterprises, rather than simply face-to-face groups; accountable, in the sense that individual specialisms have usually to produce to a high specification products that may be utilized in quite a different context. Steiner offers a basis from which further exploration of groups and tasks may take place. His categorization is not the end of the debate.

Steiner's model applies mainly to tasks in which group members feel co-operatively interdependent. Generally, cooperative groups outperform competitive groups (Deutsch 1949; Rosenbaum et al. 1980). Kelley and Thibaut (1969) distinguished between two kinds of communication processes which throw some light on why cooperative groups might outperform competitive groups. In more competitive groups, it is quite often to a member's advantage to withhold important information in order to attain a better or earlier solution than the other group members. Moreover, information exchange in more competitive groups is inhibited because its members are more likely to focus on the distribution of rewards instead of the group working at the group task. As a consequence, there is less inter-member influence and less acceptance of others' ideas, group members have greater difficulty in communicating with and understanding others and there is less coordination of effort, less division of labour and poorer productivity in more competitive as compared with more cooperative problem-solving groups. In problem-solving groups in which members have to solve the group task as well as distribute task rewards, performance may be hampered when group members are involved in bargaining about the scarce group rewards. In cooperative groups, the members' individual interests coincide with the group interest, so that maximum attention can be paid to solving the task.

The task demands and the nature of the group interact with group size. In a series of studies by Kerr and Baum (1983), larger groups were found to provide the opportunity for less able members to produce less without sanction in disjunctive tasks, while in conjunctive tasks more able people performed below their level of ability. These seem crucial considerations for production management and organizational development specialists, yet seem not to be understood when jobs and teams are being designed.

Leadership

In some ways, the crisis in social psychology was replicated in the study of leadership. Stogdill's review of published research on leadership (Stogdill 1974) summarized over 3,000 published works. Bass (1981) cited over 5,000 and *Bass and Stogdill's Handbook of Leadership Research* (Bass 1990) contained over 9,000, yet little agreement on the operational definition of leadership emerged. These reviews chart the fact that leadership research effort in social psychology diminished at the point at which popularization of leadership within management and organizational writing became increasingly fashionable. The net result is that a considerable amount of contemporary publication on the topic is largely atheoretical or draws on theory that has long since become superseded in the science.

Early studies, such as those by Bernard (1926) and Jenkins (1947), saw leadership as being a personality trait. Under this view, people with the appropriate personality characteristics are able to influence others, whereas those without the appropriate traits simply follow. Stogdill's own work (Stogdill 1948) pointed to leaders being more intelligent, having more education, being more inclined to take on responsibilities, being more active and having higher socio-economic status than followers. However, he concluded that situational factors seemed to be of major importance in determining who will become a leader. Following Stogdill's critique, psychologists moved away from considering personality as the most important issue, and explored specific leadership behaviours. The most prominent studies were conducted by the Ohio State University group, which included Hemphill (Halpin and Winer 1957; Hemphill and Coons 1957), who designed a leader disposition questionnaire intended to measure nine behaviours, the most important of which were consideration and initiation of structure. Consideration was defined as the degree to which leaders display consideration for followers. Considerate leaders display trust, warmth and respect; inconsiderate leaders are unconcerned with followers' feelings or needs. Initiation of structure was defined as the degree to which leaders organize, define or otherwise structure the job activity of their followers. Fleishman (1953) developed a behaviour description questionnaire which contained a version to be completed by managers to describe ideal leadership behaviours. The questionnaires were able to produce correlational evidence that supported their construction but were soon regarded as being oversimple. The classic study by Fleishman and Harris (1962) demonstrated that the effects of initiation of structure depended on the level of a leader's consideration, whereas of course the development of the questionnaire had proceeded on the basis that the two dimensions were independent. The study itself had included a recording of the number of grievances filed against each manager. Initiation of structure had little effect on managers low in consideration, who received quite a few grievances no matter how much structure they imposed. Couch and Carter (1953) report a low correlation between ratings of leadership and consideration. They found that consideration and initiating structure together explained less variation than a third factor which they called individual prominence, which refers to the leader's assumption of the leadership role by declaring himself or herself as the leader. Questionnaire studies tend to focus on idealized versions of the behaviours under investigation. They also focus exclusively on the leader rather than on leader–follower relationships. There is little attempt, despite calls that emphasize context, to relate the leadership studies to behaviour within groups. Steiner (1976) saw task leaders as being able to develop a group's potential productivity but beyond that the literatures that are on groups and on leadership are not well integrated. Fiedler (1978) took up a contingency approach which assumes that group productivity can be predicted only when one knows both the leader's style and his or her situational control. For Fiedler, leadership style refers to the extent to which a leader is either relationship or task motivated and is based on the leader's ratings of the least preferred co-worker (LPC). The 'high-LPC leader' or relationship-motivated leader perceives this co-worker in a relatively favourable manner. This type of leader derives considerable satisfaction from successful interpersonal relationships. The 'low-LPC leader' or task-motivated leader rates his or her preferred co-worker in a very unfavourable way, and is described as a person who derives most satisfaction from task performance.

Besides leadership style, situational control is of importance in Feidler's model. A leader's situational control has three components: leader–member relation, which may be good or bad; the task, which may be structured or unstructured; and leader's position power, which may be strong or weak in terms of the leader's ability to evaluate the performance of the workers and give them rewards or punishments. According to Feidler, leadership style and situational control together determine leadership effectiveness as measured by group performance; that is, one has to know how leadership style and situational control interact to be able to predict the effectiveness of the leader. Feidler's main hypothesis is that low-LPC or task-motivated leaders are most effective when situational control is either very favourable or very unfavourable. In contrast, high-LPC or relationship-motivated leaders are most effective when situational control is good. Thus, in extreme (favourable or unfavourable) situations, task-motivated leaders are most effective, while relationship-motivated leaders are most effective in middle-range situations. Feidler still attracts considerable attention in texts of organizational behaviour and management studies, despite the fact that there are considerable problems with his approach. The LPC measure remains poorly defined and so cannot be interpreted (Rice 1978; Hosking 1981; Vechio 1983). The extent to which the various component factors of the model are actually independent is doubted. This being the case, it is difficult to know whether what high- or low-LPC leaders are actually doing is effective.

As Turner points out, it seems likely that the way they behave will be a complex interaction of their motives, abilities and the specifics of the situation (Turner 1991), but then there is little else to be explained from a behavioural point of view. Hosking and Morley (1991: 240) define leadership as 'a more or less skilful process of organizing, achieved through negotiation, to achieve acceptable influence over the description and handling of issues within and between groups'. They see skilful leadership processes as promoting and supporting a culture of productivity. As they say themselves, their definition varies from that found within the literatures of organizational behaviour and HRM, where leadership is seen in a way in which individuals are set aside from one another and from the wider setting of the organizational relationships around them. The Hosking and Morley position is actually quite close to the propositions put forward by Peters and Waterman (1982) in their *In Search of Excellence*. Hosking and Morley's approach also distinguishes itself from much social psychology, the majority of which is data-driven rather than theory-driven accounts of what usually amount to personalized attributes, and in doing so begins to bridge the scientific and the management pictures. In some respects it is an unfortunate, if deliberate, omission that they do not discuss at least some aspects of the more traditional literature in their text, if only to test its adequacy within the new paradigm.

They identify the skills of leadership and organizing as skills within the relational processes that are grounded in helping, networking, negotiating and enabling, all of which they see as being social processes with cognitive and political aspects. 'Through their social relations they create orderings of value and power which make sense in thought and action. In the course of their conversations, participants make commitments to particular descriptions and particular lines of action. These commitments may be more or less helpful to collective . . . work' (Hosking and Morley 1991: 250).

Drawing attention to networking as an important dimension in leadership activity raises important implications, because it is through networking that power relationships are built up. Networks provide resources that can be mobilized in support of actions of particular kinds. Networks also provide a basis for gathering organizational intelligence that can be mobilized within groups. In this way, leaders interface within the organization and beyond it. The majority of social psychological studies fail to take the context of leadership this far. Meindl (1993) is one who does do this, with his ideas stemming from what he calls the romance of leadership. He calls for a radical social psychological approach to leadership which would emphasize followers as they are affected by their social contexts. 'This involves focusing on leadership as seen by group members. In this approach, the social context and network of relations within the group has to be understood and explored' (Meindl 1993: 109). A combination of examining the network processes within groups as well as between them would, it seems, answer many questions in the study of leadership.

Leadership research is being further developed in the area of cognitive social psychology. Lord and Maher (1990) point out that the relationship between performance and perception is a complex issue, since at any point perceptions are partially dependent on past performance, yet they provide a cognitive context that influences future performance. In other words, people look backward at past behaviours or past performance to form perceptions of leadership. Once formed, leadership perceptions form an important cognitive context that indirectly affects future performance at both individual and organizational levels. Lord has proposed that leadership can be recognized from the qualities and behaviours revealed through normal day-to-day interactions with others, or it can be inferred from the outcome of salient events. For example, someone who is intelligent, honest, outgoing, understanding and verbally skilled is likely to be recognized as having strong leadership qualities. The proposition is that people form perceptual prototypes of leadership which can be used both for evaluating others' behaviour and for self-evaluation (Carver 1979). Leadership is also likely to be inferred when a person is seen as being directly responsible for a favourable outcome. Success enhances the perception of leadership, while failure can limit perceptions. Weick (1995) locates leadership clearly within the social processes of sense-making. He quotes from Thayer (1988: 250–4), who tells us that the leader is:

> one who alters or guides the manner in which his followers 'mind' the world by giving it a compelling 'face'. A leader at work is one who gives others a different sense of the meaning of that which they do by recreating it in a different form, a different 'face', in the same way that

a pivotal painter or sculptor or poet gives those who follow him (or her) a different way of 'seeing' – and therefore saying and doing and knowing in the world. A leader does not tell it 'as it is'; he tells it as it might be, giving what 'is' thereby a different 'face' . . . The leader is a sense-giver. The leader always embodies the possibilities of escape from what might otherwise appear to us to be incomprehensible, or from what might otherwise appear to us to be a chaotic, indifferent, or incorrigible world – one over which we have no ultimate control.

Leadership studies are likely to continue to attract attention in the study of organizations. For some researchers leadership is still the most important process in organizational behaviour (Rahim 1981). Leaders are also likely to be pivotal in the process of change, since, no matter the theoretical position, all researchers indicate that influence is the principle defining characteristic of leadership. Whether leadership is management is a difficult question in this area, since the positioning of supervisors and managers is accomplished formally as a process of organizational activity. The extent to which group leadership and management actually overlap is probably less than might be inferred from a reading of popular texts. Of Mintzberg's (1980) ten principles of management just one is concerned with leadership – most of his roles of management are not related to leadership or even to interpersonal relationships. So, if all managers are leaders, they are many other things as well (Hunt *et al.* 1982). Nearly all theories of leadership are concerned with managerial influence. The terms management and leadership are used almost interchangeably in both the social psychology and the management literatures. Wilpert (1982) commented on a series of presentations in a symposium on leadership that was intended to address the difference between the terms, as well as to explore the relevance of leadership research for management. He commented that whilst the papers implied a difference between the two constructs, no paper described the difference and all used the term synonymously. Wilpert himself made the assumption that 'managers always perform some leadership function due to their organizational position' (p. 69). Managers are always likely to exercise broader leadership or to have influence over a wider range of issues than non-managers because of their formal organizational position and the way in which they enact within the networked social context. If the social cognitive studies are right, the structural positions held by managers will also impact on both managers' own leadership self-perceptions and the perceptions of followers.

Teams

Teams as a phenomenon raise interesting issues for social psychology, for organizations and for change. When experimentally based social psychologists go about their investigatory tasks they assign people to conditions in the experiment on a random basis, so to be able to test hypotheses without bias. The groups may be said to be compiled on a statistical basis and the behaviour that is observed in the conditions may be held to generalize beyond the immediate laboratory situation to similar behaviour in general. Groups are often not well defined by social psychologists. I well remember the very first social psychology lecture that I attended, at which Michael Argyle, having with his usual erudition covered the entire span of the discipline as it stood in the late 1960s, was asked by a rather forthright student of theology why he had not defined what a group was. Summoning a goodly measure of his appealingly shy wit, Argyle replied that the definition was easy: 'If the number of people engaged in interaction was below two then clearly there was no group. If the number were greater than fifteen then the number of people was too great to be studied by social psychologists!' Whether social psychology has progressed its definition of groups beyond the summative I sometimes doubt.

Those concerned with teamwork are sometimes at pains to distinguish between 'groups' and 'teams'.

> A team can be distinguished from a group. Or rather, in the words of Bernard Babington Smith, a team is a group in which the individuals have a common aim and in which the jobs and skills of each member fit in with those of others, as – to take a very mechanical and static analogy – in a jigsaw puzzle pieces fit together without distortion and together produce some overall pattern. The two strands of this definition – a common task and complementary contributions – are essential to the concept of a team. An effective team may be defined as one that achieves its aim in the most effective way and is then ready to take on more challenging tasks if required.
>
> (Adair 1986: 95)

Michael West, whose entire stance is firmly within social psychology, makes no such distinction in his work (West 1994), and he moves easily, and with equal sense of principle, between the literatures. There is, however, a selective and partial linking of experimental social psychology and teamworking in some texts. Tjsvold's (1991: xi) position is that:

> teamwork is an ultimate competitive advantage for it fuels the continuous improvement necessary to adapt and prosper in a turbulent world . . . Successful teams envision a common direction, recognize that their goals are united, feel empowered and skilful, explore alternative positions before deciding, and reflect on their progress . . . teamwork is not easy. It requires courage to break out of suspicious, cautious ways of working. In the mistrustful, impersonal climates of many organizations, people must give before they are assured of getting, they must reach out before they know others will reciprocate. Departments must

relinquish feelings of self-righteousness and superiority to recognize their independence. Fair division of work and distribution of rewards must be negotiated, opposing positions integrated and frustrations addressed . . . But teamwork is possible. Most of us have belonged to fun, involving, and productive teams. We wanted each other to succeed, felt bonded, and got an extraordinary job done. The challenge is not to do something that we have not done before, but to form teams under pressure to produce quickly and efficiently with people we do not know well, who are trained in another speciality, and have cultural background. Many teams spread out around the world, must coordinate by fax and computer. Hundreds of employees in different business units are asked to be synergistic. Humans have worked together for tens of thousands of years, but have little experience in the conditions of contemporary organizations.

Tjsvold draws on publications that have been introduced in a little depth already in this chapter. He takes a broad brush approach rather than a detailed one. 'Lewin proposed that interdependence was central to the understanding of groups. Fiedler characterized groups as individuals who share a common fate that in an event which affects one affects the others. Sherif and Sherif argue that group members have reciprocal roles and norms that regulate their behaviour' (Tjsvold 1991: 22). Taken at this level and combined, we are presented with a set of principles that produce a homogenized view of groups that admits to the consensual view that teamwork seems to demand from some researchers and some practitioners. There is a missionary zeal about all of this.

Effective organizational groups, as open systems, must serve the interests of the organizations from which they draw their charter and resources. Similarly, effective organizations, as open systems, must serve their customers and other stakeholders or they will eventually suffer the loss of support and resources. Groups and organizations must also serve their members to develop motivation and commitment. If persons believe that the group and organizational goals, experience, and rewards are trivial and meaningless, they may go through the motions but will not provide the effort and persistence necessary to get something extraordinary done.

(Tjsvold 1991: 23)

Teams: science, ideology or technique?

There is a deeply unitarist philosophy underlying this approach. Teams have to feel valued and know that top management will consider their ideas and recommendations seriously. They have to be able to negotiate so that they can have appropriate resources and time to complete their tasks. The reward, training and promotion systems support teamwork within and between groups. Managers and employees have also to meet the personal challenge to strengthen their attitudes and skills to work productively with each other, to learn to communicate openly, to support others and to manage their conflicts. Members of teams have to be fully aware of the team's business objectives and its organizational framework: they know what they are expected to accomplish and how they will work together to achieve it. They understand the importance of this vision for themselves and others, and are committed to pursuing it. The vision becomes something which, according to this perspective, motivates and directs. Tjsvold is not alone in his approach. The training manual for the car company Nissan, for example, has been written in similar terms.

> Organizations are about people working together to achieve a common objective. In our case it's about 'build the best quality car in Europe'. Therefore we need to develop teams, a team can accomplish much more than the sum of its individual members. Teamwork is individuals working together to accomplish more than they could alone, but more than that it can be exciting, satisfying and enjoyable. If any of us were given the task of building the English football team – we know the task would involve much more than just picking the best eleven players in England. The success of the team would depend not only on individual skill but the way those individuals supported and work with each other.
> (Nissan, *Kaizen Leader Training Manual*, cited in Garran and Stewart 1992)

Garran and Stewart analyse the passage as indicating that Nissan picks up on the notion of individuals working together and embeds it within the concept of synergy. This, they say, is an important process for all organizations, because it represents the appropriation, to the company's benefit, of what commonly happens in work organizations where workers help one another, perhaps to fulfil work quotas, or to allow someone to 'have a break'. With the team concept in operation, the use of synergy is said by Garran and Stewart to be a recognition of the importance the company attaches to the harnessing of what this

> helping out depends on – the social and psychological factors that help create group or work solidarity. It is this, they say, that Nissan rely upon via the team concept, and utilize for the company's own ends. It relies upon a carefully articulated set of definitions about both teams and teamworking: both the individual and his or her work only have a meaning in so far as it is specified by the company.
> (Garran and Stewart 1992: 97)

The team philosophy becomes controlling in the sense that the individual's relationship to others in the team is defined by the company's imperatives. Garran and Stewart tell us that this is an important political and strategic point. It is political, they say, because it is a recognition that since in reality flexibility is quite limited, workers in teams are bound to build up close relationships at work. It is strategic because of the personal and social identities in the team (the company needs to control or moderate their potentially disruptive character) and because teamwork at Nissan is conducted within the overall framework of just-in-time management, which, with its tight scheduling and controls, is extremely susceptible to social disruption. In the absence of any countervailing culture such as might be made possible with trade union representation in the Nissan plant, the system of production comes to be seen by Garran and Stewart as management by stress. The claim is that the incorporationist methods of Nissan are forged by the company's ability to trade on the social insecurities of workers who fear social isolation or personal failure. Marchington (1992: 121) finds similar experiences reported in the research literature on teamworking that emanates from the United States.

> Although there are several reports which suggest that employees find the new methods of working more attractive than traditional techniques (especially in Sweden where teamworking has been introduced jointly with the trade unions), there are also indications that it produces a more stressful factory environment. Many of the independent studies agree that teamworking, especially on car assembly lines, does induce higher levels of stress among employees. For example, Berggren, indicates that workers perceive greater time pressures in the most technologically advanced Volvo plants than in the others . . . and Black and Ackers report a similar finding from GM in the USA . . . Others, and in particular Parker and Slaughter . . . view the whole concept of teamworking as little more than a managerial technique to intensify work yet further, to 'stretch' the production system as far as it will go . . . It also helps us to remember that management's primary interest in new production techniques is not – with the possible exception of some of the Swedish experiments – specifically aimed at increasing industrial democracy and worker participation.

Teams and management

The notion of teamworking was propounded as a distinct technique by Trist and Bamforth (1951). They were simply replacing the communal basis for work organization that obtained prior to the separation of activities and the consequent isolation of work processes that follows the implementation of the scientific management approach. Trist and Bamforth's work developed the notion of autonomous teams in which significant elements of immediate and local decisions about work were left to teams. Conceptually, this approach led to a dichotomy between management and groups that if left partially worked through can be disastrous. Autonomous groups still require management, but they need it to be more distant and supportive. Planning and logistics, supply and purchasing, marketing, the overall support for group activities and so on all need to be designed so as to meet group needs, rather than groups being left to fend for themselves in significant areas that lie beyond the execution of the work itself. There are many organizations that have established teamworking in a partial way. In ongoing work in Northern Ireland's textile industry, my own research has identified the fact that a considerable number of companies have embarked on teamwork because their prime contractor has suggested it or because the management has heard of a competitor company establishing teams. In many instances these companies have set up one team to improve quality and a further team to deal with a quick response to customer needs. This has led to clashes within the company, between the teams and those responsible for them and the rest of the company, which has often been left to work on traditional assembly line principles.

Hackman's review of teamworking (1990) describes a considerable number of circumstances in which teams fail. He points to the fact that it is misleading simply to look at the internal interaction processes of groups to understand and explain differences in task effectiveness. The organization itself generates self-fulfilling and self-generating cycles for teams' success or failure. A team that believes it will be successful in an organization behaves in ways that make it so. It develops positive task perceptions and productivity norms that make it successful. A team that believes that opportunity will not be forthcoming no matter what it does will not generate much effort; nor will it capitalize on the opportunities that do present themselves (Hackman 1990: 396). How the group views its task is often as important as the objective design of that task, so expectancies and future orientation are key factors in teams' appraisal of how much of themselves to put into a task.

Hackman finds little of value to support the descriptions of teams in the social psychological literature. Personally, I find this an unhelpful stance. He says, 'much of our understanding of group formation and development has emerged from the study of learning groups or therapy. (We have already seen that this is a partial view of psychology in this area.) Such groups import little from the organizational context; nor are they highly dependent on the organization for what they need to get their work done' (Hackman 1990: 445). Taking the example of flight crews in aircraft, Hackman tells us that they 'form with an already well-developed task definition – that is, they all come to work knowing what they are going to do and possessing the necessary skills to do it. And they are part of an organization that provides most of the resources and information they need for their work. Furthermore, the organization is embedded within an environment of other agencies and organizations that further define and augment individual and collective tasks' (p. 445). Hackman's thesis continues:

> Production technology is designed to be operated by a person and not by a team. When plants are laid out the 'natural' thing to do is to array the machinery in a long line, with materials coming in one end and products going out the other. This layout, of course, is an immediate and significant obstacle to team performance, especially if the distances are great or the noise is loud . . . Real technological obstacles, such as machine design and plant layout, are reinforced by the symbolism of the machinery. We want the machines on which we depend . . . to be predictable and reliable and to require a minimum of maintenance. This ethic runs deep in production organizations and, not surprisingly tends to be applied to people as well as machinery. The production organization, like the production machinery, should be predictable, reliable, and maintenance free. Such thinking does not lead one to think of teams as the design option of choice. Teams, when they work, are flexible, adaptive, and capable of collective learning. These are different values, reflecting a different ethic about what a production organization should be . . . Even when teams are installed in production organizations, it can be a significant challenge to transform them into fully-fledged, mature social systems capable of realising their full potential as task-performing units . . . it takes expertise, hard work, and time to design, lead, and support teamwork.
>
> (Hackman 1990: 475)

Hackman concludes by identifying a number of mistakes that designers and leaders of work groups make. The first he identifies as calling the performing unit a team, but really managing members as individuals. A mixed model, in which people are told they are a team but are treated as individual performers with their own specific jobs to do, sends mixed signals to members, is likely to confuse everyone and in the long term is probably untenable. The second is to create an imbalance in the authority structure, especially when the team has authority for some parts of the work and that authority is withheld for other parts. Hackman tells us that this leads to managers and team members colluding to produce a 'clarification' which looks to be close to anarchy. The third mistake that is frequently made is to assemble a large group of people, tell them in general terms what needs to be accomplished and 'let them work out the details'. The unstated assumption is that there is some magic within group processes and that by working together members will evolve the structures that the team actually needs. Here the formal social psychological literature provides clear evidence that groups do not have special properties and that structures need to be developed that enable management of details. The fourth mistake is to specify challenging team objectives, but skimp on organizational supports. Teams in high-commitment organizations suffer in this respect when they are given stretch objectives but not the means of accomplishing them. High initial enthusiasm then becomes disillusionment.

The last mistake listed by Hackman is to assume that members have all the competence they need to work well as a team. Despite there being good reasons for giving teams scope to go about their business, a strict hands-off managerial stance can limit a team's effectiveness when members are not already skilled and experienced in teamwork. The role of the manager, according to Hackman, requires three kinds of conditions: (a) creating favourable performance conditions for the team, either on one's own authority or by exercising influence upwards or laterally with managerial colleagues; (b) building and maintaining the team as a performing unit; and (c) coaching and helping the team in real time. To these we might add addressing, as part of management, real problems experienced by the team in the course of their work. Hill (1991) has provided considerable evidence of the transitory nature of one form of teamworking, namely quality circles. Again, the enthusiasm for this particular innovation was picked up by British management from the Japanese ethos for management of human resources for continuous improvement. Hill's research strategy was to conduct in-depth case studies of eleven companies that were pioneers of quality circles in Britain. Only five still had quality circles just a few years after their initiation. Worse, of the five, one company said that its programme was at the point of collapse and two others with viable programmes said they were dissatisfied with circles. Data gathered from those companies still with circles showed no significant differences in job satisfaction, long-term commitment to working for the company, perceptions of the company as a 'fair' employer and the amount of trust between management and employees. There were significant differences in the desirability of greater participation in managerial decision-making. Non-members of circles downplayed the importance of the groups, while members endorsed them strongly. Despite the many shortcomings of the circles, Hill claims that there is firm evidence of the business benefits of quality management, with its central assumption that all activities lead to improvement in product. Principal among the benefits is a change of culture in the organization resulting from an increase in attempts to make participation work at all levels.

From this follow other changes in the organization, such as delayering and decentralization of management, as well as the enlargement of jobs at the bottom end of the organization. In looking for positive evaluation of the quality circle experience, Hill cites the increased determination to succeed over what was apparent in the past. Hence, claims Hill, total quality management might succeed where quality circles have failed. The question is whether or not allowing an organization to be driven by the experience of others, particularly when the comparison is with a country on the other side of the globe which has an entirely different history as well as a contrasting economic, social and political structure, provides an unsound basis for management. How is management to evaluate developments? One possibility is to consult appropriate scientific evidence. Kelly and Kelly (1991) indicate that social psychology offers considerable evidence of value to managers interested in producing a new framework for working relations, but that there is so far little evidence that work is being shaped so as to take advantage of what the science has to offer. They draw particular attention to the long history of social psychology's research on attitude change and to the potential for a reduction in 'them and us' positions in industry. Workers, they point out, have often lacked choice over participation in new schemes; there has often been lack of trust between the parties involved, together with inequality of status and benefits as well as lack of institutional support for schemes among top management (Kelly and Kelly 1991). Many of these issues require more than scientific knowledge: they require economic and political effort to produce a change. However, one role of scientific knowledge is to provide a basis for informed judgement and prediction of at least what variables might be important to success. If management and social psychology could come closer together in understanding the process of change, perhaps organizations would be less littered with failed innovations and the consequent impact this has on economic performance and on people themselves.

Groups: social categorization and social identity

Social identity theory is principally concerned with those aspects of identity that derive from group memberships. Tajfel (1978; Tajfel and Turner 1979) stressed that society is composed of social groups that stand in power and status relations to one another; he believed that this group structure has important implications for identity formation. Tajfel followed Festinger (1954) in proposing that identity formation rests on the process of social comparison, whereby in order to evaluate their opinions and abilities, people compare themselves with others in the course of social encounters. However, Tajfel stressed the importance of comparisons between social groups; he theorized that as well as evaluating themselves through interpersonal comparisons, people also need to assess the value of their own group in relation to other similar groups, and they do this by intergroup comparison. The process is that our own group or ingroup is compared with similar but distinct outgroups. The dimensions that are used to make these comparisons – that is, to distinguish self and ingroup from other comparable groups – are called social categorizations. These are by nature stereotypic or consensual constructions, since they mark out the agreed boundaries of group membership. Social identity is founded on the internalization of these categorizations.

Turner (1982; Turner *et al.* 1987) has linked the processes of intergroup and interpersonal comparison to two essentially distinct aspects of the self concept. He sees the self concept as consisting of all available constructions of self which fall into two different subsystems: one of these is made up of social identifications derived from the ingroup–outgroup categorization (such as sex, race, occupation and class); the other consists of personal identifications, idiosyncratic descriptions of self which derive from differentiation of self as a unique individual from other individuals.

Identity and social change

Whether the primary motivational factor governing the process of intergroup comparison, the need for positive social identity, is achievable depends initially on the relative status of groups being compared. Hogg and Abrahms (1988) show us how the power and status relations between groups bear on social identity; the dominant groups in society have the power and the status to impose the dominant value system and ideology, which serves to legitimate and perpetuate the status quo. Individuals are born into this structure, and simply because of their sex, social class or race, fall into one social class rather than others. By internalization of the social categorizations that define these group memberships, they acquire particular social identities that may have positive or negative value. Members of dominant and higher-status groups gain a positive social identity and high self-esteem from group membership; members of the lower-status or subordinate group have a less positive social identity and lower self-esteem. Here the behavioural consequences of social identification come into play. Members of low-status groups may seek to change their position and so attain a sense of positive distinctiveness, while the members of high-status groups will act to maintain superiority (Turner 1982). The nature of the action taken by low-status groups depends upon their beliefs about the nature of intergroup relations. If individuals believe that membership of the higher-status group is achievable by individual effort, they will attempt to move upwards into the dominant group by these means. This does have the effect of leaving the status quo intact, as Hogg and Abrahms (1988) point out. However, if individual upward social mobility is impossible and members of low-status groups see boundaries between groups as impenetrable, they may adopt collective strategies to create a more positive social identity for their group. These strategies are called social change by Tajfel (1978). The proposition is that there is a continuum between individual action at one end and collective action at the other, whereby the more difficult it is for individuals to improve their own personal position or status by becoming members of the high-status group, the more likely it is that members of the low-status group will join together to improve the group's status.

Tajfel uses the term 'social change' to include three kinds of activity. The first of these is assimilation or merger, which involves the adoption of the positive features of the high-status group by the low-status group who wish to join them. This strategy effectively dissolves the comparison processes which maintain intergroup tensions, by reducing the psychological distance between the two groups, so increasing the similarity. Such a strategy requires cooperation between high- and low-status groups rather than differentiation and competition. Tajfel distinguishes a second type of action which he calls social creativity, whereby the subordinate group seeks to create a new and positive image for itself. So low-status groups may create brand new characteristics for the group which effectively make it so different from the group it compares itself with that it reduces the need for any further comparisons with the high-status group and so creates a more positive social identity. Finally, rather than compare themselves with the superior group, low-status groups may seek comparisons with equivalent or more subordinate groups to themselves in order to enhance their social identity. The third strategy for social change is social competition (Tajfel and Turner 1979), when the subordinate group challenges the basis of the status hierarchy and seeks to change the relative power and status of the groups by active or passive resistance.

In the 1979 series of papers in volume 18 of the *British Journal of Social and Clinical Psychology* Tajfel replies to Taylor and Brown by both offering support for their general argument and gently suggesting that social psychology needs not just to look at its findings from experiments but also to look beyond them. The answer to developing a more social social psychology is not just as easy as taking up social identity theory.

The aim of a theory of intergroup behaviour is to help us to understand certain selected uniformities of social behaviour. In order to do this, we must know (i) of the ways 'groups' are constructed in a particular social system; (ii) what are the psychological effects of these constructions; and (iii) how the constructions and their effects depend upon, and relate to, forms of social reality . . . We need first of all a definition of a group which refers to the way the notion is constructed by those inside the system. This definition must enable us to make the transition from what we assume is 'constructed' by the individuals involved to data showing whether our assumptions were correct or incorrect . . . Secondly, it is necessary to state what are the basic conditions for 'groups' to be constructed in such a way that the consequent behaviour of members of one group towards another shows uniformities rather than a random variation from individual to individual.

(Tajfel 1979: 186)

Tajfel develops his theory from the platform of social comparisons proposed by Festinger. He also draws heavily on the work of Sherif (1966), who postulated that 'Whenever individuals belonging to one group interact, collectively or individually, with another group or its members in terms of their group identification, we have an instance of intergroup behaviour.' Tajfel tells us that Sherif's definition needs to be anchored to its two underlying concepts: 'group' and 'group identification'. For Tajfel (1982: 1–2),

> a 'group' can be defined as such on the basis of criteria which are either external or internal. External criteria are the 'outside' designations such as bank clerks, hospital patients, members of a trades union, etc. Internal criteria are those of 'group identification'. In order to achieve the stage of 'identification', two criteria are necessary, one is frequently associated with them. The two necessary components are: a cognitive one, in the sense of awareness of membership; and an evaluative one, in the sense that this awareness is related to some value connotations. The third component consists of an emotional investment in the awareness and evaluations.
>
> The empirical reality of the internal criteria is a necessary condition for the existence of a group in the psychological sense of the term; but it is not a sufficient condition for the emergence of intergroup behaviour. There can be no intergroup behaviour unless there is some 'outside' consensus that the group exists. But this in turn cannot be a sufficient condition since a classification by others of some people as a group does not necessarily mean that the individuals so classified have acquired an awareness of a common group membership and the value connotations associated with it.

The social categorisation and social comparison approach to intergroup behaviour is demanding. For experimental tests to meet all of the conditions across each of the components is a stringent set of requirements.

Between 1972 and 1975, Geoffrey Stephenson and I, together with Martin Skinner, conducted a set of experiments that sought to test some of Tajfel's propositions. Taking issues that we knew to be live within particular organizations at the time, we divided members into groups rather as Tajfel himself had done. We did not find the intergroup discrimination effects that Tajfel had done. Instead, we found either no discrimination against the experimental outgroup or a series of social processes which suggested that groupness varied according to size and the extent of disagreement (Stephenson and Brotherton 1973, 1975; Stephenson et al. 1975). One possible reading of our findings is that, given a discussion task that mattered to the group members rather than an abstract and minimal task such as those invariably given to Tajfel's participants, the groups did not discriminate. The demand characteristics of Tajfel's studies were such that people taking part in them had the option of either producing a response that was Tajfellian or abandoning the study.

We know from other studies of the power of the experiment that abandoning participation is something that most subjects are not prepared to do (Orne, 1962). In reviewing one of our studies (although he was well aware of others), Tajfel refers simply to the fact that our dependent variables produced findings that were at variance with the general run of those found within the paradigm (Tajfel 1981, 1982). The fact that the social processes that followed from the task differences indicated little support once context variables were brought into play was not handled – perhaps it could not be!

There are remarkably few tests of the intergroup relations paradigm that involve handling issues that relate to social context in a direct sense, despite the powerful intellectual call of Tajfel and his colleagues to do so. Giles (1978) has shown how language or dialect has been used by ethnic minorities such as the Welsh, French Canadians and American Blacks to assert their positive distinctiveness from the majority.

Skevington (1980, 1981) examined social change strategies in nursing, and found merger the most important strategy considered during discussions about changes in the structure of the profession. By merging low-status state enrolled nurses (SENs) with the high-status state registered nurses (SRNs) through training, it was intended that the more positive characteristics of the high-status group would be attributed to all nurses. In this case, the SRNs felt threatened by the potential loss of their highly valued and positive social identity. In contrast, the low-status SENs generally wished for change and supported the dissolving of status relations through merger. Brown *et al.* (1986) conducted a study of workgroup relations in a large paper factory. They asked people to judge their own and others groups' contributions to the running of the organization. They almost invariably favoured the ingroup when rating the groups and put their own group score highest, sometimes accompanying it with mildly disparaging remarks about the performance of other groups. When Brown and his colleagues asked them to characterize each intergroup relationship on a harmony–conflict dimension ('two teams pulling together' versus 'two groups on opposite sides working against each other'), it turned out that the resultant index of conflict was strongly correlated with the amount of ingroup bias shown against each outgroup: those outgroups with whom a conflictual relationship was perceived were reckoned to contribute less to the organization than those who were seen to be working with the ingroup. Yet intergroup relations are a significant and fundamental aspect of organizational life. Stephenson (1981) has demonstrated very clearly how the interpersonal–intergroup relations paradigm operates in industrial relations and negotiating situations. The representative actions of negotiators have to operate at the group level, and emphasis on the interpersonal aspects can be disastrous to the success of both the negotiation and the industrial relations procedure, which demands appropriate formality, beyond it. The processes to which the intergroup paradigm refers probably apply to committees as well, but these have been largely neglected, as have other forms of group working in organized settings. One problem could be that the social comparison–social categorization paradigm is too subtle in its effects for application in organizational settings. It is worse if, when it is applied, the findings that result run counter to the theory. On the other hand, the intergroup relations paradigm is widely adopted across Europe and is extremely productive in terms of fundamental research. Social psychology has identified categorization as the central process of social identity. Social identity processes are crucial to the way in which diversity operates in the networked society. We need to comprehend these processes.

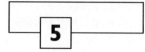

Gender and diversity

Since Max Weber's classic work (Weber 1946), bureaucratic organizations have been seen as being characterized by formal structures and by office holders who are in possession of specific qualifications. These are all factors that support conservative and conformist approaches to organizational life. All the forces that Castells identifies in the networked society militate against bureaucracy. They also range against diversity, the topic to be explored in this chapter. Bureaucracies are the likely arenas in which the processes that social psychologists have identified can be played out. This chapter begins by examining aspects of groupthink and then proceeds to look at its contrast: diversity.

Conformity *in extremis*

The case for diversity could almost be argued by presenting a description of the opposite. In the Maxwell corporation, a single man seems to have dominated decisions of all kinds by exercising fear. Rather than seeking an agreement by consensus, having looked at a range of alternatives, Maxwell's style seems to have been to shut down exploration of ideas and to drive home his own view. Whether the Maxwell style is due to his gender is a mute point. There are clearly elements of his own somewhat impoverished personal background that importantly gave Maxwell a strong motivation to succeed. As Bower (1988) tells us, 'the region of Maxwell's birthplace was probably the most primitive and impoverished on the whole European continent . . . the dollar billionaire was born into a community whose poverty and hardship would be unimaginable for those who were now to witness his ease amid wealth and power' (Bower 1988: 5 and xv).

He . . . stood calmly at the entrance of a crowded conference room. His mere appearance had silenced his audience. Over one hundred people had spotted the man who desired immortality but would compromise with glorification. Tall, bronzed and immaculately dressed (bright blue suit, white shirt and dazzling red bow tie), Robert Maxwell, alias 'the publisher,' glanced at his watch to judge whether the precise moment had struck for his next public appearance. Behind him stood four uniformed security guards. Hovering in front was his chief of staff, clasping a portable telephone. The publisher placed a premium upon instant communications. Noticeably erect on his left, attempting to peer into the room, were two secretaries. Their employer prided himself on churning out decisions at a faster rate than most can speak and required their constant attendance to transmit his thought instantly.

(Bower 1988: xv)

The results of Maxwell's style are still felt long after his death. Bower writes of the collapse of a publishing empire which culminated in many millions of pounds of pension funding disappearing from the accounts of the company owned by Maxwell

The four directors departed, relieved that the Maxwells were at last co-operating. Kevin's promise that the debt to MCC would disappear by September 'fits in with their explanation that it's just a short-term problem', Laister told Derek Hayes at MacFarlanes just before leaving for his holidays. 'All at the moment seems to be progressing satisfactorily. We're getting all the information we need and new procedures. Everything is back on the rails.'

(Bower 1995: 216)

Maxwell's whole style was one in which

the apparent reconciliation was at once exploded by Maxwell, his face turning purple. 'Stop taking notes!' he screamed at Anselmini. 'I want these conspiratorial discussions to cease. If there are any problems, please come to me rather than speaking among each other.' An outburst of verbal brutality was imminent. For Brookes, the atmosphere had become 'extremely hostile'. He would be later seen white-faced and close to tears in his office. For Laister, the meeting was appalling and surprising. Even so, as he wrote a memorandum of the meeting afterwards in Wood's office, he remarked, 'All things considered that was a reasonably successful. . .' Upstairs, Maxwell sat in fury. Anselmi, who knew so much, was clearly the ringleader of the cabal. Pole was summoned. 'I need to know Anselmi's loyalties.' Pole naturally understood. That night a diversion was installed on Anselmi's telephone: it led to a recording machine.

(Bower 1995: 216)

In addition Maxwell made use of supporters. 'Joe needs to worship somebody and gratefully devotes himself to a powerbroker. He just convinced himself that Maxwell was right on every issue' (Bower 1995: 338). This interpersonal style of leader and follower relations was reflected in the structure of Maxwell's companies.

> The frequent turnover of staff was a clear sign of an unsatisfactory working environment. Everyone was expected to adhere to the publisher's eighteen hour day, although the demarcation between waking and sleeping hours was never established. At all times they were called through the omnipresent communications network which each senior staff member accepted as a condition of service. There was no management structure. 'It resembles more a communist rather than a capitalist bureaucracy,' suggested one insider.
>
> (Bower 1995: 338)

Bower concludes that Maxwell's position during the 1980s was possible only because of the peculiarities of that era.

> The extraordinary conviction that the world's economy was destined for perpetual expansion intoxicated a swathe of bankers, brokers and lawyers. Their self-esteem dissolved any caution and sense of inquiry which they, as professionals, asserted as reward for epic salaries. Apparently sane, serious and highly paid experts were willing to be lured by Maxwell into the unknown.
>
> (Bower 1992: 510)

The Maxwell case is interesting from a social psychological viewpoint in that it draws attention to the contexts in which conformity may develop. Maxwell had established a series of companies in which many individuals were terrorized rather than allowed to put their view with confidence. Beyond that, Maxwell had enmeshed entire networks of finance and politics, including those of several countries, in what appears to be a corrupt interdependency. The interest for social psychology in organizations is that systems as well as groups produce pressure to conformity.

Groupthink

In examining conformity, social psychology frequently calls on the classic work of Janis (1982). Janis examined the documentation, memoirs and conversations derived from a series of US political events, such as the Cuban Missile crisis and the Bay of Pigs incident, both of which occurred during the presidency of John Kennedy, as well as the Watergate cover-up, which culminated in the resignation from the presidency of Richard Nixon. Groupthink is a term that refers to the psychological drive for consensus at any cost, which suppresses disagreement and prevents the appraisal of alternatives in cohesive decision-making groups. Janis produces a list of symptoms that are synthesized from research on group dynamics. First, Janis draws attention to over-estimations of the group – its power and morality. There is an illusion of invulnerability, shared by most or all the members, which creates excessive optimism and encourages the taking of extreme risks. The Maxwell illustration indicates the possibility that shared feelings may be an uneasy process for the group itself. There is also an unquestioned belief in the group's inherent morality, inclining the members to ignore the ethical or moral consequences of their decisions.

In Maxwell's case, the inherent morality was explicitly held by the leader himself, but concern was not voiced openly out of fear.

Janis draws attention to a group's tendency to 'closed-mindedness'. Here there are collective efforts to rationalize in order to discount warnings or other information that might lead the members to reconsider their assumptions before they recommit themselves to their past policy decisions. Janis gives the example of the holding of stereotyped views of enemy leaders as too evil to warrant genuine attempts to negotiate, or as too weak and stupid to counter whatever risky attempts are made to defeat their purposes. In Maxwell's case, he seemed to view those within his own camp who disagreed as the enemy. Janis identifies group pressures towards uniformity, a symptom of which is seen as self-censorship of deviations from the apparent group consensus, reflecting each member's inclination to minimize to himself or herself the importance of doubts and counterargument. Maxwell did this, according to Bower's account, by denegrating those who disagreed. Janis noted groups' tendency towards a shared illusion of unanimity concerning judgements conforming to the majority view (partly resulting from self-censorship of deviations, augmented by the false assumption that silence means consent). Janis further notes that groups may exert direct pressure on any member who expresses strong arguments against any of the group's stereotypes, illusions or commitments, making clear that this type of dissent is contrary to what is expected of all loyal members. Janis notes that as groups develop there may be the emergence of self-appointed mindguards – members who protect the group from adverse information that might shatter their shared complacency about the effectiveness and morality of their decisions. Janis tells us that 'when a policy-making group displays most or all of the symptoms . . . the members perform their collective tasks ineffectually and are likely to fail to attain their collective objectives as a result of concurrence-seeking . . . My assumption is that the more frequently a group displays the symptoms, the worse will be the quality of its decisions, on average' (p. 175). Janis indicates that his methodology does not enable him to know how widespread groupthink is as a component of all major fiascos. Some decisions of poor quality that turn out to be fiascos might be ascribed primarily to mistakes made by just one man, the chief executive. Others arise because of faulty policy formulated by a group of executives whose decision-making procedures are impaired by errors having nothing to do with groupthink. For example, a non-cohesive committee may be made up of bickering factions so intent on fighting for political power within the government bureaucracy that the participants have little interest in examining the real issues posed by foreign policy questions they are debating; they may settle for a compromise that fails to take account of adverse effects on people outside their own political arena. Groupthink sometimes plays a large part in producing large-scale fiascos. Indeed, the propositions developed by Janis seem to have wide applicability in organizations: openness and discussion are virtually to be eliminated at each stage. Maxwell was not an isolated instance: we can find other examples of individuals, groups and organizations demonstrating extreme conformity broadly in the manner that Janis describes. The Barings Bank collapse is described by the principle actor Nick Leeson (1996) as a series of processes in which individual judgement was subsumed in a broader collective which failed to make adequate checks on trading activity, still less allow alternative hypotheses to emerge even in the face of what appears to be substantial evidence that the dominant view of events is dramatically inadequate.

In the Barings case, it appears that not only were established practices set that enabled large-scale errors to go undetected, but the payment systems throughout the organization reinforced the behaviour that eventually led to disaster. Elements of what Janis calls convergent thinking are well evidenced in the procedures that lead to one person carrying the public blame for the collapse, with little other scrutiny of the general principles of the organization of the bank being apparent. One of the lessons these cases offer is that social psychology needs to go beyond the immediate framework of the group and into the structural issues that relate to the central issue. Janis provides a psychological approach to conformity in the provision of a two-factor model.

> After a leader lets it be known that he favours a particular policy alternative, the members are in the common predicament of having little hope of finding a better solution (because advocating a different alternative will evoke the disapproval of the most esteemed person in the group and of all those who uncritically support him). They will be motivated to reduce the high stress of their decisional conflict by collectively bolstering the choice made by the leader.
>
> (Janis 1982: 191–3)

Conformity in high places

Janis sees stress and esteem variables as being important, but not the only, conditions that produce groupthink, and he looks to a range of political decisions that had similar features but different levels of stress resulting from external threats. Most of the decisions he analyses are presented as broadly contextual rather than specifically structural. Janis is clearly focused on the social psychological. Fundamentally, Janis's account is short of an analysis of the power relations at work in these high-level decision processes. The result could be that we are led to consider groupthink as being a pathological response to internal processes rather than as resulting from structures that fail to maintain checks on groups in power. Yet examinations of the political structures in which the decisions he examines are reached show quite clearly that we could, if we wished, predict groupthink and conformity from the structures established around the presidency of the day. Power was being confined to the group. Several studies show how the presidency has been surrounded by lesser offices that filtered information and protected the ethos of the highest office, to the extent that the Presidential Cabinet became more or less isolated from those broader influences that could conceivably have offered alternative hypotheses.

> My primary responsibility was simply to enable the President to function most effectively. I was definitely an inside man. By 1971, Nixon was using three subordinates – Haldeman, Erlichman, and Colson – for three different approaches to some projects. I was the man for the straight, hit-them-over-the-head strategy. Erlichman, who loved intrigue, was given the more devious approach. And Colson was assigned the real underground routes. Of course, if there were no Nixon, there would have been no Colson in the White House. Colson only fed off Nixon; Nixon provided the output which all of us, including Colson, Erlichman, and myself, were ordered to put into action.
>
> (Haldeman 1978: 12–53)

The US presidency of the 1960s and 1970s and the Maxwell example are extreme illustrations of McGregor's theory X organizations in operation. It could be that the Maxwell and the Barings cases are the last of a dying era. They were might is right styles of management, which ultimately disempower people and their social practices, and they stand in sharp contrast to the needs for diversity on knowledge in the global sense. From a social psychological perspective, it may be necessary to be able to recognize the points at which conformity gives way to diversity. Hogg and Abrahms (1988) distinguish between different forms of social change and their impact upon identification processes. They compare situations in which people perceive groups as having boundaries that are fixed and rigid with those in which boundaries can be transcended by dint of hard work. In the former, it is difficult for individuals to consider alternative cognitive strategies and to cast aside negative self-images. In the latter, self concepts can be redefined in positive terms. Hogg and Abrahms relate their findings to broad social conflict situations and demonstrate how readily dominant groups can reassert their superior position in disputes raised by the subordinate groups.

Organizational needs for diversity of knowledge

Fortunately, the majority of people do not work for organizations that exhibit such difficult circumstances as those exemplified by Maxwell. However, organizations can fail to provide the conditions under which we may all feel that we are making a positive contribution. Organizations face an increased diversity of problems externally (Flood and Romm 1996), and are becoming more diverse internally and socially (Jackson and Ruderman 1995). In such circumstances, organizations cannot remain for all time within the fiefdom of one person, nor even within that of a small number of people, and survive – let alone be successful.

Within organizations, diversity can have a positive benefit for the way in which decisions are made. Diverse groups have a richer and broader base of experience from which to approach a problem. A series of studies conducted at the University of Michigan found that heterogeneous groups produced better-quality solutions to problems than did homogeneous groups. In one of the studies, 65 per cent of heterogeneous groups produced high-quality solutions (defined as new, modified or integrative solutions to the problem), as compared with only 21 per cent of homogeneous groups (Hoffman and Maier 1964). In the groupthink studies, Janis (1982) refers to the absence of critical thinking in groups, partly caused by the preoccupation with cohesiveness. Nemeth (1985) and Nemeth and Wacher (1983) found that the level of critical analysis of decision issues and alternatives was higher in groups subjected to minority views than in those which were not. The presence of minority views improved the quality of the decision process irrespective of whether the minority view prevailed. In these groups a larger number of alternatives was considered and a more thorough examination of assumptions and their implications took place. Again, this is in marked contrast to the scenarios outlined above in the Maxwell and Barings cases.

Beyond organizations: diversity in world markets

Beyond the organization, the need for diversity in knowledge sources is increasing. Markets, as well as the processes of production, for goods and services are becoming increasingly international. They are changing with increasing rapidity. Motor cars, electrical good, such as stereo equipment, and white goods, such as refrigerators, that appear to have long familiar brand names now carry a country of manufacture on the other side of the world which will undoubtedly be changed within a matter of months as different batches of the same model are produced. It is almost impossible now to purchase the exact model of a refrigerator or a washing machine that was tested in the latest consumer magazine, since the model will have been changed in minor ways as component parts in the original become unavailable in another part of the world. The changes may be minor and almost imperceptible, but may affect the specification just a little. Clothing and textiles cross the globe for both manufacture and sale. Information technology has produced a situation where airline tickets purchased in the UK are actually produced in India in a matter of seconds. New markets become available as political boundaries, such as those around China, open. Keegan (1989: 130) summarizes the situation as follows:

> Culture has both a pervasive and changing influence on each national market environment. International marketers must recognize the influence of culture and be prepared to either respond to it or change it. International marketers have played an important or even a leading role in influencing the rate of cultural change around the world. This is particularly true of food, but it includes virtually every industry particularly in consumer products. Soap and detergent manufacturers have changed washing habits, the electronics industry has changed entertainment patterns, clothing marketers have changed styles, and so on.
>
> In industrial products culture does affect product characteristics and demand but is more important as an influence on the marketing process, particularly in the way business is done. International marketers have learned to rely upon people who know and understand local customs and attitudes for marketing experience.

In the global economy in which organizations have to survive, strategies that confine information to the few are extremely costly. Skill in learning quickly is vital for everyone within organizations. Business as a whole is becoming increasingly knowledge-intensive, and long-term company profitability depends to a large extent on renewal. Transformations and discontinuity affect organizations with increasing rapidity, particularly as technologies develop and change (Wikstrom and Normann 1994).

Knowledge and diversity

Knowledge processes of various kinds are a permanent part of organizational life. New knowledge is generated by activities aimed at solving problems. New knowledge is then used in productive processes which form the basis for the offerings and commitments that the organization undertakes vis-à-vis its customers or clients. Knowledge can also be made available to customers or clients for their own value-creating processes. Wikstrom and Normann see competence, at individual and at organizational levels, as being about the way in which knowledge is utilized for particular, goal-related, purposes. They see learning as being an important means of achieving competence and knowledge. Learning can be accomplished through formal means such as training courses, or through participation in a wide range of situations in which perceiving, combining and interpreting what is happening form important parts of the process. Wikstrom and Normann (1994: 17–18) identify and analyse the emerging patterns of corporate strategy, organization and behaviour of organizations as they utilize knowledge. The patterns include: changing roles in commercial systems; more intensive interaction between the actors in the systems; customers' offerings being more flexible as well as more knowledge-intensive and function-intensive; business development being geared to the customers' consumption; and development and mobilization of the users' value creation. There are a growing number of examples of organizations moving in the knowledge transformation direction. American Airlines introduced electronic reservation systems into the travel agency business in a way which offered more than a way of improving efficiency; it could also be exploited to alter fundamentally the interactive roles between airline, travel agent and customer, which in turn would mean redefining the industry in such a way as to give American Airlines a substantial competitive advantage. The company now has in-house travel agents in large corporations, as one way to link customers, distributors and producers together in new patterns.

The Swiss-Swedish engineering company ABB is running a project aimed at halving all cycle times and so strengthening links with customers by using hotline services, guarantees and other back-up packages. Customers are actively encouraged to take part in development work, and the result is a more intensive interaction, which in turn develops a more efficient, prompt and coordinated access to various company resources, among which is knowledge.

The financial service company American Express conducts its customer relations and interactions through the medium of the plastic card that symbolizes 'membership'. By making significant investments in databases, computer networks and expert systems, it is possible for the company to achieve a very high level of prompt service, to identify a very significant market segment and to pinpoint product development practically to an individual level. The distribution system consists of a dense network of established infrastructures such as hotels, restaurants and shops, combined with the plastic card that identifies and legitimates the customer. All of this grew from a company whose financial services were originally designed to serve the travelling customer. Business development no longer focuses mainly on products and production plants, but is gradually coming to concentrate on the various processes revolving around the customer. All of this stands in stark contrast to the closed system approach to the management of organizations typified by Maxwell and Barings. Knowledge increases in organizations could well be enhanced by the processes involved in diversity. Whether the processes will be fully understood either by authors contributing to the debate on diversity or by managers has yet to be seen.

Is diversity inevitable?

The diversity debate is often presented as being initiated by the deterministic forces of demographic changes (Johnson 1991; Cox 1993). Diversity has been made an issue concerned with the population changes involved in the labour markets of Western countries. The world workforce is growing rapidly. From 1985 to 2000, the workforce was expected to grow by some 600 million people, or by 27 per cent (compared with 36 per cent between 1970 and 1985). The growth will take place unevenly. The vast majority of new workers – 570 million of the 600 million workers – will join the workforces of the developing countries. In countries such as Pakistan and Mexico, for example, the workforce will grow at the rate of 3 per cent per year, whereas growth rates in the United States, Canada and Spain will be closer to 1 per cent, Japan's workforce will grow by 0.5 per cent and Germany's workforce will decline.

The greater growth in the developing world stems primarily from historically higher birth rates. But in many nations, the effects of higher fertility are magnified by the entry of women to the workforce. Not only will more young people who were born in the 1970s enter the workforce in the 1990s, but millions of women in industrializing nations are beginning to leave home for paid jobs. Additionally, the workforce in the developing world is better educated. The developing countries are producing a growing share of the world's high school and college graduates (Johnson 1991). It is claimed that:

> when these demographic differences are combined with different rates of economic growth, they are likely to lead to major redefinitions of labor markets. Nations that have slow-growing workforces but rapid growth in service sector jobs (namely Japan, and Germany, and even the United States) will become magnets for immigrants, even if their public policies seek to discourage them. Nations whose educational systems produce prospective workers faster than their economies can absorb them (Argentina, Poland, or the Philippines) will export people. Beyond these differences in growth rates, the work forces of various nations differ enormously in makeup and capabilities. It is precisely differences like these in age, gender, and education that give us the best clues about what to expect. Women will enter the workforce in great numbers, especially in the developing countries, where relatively few women have been absorbed to date. The average age of the world's workforce will rise, especially in the developed countries. As a result of slower birth rates and longer life spans, the world population and the labor force, are ageing.
>
> (Johnson 1991: 5–10)

Johnson continues:

> The globalization of labor is inevitable. The economic benefits from applying human resources most productively are too great to be resisted.

At least some countries will lower the barriers to immigration and at least some workers will be drawn by the opportunity to apply their training and improving their lives. But more likely, many countries will make immigration easier, and many workers will travel the globe. By the end of the century, developing countries that have educated their young and adopted market-oriented policies will have advanced faster than those that have not. Developed countries that have accepted or sought foreign workers will be stronger for having done so. As the benefits become more obvious, the movement of workers will become free. The world will be changed as a result. As labor gradually becomes international, some national differences will fade. Needs and concerns will become more universal, and personnel policies and practices will standardize. As developing nations absorb women into the workforce, for example, they are likely to share the industrialized world's concern about child care and demand for conveniences. Government efforts to harmonize workplace standards will accelerate these market-based responses.

(Johnson 1991: 24–5)

There cannot be inevitability about labour market changes of the kind claimed here. Johnson does call on the European Union's activities in drawing up the Social Charter, which seeks harmonization of workplace practices, but eight years after his paper we still find the governments of prominent countries in the Union insisting on opt-out clauses and using market-oriented arguments in justification. Meanwhile, the American organizational literature is pitching the diversity argument at such a general level that managers are likely to remain inactive on that front. For example, we find R. Roosevelt Thomas providing ten guidelines for learning to manage diversity (Thomas 1990b). He advises as follows:

1 Clarify your motivation . . . only business reasons will supply the necessary long-term motivation . . .
2 Clarify your vision . . . the vision to hold in your own imagination and try to communicate to all of your managers and employees is an image of fully tapping the human resource potential of every member of the work force. This vision sidesteps the question of equality, ignores the tensions of coexistence, plays down the uncomfortable realities of difference, and focuses instead on individual enablement.
3 Expand your focus . . . Managing disparate talents to achieve common goals is what companies learned to do when they set their sights on say, Total Quality. The secrets of managing diversity are much the same.
4 Audit your corporate culture. Corporate culture is a kind of tree; its roots are assumptions about the company and about the world. Its branches, leaves, and seeds are behavior. You can't change the

leaves without changing the roots, and you can't grow peaches on an oak . . .

5 Modify your assumptions . . . The organization I'm arguing for respects differences rather than seeks to iron them out. Every culture, including corporate culture, has root guards that turn out in force every time you threaten a basic assumption . . . But you have to try . . .

6 Modify your systems. The first purpose of examining and modifying assumptions is to modify systems. Promotion, mentoring, and sponsorship comprise one system, and the unexamined cream-to-the-top assumption . . . can tend to keep minorities and women from climbing the corporate ladder.

7 Modify your models . . . The second purpose of modifying assumptions is to modify models of managerial and employee behavior . . . managers seek subordinates who will follow their lead and do as they do. If they can't find people exactly like themselves, they try to find people who aspire to be exactly like themselves. The goal is predictability and immediate responsiveness. The right goal is . . . subordinates, supported and empowered by managers who manage.

8 Help your people pioneer. Learning to manage diversity is a change process, and the managers involved are change agents. There is no single tried and tested 'solution' to diversity and no fixed right way to manage it. Employees need to know that mistakes at the cutting edge are different – and potentially more valuable – than mistakes elsewhere. Maybe they needed some kind of pioneer training. But at the very least they needed to be told that they were pioneers, that conflicts and failures come with the territory . . .

9 Apply the special consideration test . . . Does this program, policy, or principle give special consideration to one group? Will it contribute to everyone's success, or will it produce an advantage for blacks or whites or women or men? Is it designed for them as opposed to us? Whenever the answer is yes, we are not yet on the road to managing diversity.

10 Continue affirmative action . . . The ability to manage diversity is the ability to manage your company without unnatural advantage or disadvantage for any member of your diverse workforce . . . In a country seeking competitive advantage in a global economy, the goal of managing diversity is to develop our capacity to accept, incorporate, and empower the diverse human talents of the most diverse nation on earth. It's our reality. We need to make it our strength.

(Thomas 1990b: 33–41)

What we are provided with, in Thomas's offering, is a cocktail of analogy, exhortation and rhetoric. Analysis and conceptual clarity is nowhere to be seen in such papers. The exhortation and the rhetoric are valuable at the level of changing the nature of the debate about the values that support prejudice and conformity in organizational behaviour to those that support positive outcomes, but there is so little guidance to managers in the considerations put before them that the practice of management would be difficult to alter if it were to be based on detailed assessment of empirical evidence derived from the specific organizational contexts in which managers must act.

Managing diversity

The British researchers Kandola and Fullerton (1994) point out that many models of managing diversity seem to be based more on personal experience and anecdote than on anything objective. They present a model for strategic diversity implementation, which they say is the first ever to be empirically tested. Having surveyed a sample of some 285 respondent organizations across public and private sectors of the UK economy, Kandola and Fullerton developed a questionnaire that examined initiatives designed to support diversity. The results of the survey were independently analysed, and they were able to present the dimensions of their model as being found to be positively related to the successful strategic implementation of managing diversity: having a clear vision; having senior management support; auditing the organization's needs; setting objectives; communicating with the organization's workforce; establishing accountability; coordinating actions; evaluating outcomes. The importance of having a model which has been statistically validated is that organizations can be sure that they have a secure framework within which to build their strategies. Without the statistical survey, so much in this area rests upon single case study material alone. With the survey results to provide the context, Kandola and Fullerton are able to provide a context in which the generality of their claims can be supported. They then present case studies to illustrate general principles in operation. Taking the example of International Distillers and Vintners (IDV) as one organization concerned about managing diversity, Kandola and Fullerton present the IDV mission, which is to ensure that:

> IDV will be closer to its customers, to consumers and to the heart of the market. IDV will have the strongest portfolio of value-added brands, which will always be competitive within their markets. IDV people will be high-calibre, responding to professional leadership, stimulating challenges and individual opportunities, with realistic rewards to match. IDV will value the diversity contained within its global work force and build these differences into a corporate strength. IDV will exercise the

leadership role to strengthen the communities in which it is active and conduct its business in a socially responsible manner.

(Kandola and Fullerton 1994: 99)

Kandola and Fullerton report that IDV adopted a code of business, which contains specific and explicit reference to discrimination. It places the emphasis on individuals, not groups, for the way people should be treated, stressing that processes should be fair and objective. In order to make people aware of the issues relating to diversity, a senior management training programme was undertaken, which included the whole of the board as well as the chief executive, and incorporated over 200 senior managers. The workshops were used to explore diversity and see its relevance to the organization, as well as to gain feedback from senior managers as to what should be done, and what should not be done, next. Kandola and Fullerton report that at IDV the issue of diversity is not seen as standing alone, isolated from the rest of the business. Instead, it is seen as something that should run through other policies and processes. In the organization's vision and principles, other aspects of diversity are mentioned: for example, 'good ideas can come from anyone, anywhere in IDV' and 'IDV managers ensure that individual contributions to the overall success of the team are maximized and recognized'. Documents referring to the building of new brands also contain reference to diversity. For example: 'successful partnerships are built on mutual respect and the ability to listen to, understand and benefit from other people's points of view and experience', and 'we actively encourage diversity and skills, experience and personalities within the team'. Having diversity presented in different documents in different ways, and stressing the business benefits, ensures there is a greater probability that people will not only receive the message but also absorb and accept it (Kandola and Fullerton 1994: 101).

For Kandola and Fullerton, managing diversity means seeing the organization as a mosaic in which differences come together to create a whole organization, in much the same way that single pieces of a mosaic come together to create a pattern. Each piece is acknowledged and accepted, and has a place in the whole structure. The diversity consists of the visible and non-visible differences, which will include factors such as sex, age, background, race, disability, personality and workstyle. For Kandola and Fullerton, the concept of organizational diversity is founded on the premise that harnessing these differences will create a productive environment in which everyone feels valued, where talents are being fully utilized and in which organizational goals are met.

Gender, race and age in organizations

The study of gender provides a clear example of the need for diversity in organizations. The study of gender also shows how great is the task facing those wishing to see the mosaic of diversity operate vigorously.

We live in a gendered world, that gender is masculine, and is importantly also misogynist. The multiple and complex ways in which gender
operates to constrain us – men and women alike – are difficult to pin
down. Gender is both called forth and masked; at the level of organizational logic; it is particularly deeply covered; our institutional arrangements are presented as the only rational and efficient ways to proceed.
                                              (Davies 1995: 62–3)

Our sociological colleagues tell us that gender divisions lie deep within the
logic of organizing. The impact on people and on organizations is marked.
Cox reports that:

1 Nearly half of the 1,000 largest US employers have no women on
   their boards of directors ('Women on Boards', 1992).
2 A study of the 4,000 highest-paid people at the 1,000 largest US
   industrial and service sector employers revealed that only 19 were
   women (Fierman, 1990).
3 A 1990 study of the directors of regional Federal Reserve Banks
   revealed that only 3 out of 72 (4 percent) were women (*Ann Arbor
   News*, Sept 4, 1990).
4 Despite constituting nearly half the workforce and 25 to 35 percent
   of all managers, women represent only about 2 percent of senior
   managers (Morrison and von Glinow, 1990).

It should be noted that although the record of US firms on integration of
women into senior management is unequivocally poor, the record is even
worse in many other nations of the world, including Japan and Germany
(Antal and Kresbach-Gnath, 1987; Steinhoff and Tanaka, 1987).
                                              (Cox 1993: 183)

Across Europe, even when men and women do comparable jobs, women's
pay is significantly below that of men's (Rubery 1992). The UK, in common
with all other industrialized societies except Japan and Sweden, has experienced a decline in the employment of older men since the 1950s. This accelerated in the 1970s and 1980s and resulted in just over three-quarters of
men aged 55–59, just over half of men aged 60–64 and fewer than one-tenth
of men aged 65 and over being economically active in 1992. The participation of older women in the labour force has tended to increase slightly
since the 1970s (Taylor and Walker 1994).

Race has all but disappeared from the organizational literatures in recent
years. The recently published *Handbook of Organization Studies* (Clegg *et
al.* 1996) presents the point that the issue of racial and ethnic foundation of
organizational power and control is only just beginning to emerge within the
literature as an acceptable topic of investigation and debate. It has to be
accepted that little recent information exists about minority participation in
organizations.

Jones (1986) quotes two surveys of Fortune 1000 companies by the recruiting firm Korn Ferry International, which show that in the 1979 survey of 1,708 senior executives, just three were black, two were Asian, two Hispanic and eight female. The 1985 survey of 1,362 senior executive found four blacks, six Asians, three Hispanics and 29 women (Jones 1986: 66). For an indication of UK figures, it is necessary to consult the classic text by Rose *et al.* (1969), which found that:

> the majority of the population, immigrant and total, is found in the residual category 'other employees' which in effect represents the rank and file of the employed population – that is those not in authority (managers, etc.) or partly insulated from authority (professionals, etc.) . . . One way of expressing the data is to say that whilst three out of ten of the total population have succeeded in climbing out of the 'other employees' category in Greater London, only one out of twenty Jamaicans has so succeeded. In the West Midlands, the comparative picture is one in four for the total population, but only one in ten for Indians and three out of a hundred for Jamaicans and Pakistanis.
>
> (Rose *et al.* 1969: 152–3)

A similarly depressing picture was reported by Wright (1968):

> we have noted that, when first employed, coloured workers tended to obtain jobs which the white worker found too arduous, distasteful or unrewarding. In the firms visited during the interview survey, this was often the case at the time the research was carried out. For example: 'The kinds of jobs coloured workers do are knocking out and quenching the castings. Neither job is relished by the white worker. Knocking out is a sledgehammer job. It's outside work, so it is cold in winter and in summer bits of sand stick to you when you are sweating' (General Manager, Stainless Steel Ltd).
>
> 'Coloured workers are employed mainly on the lower-paid repetitious and semi-repetitive jobs such as electrode cleaning. This is the sort of job that if a white man took it, he doesn't really want a job at all. The West Indians are mainly employed on scrap crushing, a sledgehammer job.
>
> They also do the loading and unloading of pitch. The highest job done by any coloured worker is forklift truck operator' (Personnel Officer, Grange Graphite Co.).
>
> In four of the interview survey firms coloured workers were employed only in unskilled jobs.
>
> (Wright 1968: 74)

The data are rather old but make the point that there has been a longer interest in race in employment than the current literature indicates. It does, though, seem to be the case that following Rose *et al.*'s major report on race relation in Britain, researchers took up other interests. Kandola and Fullerton (1994) report the Labour Force Survey figures for 1994, which identified the picture for ethnic minorities. Ethnic activity rates for people of working age were highest for the white population (79 per cent) and those of black origin (73 per cent) and lowest for people of Pakistani/Bangladeshi origin (43 per cent). Self-employment was more common (25 per cent) among working men of Indian or Pakistani/Bangladeshi than in the corresponding white population (16 per cent). Over half of ethnic minority men and nearly two-thirds of those of Indian origin were in non-manual (mainly managerial, technical and professional) occupations, compared with half of men in the white group. Among women of working age, economic activity rates were the highest in the white population (72 per cent) and lowest for those of Pakistani or Bangladeshi origin (25 per cent). Working women from ethnic minority groups were less likely to work as part-time employees (25 per cent) than their white counterparts (40 per cent). In 1992 and 1993, unemployment rates for people of ethnic minority origin were about double those for the white population, and this difference applied after age, sex and level of qualification were taken into account. Among young people aged 16–24, participation in the labour market was much lower for the ethnic minority groups (52 per cent overall). This is largely accounted for by the higher percentage within these groups who are students. Qualification levels attained by 16–24-year-olds from most ethnic minority groups were very similar to those of young white people, though almost half of the Pakistani/Bangladeshi group had no qualifications, compared with fewer than one-fifth of the white population. People of Indian origin were the most likely to have higher-level qualifications (Self 1994, cited in Kandola and Fullerton 1994).

The picture presented by Rose *et al.* and by Wright is sustained by more recent research conducted in other parts of the world (Mills and Murgatroyd 1991). The task of examining the situation within organizations rather than within the labour market is urgent, because the available data are very incomplete. Change could have occurred but we cannot be certain. Jones (1986) issues a warning from the American scene.

> There is a problem that the statistics don't reflect. Listen to four higher level black executives who have achieved some credibility and status in the business world: 'There was a strong emphasis in the seventies for getting the right numbers of black managers. But now we are stagnating, as if the motivation was to get numbers, not to create opportunity. I know that companies have the numbers they think they need and now don't think anymore needs doing . . .'
>
> 'When you work your way up, try to conform, and even job hop to other companies only to confront the same racial barriers – well, it's debilitating. I just don't want to go through that again.'

'I went to corporate America to shoot to the top, just like my white classmates at business school. But the corporate expectation seemed to be that as a black I should accept something that satisfied some other need . . .'

'We can have all the credentials in the world, but that doesn't qualify us in the minds of many white people. They can train the hell out of us and we can do well, but they still think of us as unqualified. Old biases, attitudes, and beliefs stack the cards against us.'

(Jones 1986: 67)

It is just possible that labour market studies mask the situation facing people working within organizations. New studies on opportunity structure need to be conducted with sensitivity, since to some extent concentrating on the data that indicate lack of status for black workers can act to reinforce stereotyped views, but the data also provide an important indicator of the way in which organizational processes may operate against identifiable groups, such as women, older workers, and black and coloured people. Within a world moving towards diversity, conformity is still very evident in many organizations. What may social psychology add to the debate on gender and diversity in organizations?

Social psychology and diversity: ethnicity

In Chapter 3, we explored the central premises of Tajfel and Turner's theory of social identity. There we saw how group membership was clearly important to our own view of ourselves. However, it would be unhelpful to regard the influence that groups provide as implying that groups do more than provide a mechanism for social support and a means of reducing social uncertainty. Groups do not determine the way we think. The term 'group' may often be being used as a term of convenience to describe a medium range of social collective. Social categories are seen now as being much more fluid rather than fixed in their properties. This raises issues when we explore diversity. Use of self-labels varies as circumstances change.

The term ethnicity needs unpacking. The term may have at least three aspects that account for its psychological importance. These include: the cultural values, attitudes and behaviours that distinguish ethnic groups; the subjective sense of ethnic group membership that is held by group members; and the experiences associated with minority status, including powerlessness, discrimination and prejudice. Factors such as ethnicity may be socially constructed rather than categorical variables. Ethnicity is perhaps often thought of as culture. A common assumption about the meaning of ethnicity focuses on the cultural characteristics of a particular group, that is its norms, values, attitudes, and behaviours that are typical of an ethnic group and that stem from a common culture that is transmitted across generations.

Ethnicity is itself a complex and diverse concept and not a straightforward categorical variable. Henwood (1994) writes

> The value of Social Identity Theory . . . was that it sought to open up a space for a genuinely *social* social psychology, by focusing upon relationships between persons not as individuals but as members of groups within a stratified society . . . The theory states that by categorizing persons socially and locating oneself within this pattern of wider social relationships, a sense of social identity of selfhood – and hence a basis for social action – can be achieved. Within this approach primacy is afforded to the principles of social categorization and identification in order to undermine the view that prejudice is due to the unconscious psychological dynamics involved in the character formation of bigoted authoritarian individuals . . . or a human instinct for aggression in response to frustration . . . However, the strategy of simply excluding unconscious psychological processes from consideration would not be judged a satisfactory solution to the problem of reductionism by many anti-racist researchers today. Despite the fact that advocates of Social Identity Theory continue to distinguish it from other more individualistic and reductionist approaches in social psychology, there are some significant points of concordance with other contemporary social psychological accounts of prejudice and discrimination. First, while glossed as research on a social problem which therefore requires some analysis of social context, prejudice and discrimination are nevertheless perceived to have a psychological origin which can be traced back to the fundamental cognitive process of categorization . . . Prejudice, in this sense, is a form of prejudgement – a cognitive filing system . . . which is necessary if human beings are able to comprehend, act, and survive . . . Second, in time honoured fashion for psychology and in common with other social categories, 'race' is treated practically as an operationalizable, measurable and contrastive variable. Social psychology is a constitutive and productive social activity which occupies the same plane as everyday thought and understanding; accordingly it can be 'deconstructed' to establish what is taken for granted within it . . . This has begun to occur in social psychological research on prejudice and discrimination, with the result that hidden racist and sexist practices and assumptions are being revealed. The problem is not one of overt hostility and disparagement, nor in most cases of malicious intent, but of the 'new racism'. . . Unlike the old style racism, which tends to posit crude notions of 'racial' and cultural inferiority, the new racism asserts that differences between groups are simply natural, intractable, and non-negotiable, and that for this reason groups are best kept apart. It is

proving to be a potent means by which dominant groups can discriminate, yet apparently save face by denying racism . . . In the case of using
'race' as an experimental variable, Steven Reicher (1986) has considered the practice in research on intergroup contact, and pointed out
that it may, unintentionally, represent an example of new racism since
it takes the 'category' of race for granted. Susan Condor (1988) has also
found some striking and alarming parallels between new racism and
social cognitive research on social stereotypes. One example – of the
practice that she calls 'metalevel racism' – is of the quite fundamental
argument in social cognitive research that categories of people (e.g.
'race' and sex), like categories of objects, are more or less useful to the
extent that they allow for accurate, empirical prediction of behaviour
. . . Condor's second form of new racism, called 'reification of "race"
categories' again involves a treatment of 'race' not as a social construct
but as a highly 'visible' or 'distinctive' physical characteristic . . .
Undesirable stereotypical attributes are explained as resulting from
associations (including temporal and metaphorical connections)
between salient physical (e.g. black/white faces; thick/thin lips) and cor-
responding/social characteristics (laziness/endeavour) . . . A flawed and
rigid commitment to naive empiricism in this case reinforces a highly
racialized view that the attribution of undesirable characteristics to certain other groups merely reflects certain objective facts about them . . .
The assumption that the use of category and categorization is some neutral act of biological significance also has the effect of implying the
inevitability of prejudice (Billig, 1985). Billig also points to the lack of
universally held prejudice within society, given the existence of what he
calls 'tolerance'. The problem with this notion of tolerance is that it
implicitly assumes that there is, indeed, something about minority
groups which is to be tolerated – that majority groups have genuine
fears.

(Henwood 1994: 43–5)

These two extended quotations provide an articulation of considerable
concern for the current state of a dominant paradigm in social psychology.
The attempt to provide a social basis for social psychology appears to have
created problems of its own. It also poses problems for organizations and
their managers. Given that managers might wish to develop the mosaic of
diversity, how might they set about the task? It is likely that they will recognize the need for diversity management through the presence of different
groups within the organization who might, in turn, give expression to the
need to be heard differentially. Social audits of organizations might also suggest that groups within the organization have differing needs. The Phinney
and Henwood critiques of social identity and categorization theory would
suggest that the group level data be unpacked so as to reveal individual

characteristics and contributions. Kandola and Fullerton (1994) recommend that diversity be handled at the level of individual need and aspiration, but do not provide substantiation for their reasoning. Henwood provides substantive scientific substantiation. Handling the debate at the level of the group can create, or at least mask, other difficulties. One of the issues that faces social psychology at this point is that of recognizing the limits of utility for social identity theory. The theory has benefit in bringing contextual issues into play, but has limits in that it does not provide a basis for linking factors of context with factors at an individual level in such a way as to make clear the influence of both. As Henwood illustrates, this then hides other difficulties, such as the new racism, and reduces social understanding and the potential for problem-solving.

Social psychology and diversity: gender

While Henwood addresses the problem of race and ethnicity, Skevington and Baker (1989) address social identity and gender. They write that:

> Social identity theory has potential as a way of understanding both the nature and content of women's group identifications in the course of women's lives, and also the intergroup relations between women and men and their consequences for social action. The first and definitive paper in this area was that of Williams and Giles (1978). They saw women as being the disadvantaged gender group, whose social identity derives from comparisons with men. Because men are dominant and more powerful and women are less powerful and subordinate, group identification brings with it negative characteristics and inferior status. So women need to take action in order to develop a sense of positive distinctiveness. Williams and Giles illustrate ways in which the strategies of social mobility and social change have been employed by women for this purpose. If women accept their lot they may choose to enhance their personal status by individual means. For instance, by defining themselves in relation to their husband's occupation and position and in devoting their efforts to improving his social status, they may also enhance their own self-image. On the other hand, if women collectively do not accept their status as a group, they may take action to establish a positive social identity for the group. The aims of the Women's Liberation Movement illustrate this strategy well. Within the broad context of this movement women have fought to establish equality with men in working conditions and in legal and political terms. They have tried to modify the consensual inferiority associated with women's roles by encouraging women to make choices about motherhood and to take control over their own bodies through contraception and abortion.

Some writers redefined women's work in the home so that it is valued in the same way as work in the public sphere. Women have also asserted their differences from men in positively valued directions by organizing their groups in a non-hierarchical way. This contrasts with the organizational features often adopted by male groups, using stratification to form hierarchies and to promote leadership qualities . . . One problem is that Williams and Giles are describing the ideological intergroup relations between men and women from a theoretical rather than an empirical stance. In doing this they make the mistake of assuming that womanhood is perceived by all women in the same way, using the same consensual (and unfavourable) dimensions when comparing themselves with men. So womanhood is presented as a unified social category whose characteristics are well known and accepted.

(Skevington and Baker 1989: 3–4)

Skevington and Baker continue by drawing attention to Breakwell's (1979) analysis of social identity for women. She theorizes that it is the lack of consensus as to what actually characterizes 'womanhood' at any one time that gives rise to an unsatisfactory social identity for women, rather than unfavourable comparisons with men. To illustrate this point, Breakwell makes the distinction between external and internal criteria for group membership. External criteria are often social norms that are personified in stereotypes and have a consensual objectivity quite independent of fact. Internal criteria are composed of personal knowledge and beliefs about group membership and perceptions of how they relate to self. Breakwell suggests that for women these two facets of group membership are usually incompatible, because there are no static or consensually agreed external criteria for womanhood. Consequently, whenever a woman synchronizes the 'woman' that she is and sees herself to be with 'woman' as society says she should be, the focus is likely to change and the external criteria are amended. Whatever the precise nature of this change – whether, for instance, it is the image of the working woman that is at the forefront, or the mother, or the working mother – this incompatibility gives rise to the subjective experience of marginality, and it is this, Breakwell says, that leads to unsatisfactory social identity.

Social psychology and diversity: older workers

As far as I can discover, there are no studies of older workers from a social identity perspective. Decker (1983) found that business students rated older people lower on attitude dimensions of autonomy, effectiveness and personal acceptability, and concluded that this group would continue to face job discrimination. Slater and Kingsley (1976) found that younger employees tended to report less favourable attitudes towards older employees rather than older employers, and employers from firms consisting of large numbers of older employees tended to have more favourable attitudes towards this group. These studies have shown that older workers are perceived as being more likely to be in poorer health, less likely to stay with a company for a long period, more resistant to change, less creative, more cautious, having a lower physical capacity, less interested in technical change, less trainable and more accident prone (Taylor and Walker 1994). Warr and Pennington (1993) find that as many as 80 per cent of British personnel managers report that age discrimination is a problem in their area of work. Furthermore, many organizations employ older people primarily in jobs, which provide only limited psychological and financial rewards (Warr and Pennington 1994). Yet research evidence runs counter to the expected picture for older workers. Warr tells us that:

> The overall finding from more than 100 research investigations is that there is no significant association between age and work performance. The average correlation coefficient is about +0.06, but separate correlations in the literature range from −0.44 to +0.66 . . . It is clear from this wide range that the importance of age varies between different jobs and between different aspects of performance. However, the general pattern is clear: in overall terms, there is no difference between the performance observed for older and younger staff in the same job. Incidentally, in almost every case variation within an age-group far exceeds the average difference between age groups.
>
> (Warr 1996)

Taking three principal groupings within the diversity model, we can see that each has to face a range of negative images. For each group, there is substantial research evidence that the negative argument is based on a false premise. Maccoby and Jacklin's (1974) extensive two-volume treatise on the psychology of sex differences, Harding's (1993) impressive edited work on race and gender and Salthouse's (1991) account of his own substantial work on the cognitive effects of ageing all provide convincing in-depth argument that there is no objective evidence to support stereotypic and prejudiced views of women, black people and older people. It is possible to conclude that social stereotypes and categories are just that – stereotypes and categories that are socially constructed. While we continue to respond by providing evidence that they objectively fail to be justified, psychology is doing just half of its work. There is a cry yet to be heard from the deepest depths of the soul of science that a positive message needs to be developed. This is just a little difficult when the scale of the evidence is balanced to display no gender or race differences in ability and few that matter regarding age. Can we expect to reach the point that James Wertsch draws our attention to: 'Let us rejoice in our multi-voicedness' (Wertsch 1991); in other words, can diversity be celebrated and enjoyed?

The management of diversity

From the perspective of the management of diversity, there are clear business imperatives towards the positive engagement of difference. Cox (1993) reports that:

> The Asian segment of the population is growing at a rate that is ten times that of the overall population. Moreover, research on consumer behavior has consistently shown that sociocultural identities do affect buying behavior. For example, Redding (1982) outlines the eight characteristics of how a Chinese manager approached a business transaction:
>
> 1 Desire for wealth for security reasons.
> 2 A strong consciousness of family obligations.
> 3 A sense of being Chinese, which may manifest itself as anti-other feeling.
> 4 Sensitivity to 'face' that often manifests itself as a concern over the rank of the person sent to deal with him or her.
> 5 A desire to avoid conflict.
> 6 An emphasis on building friendships in business relationships.
> 7 A tendency to see things as a set of alternatives rather than a universal set of guidelines.
> 8 The assumption that interpersonal trust is of great importance, which manifests itself, for example, as disdain for the 'contract type of relationship'.

Redding notes that this thinking diverges in many respects from the typical Western approach to business, and goes on to discuss implications for marketing practices in dealing with Southeastern customers. As a second example, Redding reports studies of characteristics relevant to buying behavior among 145 mainland Chinese, Hong Kong, and Canadian executives which found that culture had predictable effects on decision-making behavior. Among the studies specific conclusions were the points that culture affects problem identification and the objectives motivating choice in decision situations. In view of the effects of culture on consumer behavior, selling goods and services in the increasingly diverse marketplace should be facilitated by a well-utilized, diverse workforce in several ways. First, there is the public relations value . . . of being identified as managing diversity well . . . Second, firms may gain competitive advantage from the insights of employees of various cultural backgrounds who can assist organizations in understanding the cultural effects on buying decisions and in mapping strategies to respond to them. A third, somewhat different example, is Maybelline's Shades of You line of cosmetics developed specifically for women with darker skin colours. Introduced in 1991, the product line did 15 million dollars of sales, beating the industry standard for a major first-year success by 50 percent . . . This example, illustrates the potential value of market segmentation based on culture identity groups.

(Cox 1993: 29–31)

Moving to consideration of older workers, it is typically found that job satisfaction is significantly higher among older workers, particularly when the focus of investigation is on the nature of the work itself, rather than with aspects of the organizational context.

Satisfaction with pay is often found to be positively associated with age, but less so with promotion, co-workers and supervision. In a study of human service workers, older people reported lower levels of burnout in terms of emotional exhaustion and depersonalization. All of this is perhaps because older workers have moved to situations in which the aspects of work that they value are present (Warr 1996).

Davies (1995), in exploring what she calls cultural codes of gender, contrasts key features of the 'masculine' and the 'feminine' voice. To the feminine voice she ascribes the codes of relation (in contrast to the masculine separation), connectedness (in contrast to boundedness), responsibility to others (in contrast to responsibility to self), selflessness (in contrast to self-esteem), self-sacrifice (in contrast to self-love), concrete contextual thinking (in contrast to abstract, rule-governed thinking), understanding/use (in contrast to mastery/control), emphasis on experience (in contrast to emphasis on expertise), skills/knowledge as confirmed in use (in contrast to skills/knowledge as portable acquisitions), reflective (in contrast to decisive), accommodative (in contrast to interrogative), group-oriented (in contrast to hierarchy-oriented), loyal to principles (in contrast to loyal to superordinates) and facilitative/expressive (in contrast to agentic/instrumental) (Davies 1995: 27). Management needs to ensure expression of both voices if it is to avoid conformity and celebrate diversity.

As organizations move from being hierarchical and remote in their decision-making processes to being concerned with the localized empowerment of teams based on problem-solving, it is possible to see that what are here described as masculine cultural codes will be de-emphasized, while feminine cultural codes may become the favoured pattern for successful adaptation in the changing world environment. The reflective and the connected, the accommodative and the group-oriented features ascribed to the feminine cultural codes seem likely to be successful in the consumer-oriented demands of today's world markets. The codes are not presented as things that women have that men do not. The point presented is that difference can be celebrated. Further, gender is to be understood at many different levels (Davies 1995: 30) – for the purposes of the current thesis, the levels are the individual, the group, the organizational and the cultural. Social psychology has to articulate the relatedness of and the connections between each level. Management has to find ways of enabling and expressing the values of each so that organizations become 'great places in which to work – for everyone' (Kandola and Fullerton 1994).

Multiple voices and multiple groups: the expression of diversity

Culture can be a focal concept in framing the positive aspects of diversity, but there is a need to ensure that our conceptions of the social collective and the individual are adequately linked. The points that Kandola and Fullerton (1994) have made about the need to enable individual perspectives to develop through the management of diversity would be lost if managers were to assume that every member of a group thought in the same way or sought to contribute in an identical manner. Culture can be seen in terms of highly variable systems of meanings, which are learned and shared by people (Rohner 1984; Ferdman 1995). There is some advantage in focusing specifically on psychologically relevant elements of culture, such as roles and values (Betancourt and Lopez 1993), since some descriptions of culture (Hofstede 1980; Triandis 1994) provide generalized pictures of large-scale groups without providing guidance as to the degree to which such accounts might apply to given individuals. Individuals resist overgeneralizations about them and this, according to Ferdman (1995), makes it difficult to frame cultural differences positively. The framing of language is crucial to the celebration of difference, whether psychologically or sociologically. That language signifies difference has been the distinguishing contributions of semiotics since Saussure (1857–1913). The South Australian Department of Labour (1992) presents an encouraging picture to those involved in job evaluation for women, which is intended to support them in using terms that present their contribution as positive rather than denigrating. For example, 'I am responsible for the presentation of the company and its image to visitors' rather than 'I am just a receptionist', 'I prepare the organization's high-level reports' rather than 'I am only a typist' place high value and encourage the processes of personal valuing of work that might otherwise be invisible and unnoticed by both the job holder and the evaluator.

James Wertsch (1991) develops the links between language, culture and our psychology in a chapter that he calls 'The multivoicedness of meaning'. We seldom explicitly consider the term 'literal meaning'. Instead, we contrast it with notions such as 'figurative meaning' or 'metaphorical meaning'. Wertsch tells us that

a small group of scholars such as Goffman (1976) and Rommetviet (1988) have recognized that issues concerning literalness of meaning range all the way from folk lore linguistics to axiomatic features of formalized semantic theory. They recognize that the idea of literal meaning is grounded in what have become everyday practices in the western world having to do with literacy and modern scientific rationality.

These have now come to form such a pervasive part of modern life (especially among those who *write* about literal meaning) that it is now very difficult to recognize that 'the assumption that there is such a strict and literal meaning of an expression turns out to be an ethnocentric assumption' (Taylor 1985, cited in Wertsch 1991: 84). Socio-linguistics informs us that speech forms privilege a particular view of language and of language activity, and this makes social communication both possible and a problem. If even the fundamental term 'literal meaning' has become so embedded in ethnocentric assumptions, how much more have terms that express race, gender and age become entwined in our cultural and linguistic histories? In a world in which everything can be placed in the analytic and critical arena, managers themselves face an interesting task in managing diversity, for absolutely nothing can be taken as given and even less can be taken for granted. Yet, as Wertsch and those upon whom he draws tell us, the importance of language lies in its dialogic activity, not in its structure and form alone. It is through dialogue that our own minds (our psychologies) link, form and are formed, by and with others and hence cultures.

Giles and Johnson (1981) note that social identity theory is a dynamic perspective, which also has the potential for considering ethno-linguistic change. In particular, a negative social identity would be expected to act as a motivating factor in social change, as a means of attaining a more satisfactory social identity; a dominant group, which has satisfactory conditions for its ethno-linguistic identity, would desire to maintain the status quo. Albo is cited by Giles and Johnson as having studied the effects of group assimilation on two subordinate collectivities in the Andes. As the subordinate ethnic groups attempt to assimilate into the dominant Spanish-speaking group, their ethnic languages become restricted to certain domains of usage. This results in their language lacking neologisms for technical advances etc., since Spanish words are used instead to denote prestige. For example, the Spanish word is adopted for a modern kitchen, whereas the ingroup word is used for a traditional kitchen, and Spanish words are preferred for telling the date or time, while native numerals are allowed for counting sheep. The frequency of borrowing Spanish words varies with the topic: for example, only 11 per cent borrowed words for a theme such as 'fear of spirits', but over 40 per cent borrowed Spanish words in discussions of politics or modern medicine. Thus, impoverishment of speech of the subordinate groups' language will be impossible on certain topics.

The strategy of upward mobility is not always ultimately a successful means of attaining a more satisfactory social identity. Indeed, rather than producing the desired effect, it may instead lead to anomie and a loss of cultural distinctiveness for those individuals who still value their ethnic group membership and see language as an important dimension of it. Thus, acquiring another ethnic group's speech style can lead sometimes to 'subtractive bilingualism' for an ethnic group with an inadequate social identity. Further, the dominant group frequently does not fully accept the subordinate group, even after it has attempted to assimilate, as this in turn diminishes the dominant group's own psycholinguistic distinctiveness (Giles and Johnson 1981: 220). A range of strategies to respond to the issue of social identity and the problems created by status imbalances are discussed by Giles. But the keystone for social identity theory and for diversity is that in organizational life we are all members of more than one group at a time. We are members of a multiplicity of different groups. People are part of many types of groups at the same time. The meaning that we give to any particular group membership may well relate to the constellation of our other social identifications. Ferdman (1995) reports a study of how people of Mexican descent born in the United States (Chicanos) and immigrants to the United States born in Mexico (Mexicanos) constructed their social identities quite differently, such that each had different associations among family, class, gender, nationality and ethnic identities. Among Chicanos, but not among Mexicanos, these identities were correlated with the reported amount of contact with a variety of other groups. Hurtado *et al.* (1993) point out that:

> Different social experiences, even among people who share an objective categorical membership, can encourage the perception and establishment of subtle and detailed group distinctions. Mexican descendants recognize that some members of this category are farm workers, others working class; some are Catholic, others Protestant, some are recent immigrants, others third-generation. They go on to use these distinctions to construct different social identities.
>
> (Hurtado *et al.* 1993, cited in Ferdman 1995: 45)

Rodriguez-Scheel (1980) presented Chicanos in Detroit with a set of labels and asked each respondent to select one label to identify himself or herself. Non-ethnic categories – for example, occupation, family-related, racial, religious and/or linguistic – were picked at least as often as ethnic labels. As Hurtado *et al.* (1993) concluded: 'To isolate one criterion as capturing the essence of ethnicity is to artificially limit and simplify its nature and to represent the Mexican-descent population as a homogeneous aggregate.' In a study of Hispanic managers, Ferdman and Cortes (1992) point out:

> The findings . . . highlight some of the ways in which the individual expression of group-level cultural features is modified by and interacts with other variables. Some of these include organizational demands, minority roles, specific situations, and both organizational, and individual perceptions of ethnicity. For both the Hispanic managers at

XYZ, as well as for the organizational researchers, it is difficult to 'see' culture at the individual level. Nevertheless, as the patterns we found indicate, group-level patterns are present in individual behaviour. That we can abstract such group-level features, however, does not mean that we then directly apply them back to individuals. The Hispanic managers at XYZ varied widely in their specific behaviour and outlook, as well as in how they thought about culture.

(Ferdman and Cortes 1992: 273)

When we focus at the individual level and take seriously the multiplicity of group memberships of any particular person, it becomes unnecessary to separate the person from the group to view others and ourselves as unique. While I particularly identify with others – for example, I am English and male – the specific expression of that group membership is defined by its coexistence with the variety of my other social identities – for example, I am a university professor, a psychologist, a father, a son and so on. I can think of myself in terms of a number of social identities that contribute to and form part of my individual uniqueness, whereas Turner *et al.* (1994) put a contrasting position for social identity: 'as shared social identity becomes salient, individual self-perception tends to become depersonalized. That is, individuals tend to define and see themselves less as differing individual persons and more as the interchangeable representatives of some shared social category membership' (Turner *et al.* 1994: 455). Ferdman (1995) puts the alternative position in considering the links between group differences and individual uniqueness, where the emphasis is on the personalization of group perception. England – or perhaps it is Britain – has not been much loved in recent centuries by either Ireland or Scotland. As an Englishman who has lived and worked in Northern Ireland and Scotland, I may de-emphasize my Englishness as much as I can, simply by not endorsing certain aspects of the expected stereotypical response. My class and my political background help me to do this. My professional status does not help much in that particular respect, except when I am in professional company, but my family status does; and so on. When I am with my professional group, my nationality is not a concern. This is often not the case for many black people or for women working in organizations. The respective groups experience high levels of racist and sexist harassment and abuse, and experience pressure on their performance at work because of the way in which their social identities are perceived by the dominant groupings in the organizational settings (Davidson 1997).

Managing age and diversity

It would be easy to take the view that diversity will be forced on organizations by an economic imperative or that it is simply an expedient that is made necessary by a politically correct world. The argument that I wish to develop is that employing people from a variety of different ethnic backgrounds can bring organizations closer to clients and customers in a global economy, and that employing women is likely to provide an organization with a culture that can meet the needs of the future as well as the present. I have said little about older people so far, except to note that they too experience difficulties in terms of equality of opportunity. This omission results from the fact that the research work on social identity and categorization, which has been the main focus for theory in this chapter, seems not to have addressed the issue of age. We need to look elsewhere and to extend the theoretical argument.

In a short review of adult intelligence that I published a few years ago (Brotherton 1991), I noted that even Binet and Simon (1908) had been puzzled by the notion held by philosophers of the day that cognitive development is either fixed or in decline from a very early age in life. I wrote that:

> The issue of the measurement of decline has always presented a puzzle to observers of the scene. At a common sense level, it might be asked how do adults, who are said not to be in a position to benefit from increasing intellectual development, manage to perform adequately and competently in their everyday lives. The puzzle received considerable attention in the contemporary cognitive development literature.
>
> What emerges from enquiry is a new, if still often cautious, optimism. The long held belief that intellectual decline increasingly marked the passing of years is now strongly challenged (Baltes and Schaie, 1976; Willis and Baltes, 1980; Labobouvie-Vief, 1982). However, the position is also modified by those who present detailed methodological critiques (Horn, 1982; Horn and Donaldson, 1976). Everyone it now seems, agrees that intelligence *changes* in adult years – but there is little agreement about how it changes . . . the weight of evidence still favours the position that with increasing age adults do seem to process less information in a progressively slower, less efficient manner. However, this is largely true only for areas of information that are well outside the established expertise of the individual. Practice, experience, or familiarity with the task, will assist the performance of older adults to a level that is comparable to that of a younger person. Similarly, information which is related to the rich personal history of the individual is much better remembered than information which is isolated, factual, and not part of any formal and personal knowledge structure.
>
> (Brotherton 1991: 3–4)

What older employees have to offer is expertise. It is likely that they will use expertise in specific areas to compensate for the fact that their information-processing skills are not as fast as once they were, but the quality of their input in this relatively more specific area may be much more secure than that of younger people. Where knowledge can be represented in a manner that is ecologically relevant, older people outperform younger people. Where knowledge has been attained under conditions that demand considerable personal resources in terms of individuals coping with problems that face their personal and intellectual development, personal thinking styles are considerably extended (Rybash *et al.* 1986). This mode of thinking leads to the ability to construct new theories of how issues might be handled by experimentation and in new forms. Older people, women and black people jointly and severally have much to offer. We are beginning to see organizations that had once delayered and downsized now having to recruit afresh because they had reduced their labour force beyond the point where knowledge could be shared within the organization. Some organizations have begun to recruit older workers because of their reliability and their special knowledge in particular sales situations. One result is that companies adopting this policy are seen as making a special and a noteworthy contribution by customers. Positioning in the market place is positively affected by diversity policies. Diversity has positive benefits and positive potential; it is not simply about avoiding the negative.

The conformity and the groupthink models that this chapter began with draw attention to processes that lead to our failing to see that knowledge and information reside with the groups that comprise the organization, not with the chief executive alone. The notion that cognition is bounded by the individual brain or mind is reinforced by much psychology (Resnick 1991), but it is not helpful when we come to attempt to understand organizations. People build their knowledge structures on the basis of what they are told by others, orally, in writing, in pictures and in gestures. Our daily lives are filled with instances in which we influence each other's constructive processes by providing information, pointing things out to one another, asking questions and arguing with and elaborating on each other's ideas. All of this happens in life in general, as well as in organizational life in particular. Recent theories of situated cognition are challenging the view that the social and the cognitive can be studied independently, arguing that the social context in which cognitive activity takes place is an integral part of that activity. These theories argue that every cognitive act must be viewed as a specific response to a specific set of circumstances. Only by understanding the circumstances and the participants' construal of the situation can a valid interpretation of the cognitive activity be made. The organization's culture as well as the general culture of society beyond the organization will be an important influence on the way particular problems are approached by particular teams, groups and individuals. As Resnick writes:

> The social, then, pervades even situations that appear to consist of individuals engaged in private cognitive activity. It is only through social construals and task representations that the social intrudes on the

ostensibly individual. In real life – in contrast to the classroom and the psychology laboratory – mental work is rarely done without the assist-ance of tools such as external memory devices and measurement instru-ments to tables of arithmetic conversions and dictionaries and thesauruses, and maps. Cognitive tools embody a culture's intellectual history; they have theories built into them, and users accept these theories – albeit often unknowingly – when they use tools . . . Theories, implicit and explicit, both enable and constrain thinking, just as physi-cal tools do . . . What individuals reason about, the knowledge they bring to a cognitive task, provides the interpretative frames or schemas that allow reasoning and problem solving to proceed . . . beliefs, indi-viduals' schemas for reasoning, are not purely individual constructions; instead they are heavily influenced by the kinds of beliefs and reasoning schemas available in the individuals' surrounding culture.

(Resnick 1991: 7)

Celebrating diversity in organizations

Given the impact of culture on the way in which problems are faced, the issue of conformity creates a multiplier effect on the constraints that follow from that management style. There are profound problems in organizations that do not recognize diversity. In the global market place, management requires a diversity of people to handle the wealth of issues being faced within organizations at all levels. Diversity can be planned and managed. It can be seen as a positive benefit in itself and as a means of guarding against the closedness of conformity and fear. Diversity will flourish in an open organization that seeks to learn from its people and from its environment. The diverse organization is likely to see transparency in its operating meth-ods as a prime objective. It will seek to learn from errors and challenges rather than seek to hide them, deflect them or bury them. Managing diver-sity positively should make work enjoyable for people, as well as producing organizations that flourish. All these processes seem increasingly necessary as the pace of change in the networked society increases. Castells draws attention to the problem that people drawing back from the networked society retreat into narrow forms of identity, such as racism or funda-mentalism, which again come to have meaning for individuals. The net-worked society is not of itself going to create a more diverse world. It will, though, make conformity a difficult stance to maintain. However, it does offer a possibility that the greater access to other cultures will enhance the celebration of diversity. On the other hand, as Castells reminds us, the networked society is developing against the background of conflicting expressions of large-scale cultural expression. The tensions between groups and cultures grow stronger as the networked institutions themselves advance. This produces a fierce cauldron in which the elements of social change are refined. The heat is no less fierce for social psychologists or for managers involved, whether through understanding or acting upon these imposing processes of social change.

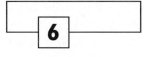

Social psychology and technology

The extent to which we may identify with work through the mediation of technology has been a preoccupation for all of social science. The issue is taken up by Castells, who makes it clear that the division between work and self could intensify further in the networked society.

Technology provides opportunities and it provides risks. In this chapter, we shall see that when there is a lack of balance between social processes and technology there is a high potential for things going wrong – sometimes tragically wrong. Social psychology has made important contributions to our understanding of how organizations are shaped by technological advances, and how advances may be harnessed more effectively to the furtherance of organizational goals. To illustrate the importance of considering links between social psychology and technology, illustrations from accident research are presented. The chapter then considers issues raised by the communication technologies for use in a variety of organizational circumstances. The chapter considers the design process and the need for it to be closely related to people, their needs and their influence.

Organizational and technological choice: the case of accidents

A little after 11:25 a.m., the terminal countdown began. STS 51-L was launched at 11:38 a.m. EST. The ambient temperature at the launch pad was 36 degrees F. The mission ended 73 seconds later as a fireball erupted and the Challenger disappeared in a huge cloud of smoke. Fragments dropped towards the Atlantic, nine miles below. The two SRBs careered wildly out of the fireball and were destroyed by an Air Force

safety officer 110 seconds after launch. All seven crew members per-
ished.

(Vaughan 1996: 333)

Vaughan describes one of the most momentous disasters in space flight history – the loss of the space shuttle *Challenger* and its crew, Richard Scobee,
Michael Smith, Ellison Onizuka, Judith Resnik, Gregory Jarvis and Christina
McAuliffe. Christina McAulliffe's assignment had been to teach elementary
school students from space, and her death, before the massive media coverage of the launch, gave a special aura to the disaster in the memories of all
those following the mission.

The official reason for the disaster was the failure of rubber O-rings that
sealed the joints of the fuel tanks on the shuttle's booster rockets. However,
Vaughan's analysis indicates that although the original design of the O-rings
was challenged when the first signs of danger occurred, the workgroup's
beliefs in the safety of the design was sustained. The O-rings were made of
rubber. Rubber becomes less flexible at low temperature. The *Challenger*
launch took place at low temperature. However, the managers made their
calculation of risk based only on data retrieved from launches in which a
problem with the O-rings had occurred. Had they included the data from
launches in which there had been no problem, they would have noticed that
the probability of failure at very low temperature was very much higher.
They had not included information in their calculation that was available to
them. In a sense, this looked again as though it was an example of 'groupthink'. However, many of the features outlined by Janis (and covered fairly
comprehensively in the previous chapter) were not present in the *Challenger*
launch decision. The structural features of the NASA groups were entirely
different. The avoidance of important data was only apparent after the
tragic event and not apparent as part of the ongoing process and so on. A
central problem concerned responsibility for risk assessment in unfamiliar
circumstances. Indeed, actually recognizing that the circumstances were
unfamiliar was a problem for the groups involved.

The uniqueness of the shuttle design, its components and its mission made
calculating risk a fact of life. From the beginning of the space shuttle programme, the assumption was that risk could not be eliminated. It could be
calculated, it could be predicted, it could be regulated, it could be managed,
but after everything that could be done had been done, certain residual risks
would remain.

> Risk assessments were the outcome of engineering analysis done by
> what I am calling work groups: managers and engineers at the bottom
> of the launch decision chain whose primary daily responsibility was
> technical decision making for the shuttle component to which they were
> assigned. Work groups were headed by Project Managers responsible
> for each of the main shuttle elements – the Main Engine, External Tank,

Orbiter, and SRBs. Project Managers worked closely with the managers and engineers at their space center and with the prime contractor's managers and engineers assigned to that particular element.

(Vaughan 1996: 79–80)

Vaughan presents a picture of NASA in which the daily determination of acceptable risk and the pre-launch decision-making of processes were characterized by engineering disagreements that had to be negotiated. They originated first because the shuttle design was unprecedented and its operation extremely complicated. But Vaughan indicates that disagreement was built into the organizational arrangements of the government/contractor relationships. Moreover, she points out, 'Flying with a design that violated industry standards was not deviant in the work group culture. In fact, deviation from industry standards is accepted practice in the aerospace industry' (p. 114). However, 'Signals of potential danger tend to lose their salience because they are interjected into a daily routine full of embellished signals with taken-for-granted meanings that represent the well-being of the relationship. A negative signal can sometimes become simply a deviant event that momentarily mars the smoothness of the ongoing routine ... Small changes – new behaviours that were slight deviations from the normal course of events – gradually become the norm, providing a basis for accepting additional deviance' (p. 414). This makes management difficult – not least because it is difficult to recognize that circumstances are new.

Vaughan, after an exhaustive investigation of primary and secondary sources emanating from NASA and its contractor companies, could find no evidence of ill-will or of wrong-doing. The work system and its groups eventually produced a situation in which large-scale disaster became unavoidable.

The *Challenger* disaster raises interesting questions about the interplay between social and technical forces. It is possible to argue that from a scientific point of view far more could be learned at lower cost and with greater safety if space flights were unmanned. The political context in which space exploration has taken place has largely been one of extreme international competitiveness. National supremacy seemed a more important value than the pursuit of knowledge or the advancement of technology throughout the space programmes (Heppenheimer 1997). Political considerations demanded that flights be manned.

Nevertheless, it would be wrong for us merely to assume that technology dominates in its interplay with social forces. Latour (1996) documents the fate of 'Aramis', a guided transportation system intended for Paris. The system represented a major advance in personal rapid transit: it promised the combined efficiency of a subway with the flexibility of an automobile. The system failed to be implemented because its couplings proved too complex and expensive. However, the complexity and cost issues became political issues in themselves both between contractor and subcontractor and between contractor and local and national administrations. In the end, the political will failed and the project was ended in 1987.

Turner and Pidgeon (1997) review a number of disasters, such as the Aberfan colliery tip avalanche that engulfed a school and killed 144 people, the majority of them children. In each case, the precise pattern of events and their major technical components were different, yet Turner and Pidgeon discern a number of organizational similarities. In each case, the accurate perception of possibility of disaster was inhibited by cultural and institutional factors.

> All organizations develop within them, as part of the equipment which they use in operating organizationally upon the world, elements of continuous culture which relate to the tasks which they face, to the environment in which they find themselves, and to the manner in which those within the organization are to interact with each other and with any equipment they may use. Part of the effectiveness of organizations lies in the way in which they are able to bring together large numbers of people and imbue them for a sufficient time with a sufficient similarity of approach, outlook and priorities to enable them to achieve collective, sustained responses if a group of unorganized individuals were to face the same problem. However, this very property brings with it the danger of a collective blindness to important issues, the danger that some vital factors may be left outside the bounds of organizational perception.
>
> The Aberfan Inquiry makes it quite clear that the pervasive set of beliefs and perceptions within the coal industry, was for very good reasons, oriented almost wholly towards the problems, difficulties and activities of underground mining, and away from tips as being in any sense important for those involved with mining . . .
>
> At Summerland a crucial set of stairs was referred to and thought of as 'service stairs' rather than as 'emergency stairs' and a description of the project by the architect referred to it as 'not a building, but a weather-proof enveloping structure' which the Commission found to be both confusing and misleading to a client.
>
> (Turner and Pidgeon 1997: 46–7)

Some of the issues that were material to the eventual disasters had in each case been observed by many of those well acquainted with both the everyday operation of the eventual disaster site and the hazard itself, yet they had failed to act upon their concerns in a way in which the management of the situation could have been accomplished. Turner and Pidgeon present detailed analyses of perceptual errors and omissions of action from a multiplicity of perspectives. Their summary discussion is generally informative.

Turner and Pidgeon's analysis pays particular attention to disaster situations, and they say that when hazards arise they will be spotted more readily if they can be detected within existing communication channels and handled as a matter of routine by those who have executive responsibility. How likely it is that the normal channels will operate so as to handle hazards effectively is a matter of debate. Charles Perrow (1984) held the view that major accidents arise from the interaction of a chain of unanticipated errors and misunderstood events in complex and ill-structured situations. Perrow presents an analysis that focuses primarily on the prior structural properties of complex technical systems and on two characteristics. The first of these is systems complexity, or the potential for unforeseen interactions to occur. The second is that of 'coupling', or the extent to which the interconnected structure of a system facilitates the rapid and uncontrolled propagation of undesired events. Perrow argues that where systems are very complex and closely coupled, accidents are inherent in their design; systems of this kind generate what Perrow calls 'normal accidents'. High complexity is associated with such factors as tight spacing of equipment, very close production steps, common mode connections of components, limited awareness of interdependencies because of personnel specialization, limited understanding of some processes and so on. Tight coupling is associated with such factors as unacceptability of delays in processing, invariant sequences of operation, only one method to meet the goal, little slack possible in supplies, equipment or personnel etc.

As Reason (1990) points out, tightly coupled systems have become increasingly opaque to the people who manage, maintain and operate them, particularly if the systems are also, as Rassmussen (1988) indicates, 'defended in depth'. That is, several independent events have to coincide before the system responds by visible changes in behaviour. Reason cites the work of Bainbridge (1987: 272), who has 'expressed in an elegant and precise form many of the difficulties that lie at the heart of the relationship between humans and machines in advanced technological installations. She calls them "the ironies of automation". Many system designers view human operators as unreliable and inefficient and strive to supplant them with automated devices. There are two ironies here. The first is that designers' errors make a significant contribution to accidents and events. The second is that the same designer who seeks to eliminate human beings still leaves the operator "to do the tasks which the designer cannot think how to automate".' Reason then points out that from the point of view of operator attention, the situation has become less than optimal because the belief will have been created that the system does not fail. This makes it difficult for vigilance to be maintained for more than very short periods, as well as making training problematic because elaborate descriptions of situations that occur rarely become demanded. There seems an inescapable need to bring the designer and the user closer together in determining the specifications for work in technological systems. Many of the formal processes for accident enquiry seem to militate against the possibility of developing a more rigorously integrated approach to the design, operation and management of systems. The consequence of focusing on each event in isolation presents us with systems that make increasingly less sense.

I travelled from East Midlands Airport to Belfast sitting next to someone who was an accident investigator and was still examining the Kegworth air tragedy. I asked him how the investigation was going. 'Pilot error' was his response. The pilots had taken delivery of a new plane with a totally new engine design. I understand that the pilots had little training with the new plane because it was considered to be only a modification of a previous model. In mid-flight a fault with an engine occurred, and the wrong engine seems to have been shut down – leaving the plane with no power. The plane crashed just outside East Midlands Airport, killing some 35 people who were on their way from London to Belfast. Apparently, the pilots had received only the most rudimentary training in what was a new system. I told my fellow passenger that the coroner's report had indicated that a considerable number of deaths and injuries had occurred because of whiplash, and that these could have been avoided had seats been rear, rather than forward, facing. Some where strangled by their own clothing as the plane hit the ground. Many people had lost their eyesight because their spectacles smashed into them on impact. I found this particularly distressing, because Central European Airlines had a procedure that required that passengers take off spectacles and loosen ties when the emergency was signalled. British airlines still do not adopt this procedure. They also claim that passengers do not favour rear facing seating.

The judgement 'pilot error' seems to a social psychologist like the fundamental attribution error. Heider (1958) first drew our attention to the distinction in the formulation of potential causal factors as being internal to the actor (ability, effort, intention etc.) or external to the actor (task-related factors, luck etc.). As Hewstone (1989) points out, this distinction is fundamental to social psychological research on perceived causality. The more a person was seen as causing an action, the less the environment was perceived as causal (and vice versa). Of course, it is possible that investigators are aware of social psychological research in this area, and that legal considerations drive them towards a finding that reduces the possibilities of a large insurance claim or a huge public relations problem. However, attribution is problematic at a social psychological level and ought not to be ignored – particularly when the outcome is to ignore a more satisfactory outcome for systems and their users. As we have seen, technology provides a major interface between the organization and the environment in which it operates. The second factor in the equation is that technology and social groups interact because technology shapes and distributes the tasks that groups undertake within organizations.

Technology shapes group performance

The classic work in sociology is by Robert Blauner (1964), and it marks a starting point to the empirical and theoretical investigation of the groups and technology interaction. Blauner defines technology as a 'complex of physical objects and technical operations (both manual and machine) . . . Primarily the machine system' (p. 6).

Technology determines the extent of powerlessness that a worker experiences. It does this directly because the nature of the machinery determines the amount of control a worker can have over his or her work process. Meaningless is the consequence of the division of labour or work organization in a factory. Isolation or social alienation is indirectly influenced by technology, which 'determines a number of aspects of industrial structure that affect cohesion and integration: the occupational distribution of the work-force, the economic cost-structure of the enterprise, the typical size of the plant, and the existence and structure of work groups' (Blauner 1964: 25).

On the basis of some case studies of different factories and the reinterpretation of an early national survey of workers' attitudes, Blauner argues that empirical evidence shows how four distinct patterns of alienation exist and how these are related to four different types of technology. Craft work in the printing industry minimized alienation by allowing workers control over work processes, providing 'whole' tasks which were meaningful, creating the conditions for a social community based on the feelings of occupational identification of skilled craftsmen and fostering self-esteem.

Machine-minding or assembly work in large batch and mass production industries, such as textiles and automobiles, maximizes alienation, because workers are powerless in the face of machines, they have meaningless work and they are isolated in large and anonymous factories, which have occupationally undifferentiated masses of unskilled workers who have no little chance of forming sociable groupings on the shopfloor, while their work tasks deny them any sense of self-esteem at work. Automated work in continuous-process oil refineries and chemical plants reduces alienation to the craft level. The work is routine for much of the time, but periodically demands the use of skill and initiative during emergencies, when workers control the plant, and, even during routine working, provides a greater variety of tasks and responsibilities and more personal involvement than machine-minding in other industries. Continuous-process plant provides workers with an overall view of the production process and allows them to understand their contribution to the final product. Managers can use the extent to which groups become cohesive so as to integrate individual workers into the company. Groups then become important in the motivational processes of organizations. Jobs are arranged in a hierarchy of skill, which allows people to develop their abilities and supports a normative structure favourable to the firm, for those in higher positions have internalized the goals of the enterprise and express its values.

The final theme in Blauner's argument is the claim that his four technologies, a cross-section of technological types in American industry at one point in time, in fact represent stages in the progressive development of technology itself. According to Blauner, technology evolves historically: from craft work, where products are unstandardized, mechanization is low and hand work predominates; through intermediate machine-tending and assembly-line stages, where products are more standardized, mechanization is higher and operators either 'mind' machines or assemble parts on a moving line; to automated work, where products are highly standardized, mechanization is so complete that operators simply monitor instruments, unless the process develops faults, in which case it requires operator initiative, and work tasks are done by teams of workers. So the long-term trend is for craft work to decline and automation to grow, ultimately even to replace the intermediate stages of technology. Because alienation is low in the technological extremes of craft and automated continuous-process work, but high in machine-tending and assembly-line work, Blauner concludes that alienation can be visualized as an inverted U-curve: alienation grows with the shift from craft to intermediate technologies but declines with automation, which Blauner regards as the technique of the future. There has been much criticism of Blauner's evidence, and his apparent 'technological determinism', but general support for the broad notion that technology helps to structure social relations on the shopfloor and elsewhere in organizations (Hill 1981). To be sure, it would not be helpful to see technology as determining social relations. As one commentator puts it:

> The socio-economic context impinges on the development, selection and application of technology just as much as the other way round. Technology is not autonomously given but developed to suit socio-economic purposes. Technical and socio-economic arrangements, including training and qualification structures, thus determine each other. Reciprocal determination then means that outcomes are ambiguous.
>
> (Sorge 1984)

Hill criticizes Blauner's fundamental methodology, which was based on a mixture of case studies drawn from secondary sources and from outdated survey findings. Indeed, when the Blauner variables have been followed through with more rigour, other factors such as organizational size have been found to have a more consistent impact on employee attitude (Stephenson et al. 1983). Technology itself is not a single entity and certainly does not have unvarying effects, but, as Blauner's study demonstrates, takes different forms in particular circumstances.

Technological variations and their social psychological impact on organizations: acceptance of change

Present-day information technologies cover a huge range of activities, from robotics and computer-integrated manufacturing to advanced telecommunications and decision support. Neither culture nor social context is a single form. Training policy impacts at a societal level on the development of skill and on the extent to which technology can be advanced. Advancement in technology and its associated skills can happen at different paces and with various degrees of smoothness. As Warner (1986) points out, the relationship between technological change and skills is a complex one, insofar as the latter acts as a constraint on the former. It is likely that high levels of technological change will be increasingly associated with hybrid (or mixed) skills, where workers and managers will have less specialized training and broader ranges of taught capabilities to cope with the evolving technological challenges. Low levels of technological change may be found with low skill levels. Warner proposed that the greater the degree of technical change, the greater the need for hybrid skills, with broader rather than overly specialized training: the more diverse the training, the greater its length; the greater its length, the higher its cost (Warner 1986).

Many years later, Warner's agenda is still being worked through. The call is for 'well rounded employees who can work with people and with machines'. The call is for further and more inclusive training, as well as for greater investment in technology. At the level of the organization, Child has observed that: 'Managers will normally have several goals in mind when introducing new technology into companies' operations. The emphasis between these is likely to vary according to the priorities and purposes of their organization and the context in which it operates' (Child 1984). On the other hand, Blackler has described much of what management did in respect to technology as 'muddling through', although he later notes that managers were learning from their mistakes (Blackler 1988). Yet despite this, employees and their representatives have been largely accepting of technological change. This contradicts accepted wisdom, as Daniel's (1987) analysis further suggests:

> 'We all know how profound and pervasive is resistance to change at the level of our social structure. We have been brought up on the literature'. So said a distinguished social psychologist at a meeting I attended when drafting these conclusions. In the light of the results of our present research it appears that the literature is wrong or has become out of date, so far as technical change is concerned. Certainly, the stream of thinking that suggested that workers and their trade unions could be expected to be resistant to technical change has been shown to be inadequate by our results. In summary we found that British workers

generally experience and accept a very high level of major change. Major change affecting manual workers is common, and change affecting office workers is even more so. We found no evidence in our study of 2,000 workplaces that the rate or the form of change affecting either category of employee was inhibited by trade union organization. Technical change was generally popular among the workers affected, but both shop stewards and full-time union officers tended to support changes even more strongly than the ordinary workers they represented. Where there was resistance to change by workers and union representatives, it was most frequently provoked by organizational changes introduced independently of any new technology. Even so, there was no sign that the general effect of trade unionism was to act as an obstacle to any form of change. On the other hand, it did appear that systems of management or the nature of management structures were associated with the propensity of workplaces to innovate. So great has been the support of workers and trade union representatives for technical change that management have not had to use consultation, participation or negotiation to win their consent to change. Even major changes have been introduced with surprisingly little consultation.

It has been rare for technical change to be subject to joint regulation. Both manual workers and office workers have tended to derive benefit from technical change in terms of increased earnings and more skilled, more responsible and more interesting jobs. The workers directly involved in the introduction of advanced technological change have tended to be insulated from any damaging consequences of the change as regards employment. Managements have developed methods of reducing the size of workforces that are relatively painless.

As I argued in 1988, it is now time for a new agenda in psychological research to take us forward from the narrowly based view that workers resist change (Brotherton 1988). This is a view that has currency with managers (Northcott and Rogers 1985) but, as Daniel clearly demonstrates, has little support empirically.

In the United States, the picture has been somewhat similar. The relation between management and worker has been one in which technological change has brought the opportunity to bargain for shorter hours, greater training and job upgrading (Cornfield 1987).

Agricultural groups

Reviewing the American scene underlines the picture of the scope and variety of technological change.

In the early 1960s for example, the breeding of new tomato varieties,

durable enough to withstand the rough and tumble of mechanical harvesting, made it possible for growers to cut the labour force by two-
thirds, increase yields, and achieve greater reliability in the timing of
deliveries. Tomatoes once picked and sorted by hand, are now uprooted
and 'de-stalked' mechanically and sorted with the aid of electro-optic
sensors. Equally impressive, in the early 1970s scientists and engineers
employed microelectronics to devise harvesting machines which can
'select' mature lettuce heads for cutting, thus allowing multiple passes
through a field as the crop ripens.

(Thomas 1987)

The spread of the new mechanized methods took place against the background of employer–union battles over control of the work, the conditions
under which it was done and the wages that were paid. Without those
battles, technology would have taken hold much more rapidly. However,
once fought, a much greater concentration of production took place.

Printing

The US printing industry saw within the span of a decade 'the remembrances
of our preindustrial past and the prefiguring of the future of an automated
society'. The industry spawned a craft consciousness whose essential ingre-
dient is 'the ability of labour as a collectivity to control the destiny of the
craft', what Jackson calls the 'conceived interests of a work group'.

Craft consciousness is an ideology grounded in the concrete experience
of the occupation and the ability of its incumbents to maintain their
indispensability to the labour process against the encroachments of
market forces, technological change, and other circumstances. For
generations the printing trades exemplified a high degree of craft consciousness. But as the result of technological changes there has been a
decline not only in craftsmanship, but also in the crafts consciousness
of newspaper workers. This tendency is most evident in the growing
inability of craft unions to control the impact of new technology on
their employment and the nature of their work.

(Kalleberg *et al.* 1987)

Insurance

In the American insurance sector, the rising volume and complexity of business transactions and their records led to a continuous demand for clerical
workers through the late 1940s. However, office automation slowed the
overall growth rate of the insurance clerical workforce. 'The American
insurance occupational structure is changing in three ways. First, clerical

occupations are declining and becoming more homogenous. Second, computer occupations are emerging and differentiating into a skill hierarchy. Thirdly, insurance specific, higher-skill occupations are growing while their lower-skill counterparts are being eliminated by office automation' (Cornfield *et al.* 1987).

Educational groups

Peterson reports that

> The increasing application of computerized instructional information management systems in [US] elementary and secondary schools is beginning to transform relations between teachers and principals . . . the technological change is . . . Affecting the norms of the occupation, the process of supervision, and the professional control of classroom processes. Computers are reducing the professional autonomy of teachers as well as the application of computers to educational functions, teacher–principal relations are becoming strained; teachers are increasingly fearful of the . . . Monitoring powers of administrators. The deployment of the new technology reduces teacher control over the selection of the curricula, instructional materials, pacing, and student assessment.
>
> (Peterson 1987: 137–8)

Teachers' general belief about the technology of teaching and the structure of the curriculum reinforce and support extensive professional autonomy. Teachers often view teaching styles and behaviours as an outcome of their own psychology, personal idiosyncrasy and social skill. The teaching–learning process is perceived as an indivisible whole which others cannot understand or evaluate by empirically studying and assessing its component parts. Given the unclear technology and professional norm of autonomy, educational goals are generally diffuse and multiple. When educators and the public discuss the purpose of schooling they use terms which are often fraught with ambiguous, global concepts that have few behavioural indicators. Schools are expected to produce everything from literate and numerate individuals to good citizens, from professional athletes to heart surgeons. The administrator and the teacher inhabit largely different worlds. The development of computers in education has changed the balance between the two spheres. But it has not done this in any mechanical way. Collaboration between administrators and teachers together with technologists has produced a significant change in the culture of the organization.

> When computers are used to teach new information, to practice skills, and to manage instruction, teachers face a new set of norms about their work and the autonomy they have traditionally enjoyed. Embedded in the computer programs are traditional decisions teachers make about

the form, sequencing and pacing of material as well as the ways students will be assessed and rewarded. Whilst research demonstrated initial conflict over these issues it has also shown clearly that when consultation over computerization as a whole and of administrative issues in particular has taken place then problems have been minimized. Participatory consultations over computerization have produced situations in which supervisors have helped teachers to see how data can improve student performance; use student performance data in the context of there having been an opportunity to assist student progress; involve teachers in the decisions regarding the use of the data itself; and provide assistance to teachers whose students are achieving at less than acceptable standards. Under these conditions computerization may . . . be accepted by subordinate and superior alike. Without concomitant increase to engage in decisions and policy making and without the understanding that student performance data will help them to improve student learning, teachers will increasingly find working in schools less satisfying and more stressful, and their involvement with principals may become more strained as their autonomy over basic work processes declines with increased supervision and evaluation.

(Peterson 1987: 150)

For Peterson, the future of labour relations in education will be affected not only by computerization, but, more importantly, by the amount of control enjoyed by teachers and administrators over the implementation of computers.

Medical practice

In a series of penetrating analyses of medical practice in Finland, Engestrom (1990) has demonstrated the need not only to consult but to do this in a way which links the history of a system with its current activity. He does this by recording and analysing the use of computer-based records of consulting sessions, then taking these through detailed discussion with the practitioners, indicating as he does so the contradictions in the system. The computerization of records has enabled the information held on them to be shared more adequately with the patient and with other members of the medical team. This has reduced many deeply rooted problems in patient–doctor communication, and increased satisfaction with consultation processes. It has also shifted the basis of doctor power from being wholly based in the person to being distributed socially within the team and between the team and the patient. Much of Engestrom's intervention research consisted of him, and his research colleagues, showing how the very process of computerization placed the record in the ongoing arena of the consultation. In turn, this empowered both doctor and patient to come to a more humanly based understanding of the patient's condition and lifestyle than had been possible when, under the pre-computerized system, records were manually produced following a consultation. Doctors need Engestrom's research assistance to point out to them that the records had once simply been an administrative chore. Now, under the computerized system, they were useful in themselves in what had become an innovation.

McGrath and Hollingshead's TIP theory

Technological change transforms the culture and the patterns of inter-action that are available in the social situation. It does this in different ways according to the historical development of the particular tasks that involve the specific groups of workers, administrators and managers within organizations. The more that psychologists gather evidence on the way in which these processes take place in context, the more it becomes apparent that there is a set of dynamics at work that transcend the immedi-ate situation implied within the particular context. Whether these pro-cesses can be captured experimentally by social psychologists becomes an issue for further exploration. Whether the managers in organizations can capture the processes becomes a challenge. What is certain is that much of the change process can be made predictable – it does not have to remain the subject of resistance or the source of error and failure, still less of dis-aster.

One of the bravest attempts to bring social psychology into line with the challenges faced by new technology has been the work of McGrath and his colleagues (McGrath 1990; McGrath and Hollingshead 1994). They pick up from Steiner's analysis, which was presented in detail in an earlier chapter. They present a general approach to groups, called time, interaction and per-formance (TIP) theory. The approach needs to be set out in some detail for the arguments that follow to be appreciated.

TIP theory regards groups as continuously and simultaneously engaged in three major functions; production, member support, and group well-being. These functions represent, respectively, contributions of the group to its embedding organization, contributions of the group to its participating members, and contributions of the group to its own con-tinued functioning as an intact social unit.

Groups carry out those functions by means of activities in one or another of four modes . . .

Mode I: Inception of a project (goal choice);
Mode II: Solution of technical issues (means choice);
Mode III: Resolution of conflict (i.e. of political rather than technical issues); and
Mode IV: Execution of the performance requirements of the project.

Modes transcend functions, and there are parallel but distinguishable forms of the modes within each of the three functions. Furthermore, the modes are not a fixed sequence of phases, but rather four potential forms of activity by which each of the functions can be pursued in relation to any given project. Groups carry out their projects by means of time/activity paths that consist of mode/function sequences. Every (completed) project involves at least Modes I and IV for the production function (i.e. the group gets a project and executes it). Any given case may or may not involve Modes II and III for the production function (i.e. attempts to solve technical issues or resolve political issues). It also may or may not involve some or all modes of activity with respect to the member support and group well-being functions (e.g. a redistribution of task roles, a reallocation of status or payoff relations, and recruitment and socialization of a new member).

TIP theory deals with temporal aspects of group interaction and performance at several levels. It concerns the flow of work at the relative macrolevels that are sometimes discussed in terms of performance or stages of group development . . . These have to do with the group's ability to match time units and activity requirements of its projects in a smooth and co-ordinated pattern. The model also deals with temporal factors at a more microlevel, having to do with co-ordination or synchronization of activities . . . There is an emphasis in TIP theory on processes that bring about entrainment and mutual entrainment (that is co-ordination and synchronization) of temporal patterns of behavior within groups. TIP theory also deals with temporal factors at a still more microlevel involving the flow of information, uncertainty, redundancy, and the like, on the one hand, and the dynamics of interpersonal interaction amongst group members on the other . . . At this level, the model considers each activity of a group member in terms of its contribution to the group's production, well-being, and member support functions. It specifies how particular observable behaviors relate to smooth or disrupted interaction processes, high or low rates of productivity, or high or low quality of task performance. In TIP theory, natural groups are involved in a complex set of activities. At any given time, any given natural group is likely to be engaged in more than one project, and to be pursuing each of those projects by means of some sequences of modes of activity with respect to each of these three functions . . . The performance of a given group in an organization is contingent on a number of sets of factors having to do with (a) attributes of the group's members; (b) the group's composition, structure, and patterns of interaction, as well as its developmental history; (c) the group's assigned or selected tasks/projects/objectives, and the tools and procedures by which it will carry out those tasks; and (d) the group's organizational, physical and temporal environment.

TIP theory is a general theory of groups, rather than one developed for study of technology in groups. The propositions of TIP theory provide a solid foundation for a fairly comprehensive conception of the flow of inter-action and information in work groups in general. Nevertheless, that theory does have certain important implications for technology and its uses. Indeed, in one of its presentations (see McGrath 1990), TIP theory con-tained a set of propositions that were tentative hypotheses about the impact of technology on the flow of work in groups. These propositions included:

1 Specifications of ten hypothetical or implicit rules by which ordinary face-to-face interaction seemed to be structured, and discussion of a variety of ways in which the structure of communication under various forms of technologically mediated interaction is likely to violate or ignore these rules.
2 Identification of seven categories of technology that potentially could be used in work groups. The categories were ordered along a dual continuum that simultaneously reflects, on the one hand, the time-and-space bridging expansion of communication connections, and, on the other hand, the constriction of modalities by which communication can take place. This dual continuum has conflicting influences on the flow of work in groups.
3 Specification of several major classes of effects on informational, temporal and interactional processes, some positive and some negative in direction, that are likely to result from technology in groups.

Group interaction and performance is greatly affected by the type and difficulty of the tasks that the group is performing. Furthermore, the effects of technology on group interaction and performance interact with task type . . . All group tasks can be categorized as one or another of four main types . . . [that] are identified by the main performance processes that each entails: I, to generate (ideas or plans); II, to choose (a correct answer or a preferred solution); III, to negotiate (conflicting views or conflicting interests); and IV, to execute (in competition with an opponent or in competition against performance standards) . . .

From an information processing point of view, these task types differ in terms of the degree to which effective performance on them depends only on the transmission of information among members of the group, or also requires the transmission of values, interests, personal commit-ments, and the like. They differ, that is, in the degree of 'media richness' (Daft and Lengel, 1986) required for their accomplishment. It is likely that the effects of any given form of computer mediation will depend on the type of task that the group is doing (as well as on various charac-teristics of the group itself) . . .

Many forms of technology for collaborative work in groups . . . mediate intragroup communication, and, to some degree, place limits on, and structure the communication process itself. They necessarily limit channels and modalities by which members can communicate with one another, and to some degree limit the syntactical forms by which members can communicate via those available channels. Even the 'unmediated' interaction of face-to-face groups imposes some limitations and structuring on group communication processes and other aspects of group work, often by implicit though powerful social norms.

Many technologies for work groups . . . Structure task performance as well as intragroup communication. There are a variety of other ways in which some technologies limit and structure the group's performance: by removing one or more of the performance processes from the group's performance responsibility; by structuring the amount and form of information available to the group; and/or by structuring the form and sequence of responses by which the group can do its work.

(McGrath 1994: 62–8)

McGrath says that decision support systems are one case in point. They often embed tools for structuring the generation of ideas, for setting an agenda, for attaining consensus and so on, in addition to providing a system by which group members may communicate with one another. Furthermore, such systems sometimes impose highly constrained response formats on the group (e.g. requiring them to pick a single answer from a set of pre-established alternatives, rather than allowing the group to generate and modify its own alternatives, then choose the form and pattern of response by which to convey that choice).

Communication technology and group performance

McGrath surveys the literature on groups and technology and finds that much of it is deficient in the terms specified by TIP theory.

The theory underlying our work argues that, for the most part, groups are considered as continuing, intact social systems engaged in one or more relatively macro-projects, any one of which is likely to extend beyond the temporal boundaries of a single meeting . . . Yet the research literature on computer-mediated groups is quite the opposite: By far the majority of studies of computer-mediated groups deal with single-meetings of those groups. Often they deal with groups that exist only for single meeting; a considerable portion of the literature deals with groups whose members are using that computer-mediated system for the first (and only) time.

(McGrath and Hollingshead 1994: 76)

McGrath's review of the experimental social psychology literature comparing computer-supported groups with face-to-face reveals a very uneven picture.

Ten studies found the distribution of participation among members to be more equal with computer-supported groups, but four studies found no differences. One study found participation to be more equal with computer-supported groups in which status differences had been reduced. Several aspects of the amount and content of participation were studied: computer groups had less overall participation in ten studies (no differences in two studies); more uninhibited communication in seven studies (no difference in three studies); more communication displaying positive affect in two studies; less argumentation in two studies; less social pressure in two studies; more of it in two studies; and no difference in five studies; more task irrelevant communication in two studies, more task-relevant communication in three studies; and no differences in two studies and more in one study; and less speculation in one study. Computer groups anonymity had more critical communication in two studies, and more supportive communication in one study with no differences in one study.

Computer-supported groups had a higher degree of consensus in four studies. A facilitator or a designated leader improved the level of consensus in two studies and a higher level of support improved consensus of computer groups in one study. Computer-supported groups had a higher level of conflict than manual (that is, groups with non-electric decision support systems) groups in three studies. One study found that computer-supported groups managed conflict better, one found that manual groups managed conflict better and one found that manual groups managed conflict better during two initial sessions, but that computer-supported groups managed conflict better during the final sessions. Computer groups were less likely to have emergent leadership (two studies), but were more likely to have decentralized leadership (one study) and less stable leadership (one study). Computer-supported groups tended to de-emphasize personal relations and experience less interpersonal attraction (two studies). However, one study found that computer-supported groups developed in a relationally positive direction over time and found no significant differences between computer and face-to-face groups.

(McGrath and Hollingshead 1994: 86)

Groups using computers had longer task completion times (or decision times) in 12 studies (no difference in 1 study). Dispersed groups took longer in 1 study, shorter in another, compared to groups in a decision room. Computer groups generated more solutions in 13 studies (no difference in 1 study); more task solution proposals (3 studies); more correct solutions in 1 study, but more errors (3 studies). Computer groups whose members were anonymous generated more solutions (3 studies), and computer groups were instructed to be critical had more unique solutions (1 study). Larger computer groups generated more ideas per member than did smaller computer groups . . .

Use of a computer-aided communication system in a work group is likely to lead to a pattern of participation that overall is less in amount but more equally distributed among members. There is apparently more equal participation in computer-aided groups, although with some exceptions and with most studies simply not reporting on that variable. In virtually all cases, the equalization of participation occurs because there is a great reduction in the total number of acts in computer-mediated as compared with face-to-face interactions. The computer does not simply reduce the participation of loquacious group members nor does it simply increase the participation of quiet group members. All of these studies have ignored how group process is distributed over time (i.e. a problem-solving phase analysis), and over the group's functions, modes and tasks.

In computer groups, there is less argumentation. On the other hand, in computer groups there may be more uninhibited communication, so-called flaming (especially in computer conferences), and more positive socio-emotional communication. There seems to be more task relevant and irrelevant communication, and relatively more influence attempts . . . Computer systems may serve to surface conflict more effectively, although they may or may not have structuring procedures that help groups work through conflict over time . . . It is apparent that any generalization one might make from these results is very shaky. Whereas each individual study may be methodologically strong and sound (many are and some are not!), the body of literature as a whole is burdened with a triple or quadruple confounding of communication system, task type, and research strategy. Furthermore the literature virtually ignores all group member variables. Finally, there is a wide variation in dependent variables, and they tend to cluster within the confounded task-media strategy clusters.

The vast majority of the research on which these conclusions are based is static; that is, it involves *ad hoc* groups using computer systems for a single session, often for the first and only time, compared with face-to-face groups (whose members have been using the 'technology' all of their lives.

(McGrath and Hollingshead 1994: 89–90)

The lessons of McGrath and Hollingshead's work

McGrath appears on first reading to be presenting us with a very unclear meta-analytic perspective developed on a framework that has little internal coherence. McGrath's very transparency allows the discrepancies in knowledge about computer-based work to be more than evident. What is of concern is not that there are gaps in knowledge at critical points, but that much of the evidence is drawn from studies of systems that are themselves held as exemplars in the organizational settings they represent. The studies are not drawn from naive newcomers commencing a hesitant journey. Educational establishments across Britain and Europe find these examples before them on a daily basis. McGrath's examples are taken from some of the world's principal research and educational institutions, heralded as blazing a trail to be followed by others. These are studies drawn from Carnegie Mellon, from MIT, from the Rand Corporation in association with Claremont Graduate School, from Bell Communications in association with the University of Arizona and from Texas A & M. Any prospectus of advanced educational technology would be proud to include any one of these institutions – McGrath calls on them all and the composite picture that emerges is less than happy. The picture that we have available to us as a result of McGrath's work is one in which future studies can be conducted with a view to developing the picture with much greater eventual clarity. It is also possible now to see something of the demand characteristics of computer-based technologies in interaction with the prime user groups. The framework presents a technically driven and communicatively rich picture.

In time, it will be possible for managers and social psychologists to come together in making choices of communications technology that facilitate an optimal configuration for the tasks that are to be undertaken by groups in their organizations.

Technology and human needs

Until very recently, the notion of organizational choice would have underpinned the debate about technology and social system. The basic assumptions of the systems approach were that people possess to a larger or smaller degree a set of needs that must somehow be satisfied by the work process, and it is up to a sensitive design to assist in the achievement of this. Emery (1978), for example, presents six human needs which he says should be borne in mind in any systems design activity.

1 The need for the content of the job to be reasonably demanding in terms other than requiring sheer physical endurance.
2 The need for people to learn, develop and grow on the job and to be able to carry on doing so.
3 The need for a degree of social support and for the proper recognition of effort.
4 The need for a certain amount of decision-making which the individual can exert.

5 The need to be able to relate what is done at work and what is produced to the person's own social life. Work should have inherent meaning and confer human dignity, not degrade people.
6 The need for the worker to feel that the job leads to some form of describable future.

Some of the issues raised by this form of presentation of needs were touched on in Chapter 2. It is clearly difficult to translate this form of expression into job and system design elements because its logical status is closer to moral than to practical philosophy. It is perhaps no accident that the cornerstone of socio-technical systems design is the participative approach known as ETHICS – which is the acronym for Effective Technical and Human Implementation of Computer-based Systems (Mumford 1983).
   The approach demands seven steps:

1 Diagnose both the human and the social needs. If necessary, issue a questionnaire in order to evaluate job satisfaction and employee needs which the new system should be designed to meet. Discuss the results with employee groups.
2 Next, specify first the social then the technical objectives, and then all technical requirements and constraints.
3 Set out the possible technical solutions. Evaluate these against the ability to fulfil technical objectives. Next, establish the possible social objectives and evaluate the ability of each to fulfil the specified social objectives.
4 Compare the social and the technical solutions, assess the compatibility of each social solution with each technical solution. The result should be a list of genuine, achievable 'socio-technical' solutions.
5 Rank the socio-technical solutions by evaluating each against the social needs and the technical objectives in stages 1 and 2.
6 Prepare detailed work design to assess the types of job that will result.
7 Accept the best possible socio-technical solution.

   Essentially, ETHICS is consensus management that requires a status hierarchy to make it operate. It has become yet another management strategy that has perhaps left the approach to the mercy of incorporation into the forces of Taylorism, rather than enabling it to stand as the radical alternative. What is clear is that the approach is several levels of abstraction away from the detailed analysis developed by McGrath. This level of generalization has made it difficult for both social psychologists, particularly those who are rooted in experimental method, and managers to link the socio-technical approach to specific actions.
   Hackman and Oldham's (1975) job characteristics model takes us a step closer in specifying core job dimensions, critical psychological states and personal and work outcomes across five explicit dimensions. These are: skill variety, task identity and task significance, leading to experienced

meaningfulness of work and high internal work motivation; autonomy, leading to experienced responsibility for outcomes of the work, high-quality work performance and high satisfaction with the work; feedback, leading to knowledge of results of the work activities and low absenteeism and turnover, both of which are seen in the model as being employee growth-led strengths. Skill variety refers to the degree to which any job needs a variety of different activities, skills and talents. Task identity means the degree to which the job requires the job-holder to complete a whole, clearly defined unit or piece of work. Task significance is the degree to which the job has positive impact on other people, whether they are inside or outside the organization. Autonomy should give the job-holders feelings of freedom, permit them to use their own discretion and to be free to schedule their own work. Feedback means that job performance can be readily related to results.

Hackman and Oldman's model is very well supported by empirical evidence, although it has seldom been tested exhaustively in any one organizational setting. There are few studies that demonstrate the impact of technological change on the factors covered by the model. Kahn (1987) conducted a longitudinal study of the work of travel agents – an industry transformed by the impact of information technology. Within a period of five years, over 80 per cent of travel agents gained access to interactive videotext and the world's largest travel and timetable databases. Using a questionnaire based on the job characteristics model of Hackman and Oldman, Kahn (1987) found that job satisfaction was directly related to the power of the facilities used. The simplest facilities elicited the lowest satisfaction; the most complex the highest.

Designing and evaluating technology

Eason sets out the much needed procedures for evaluating change in systems.

When a significant part of the working technical system is available it is possible to conduct evaluations which will predict the kind of user-task performance to be expected when the system is in use. User trails can now be sufficiently realistic to permit measures of quality and quantity of performance to be taken, as well as subjective ratings of functionality and acceptability. It is at this stage that products are typically tested in usability laboratories and analyses offered of the kinds of problems users encounter, the errors they make etc. The validity of such tests depends on the quality of the technical system, but also upon the degree to which the subjects, tasks and settings are representative of the circumstances in which the system will be used. If these are not reasonably realistic, generalisation of results may not be appropriate. Ideally, if the technical system is to be tested in the laboratory, attempts should be made to create a simulated version of the real setting. It is common for usability studies to be undertaken on individual subjects working through a range of system-oriented tasks, for example, moving a paragraph in a text processing system. Systems are often designed to support people working in teams and to assess such a system needs multi-user trials in which subjects work through the organizational tasks they share with one another, for example, preparing a complete document from origination to distribution. Simulations that permit multi-user trails have long been a feature of the development of major military systems . . . and this approach can equally be used in the development of systems for the commercial world.

When the technical system is completed a field trial is often undertaken before widespread implementation takes place . . . These are often perceived as technical proving trials but they can of course be major opportunities to explore all the user issues that relate to the system. If the trials permit real users to use the system (for simulated or real tasks) then data about usability, acceptability and user-task performance can be obtained. In addition the process of establishing the trial and the kinds of organizational problems encountered can be very useful evidence . . .

Once the system has been implemented and some degree of 'steady state' has been achieved an evaluation of the system can be performed which examines all issues covered within the design cycle. If appropriate performance measures have been taken a before-and-after comparison of the performance of the system is possible . . . In addition to providing evidence of the success of the system, these evaluations also provide a way of validating the evaluations undertaken during design, i.e. was it as usable as the laboratory studies suggested?

(Eason 1988: 202)

The ergonomics approach separates out the system from its user and from its social situation. The presentation of the critical stages is entirely disconnected from context. The evaluation is abstract. It is not just Eason whose work supports such an approach. Ehn and Kyng (1984) point out that 'many systems that are designed to reduce the need for skilled and experienced workers do so because the designs are based on a rationalistic world which tends to make designers view the application from the top of the organization, view the organization as a structure, whose important aspects may – and should – be formally described; reduce the jobs of workers to algorithmic procedures, and thus, view men and computers as information processing systems, on which the described data-processing has to be distributed' (cited in Greenbaum and Kyng 1991: 9). The points resonate with the observations made by Reason in respect of the designer's role in systems hazards.

Eason is providing the standard advice developed by ergonomists. The advice is technically sound and based on years of careful, but narrowly focused, science. It was the advice given to system designers across several generations of development and implementation. Yet even at the short distance of a decade it feels greatly out of touch with the world that most managers and people working with information technology experience. What is missing is any possibility of capturing the social dynamics of the sociotechnical system. The presentation places the social on the same dimension as the engineering specification, and thereby reduces its importance.

Alternative perspectives to technological design have been developed in Scandinavia and the United States by anthropologists who found the ergonomics approach too limiting and who found inspiration in the work of the psychologist Lev Vygotsky. It seems justifiable to include brief reference to this perspective in a text that is attempting to focus on social psychology.

An activity theory perspective on design

Susan Bodker (1990) takes human activity as the approach to user interface design in personal computing.

This approach takes its starting point in human activity and allows us to deal with both communication and relations to objects as aspects of this activity. Using this approach, computers can be considered anthropologically as belonging to the same category as other artefacts. Human activity is part of the social activity of various groups and it has a purpose that contributes to the goal of the collective activity. The person is part of the practice of the group. Human activity is also a personal activity, the person has a repertoire of operations that are applied in conscious actions. While an activity is being carried out, certain shifts in levels of action occur due to conceptualization and operationalization.

Each action performed by a human being has not only intentional aspects but also operational aspects. Likewise, the artefacts employed in the actions support these aspects. When the person uses some computer-based artefact in this activity, the most fundamental level of operation is an adaptation to the physical aspects of the user interface. In addition, the handling aspects serve to operate the artefact. And the subject/object-directed aspects support the development and use of a repertoire of operations toward subjects or objects through the application . . . In design we face a number of potential conflicts: Computers are inherently active externalized artefacts but sometimes we want to design computer applications that are passive externalized. Design is a social activity in which we need to communicate about operational aspects of the instrumental side of human activity. Design of user interface means the conceptualization of former operations as well as the creation of conditions for new operations . . . Design means dealing with the practices of the involved groups. Design is fundamentally a collective activity in which the various practices of the participants meet in the process of mutual learning. This meeting creates conflicts that create new possibilities in design.

(Bodker 1990: 47–9)

Designing technology, for Bodker, is a continuous and involved process that takes the competent user as the basis from which development of systems must start and to which it must remain connected. The approach stands in sharp contrast to the human factors and ergonomics approach – as well as to much traditional cognitive science. The activity perspective seeks to work with subject and object to produce a new outcome. It does not seek to separate subject and object, ignoring one or the other and ending with an outcome that is constantly unsatisfactory.

Bodker and her colleagues utilized the activity perspective in developing a series of prototypes that were built of pluggable standard components and pieces of code written in high-level language. The pluggable components range from simulation of a slide projector, fourth-generation type components, support for simulating pieces of underlying programs, support for simulating the capabilities and style of different computers and so on. All of these components can be changed and adjusted to the specific use situation. Furthermore, the video signals can be used as means of simulating parts of a computer application. The prototypical system as a whole enables people to simulate part of the computer's part of the interaction.

Bodker develops activity theory in a technique called cooperative prototyping. This uses the HyperCard environment to establish a design process where users participate actively and creatively. Among the experiments she designed was a patient case record system for municipal dental clinics.

This patient record system combines administrative information with treatment-oriented information, utilizing direct representation of teeth on the screen. The users are mainly dental assistants working in the clinics of schools. They have little or no previous computer experience. The experiments showed that it was possible to make a number of direct manipulation changes of cooperation with the users, in interplay with their fluent work-like evaluation . . . the prototype used in this way becomes a valuable input for a process aimed at implementing a good tool for the dental assistant.

(Bodker 1991: 150–1)

When set out in this way, the activity perspective stands in sharp contrast to the traditional ergonomics perspective outlined by Eason. The activity perspective puts the user into the front seat of development from the outset, rather than bringing the system to the user as an almost completed project. The approach takes people as being knowledgeable about their work as the starting point for designing systems. It takes people active in situations to be the determining factor for design and collaborates with them in producing the system. It does not take people as passive recipients of a technology that has to be forced into adoption.

Situated activity and systems design

The activity perspective has been usefully extended by the work of Lucy Suchman.

> Actions are always situated in particular social and physical circumstances, the situation is crucial to action's interpretation . . . [She explores] . . . the relation of knowledge and action to the particular circumstances in which knowing and acting invariably occur . . . The contingence of action on a complex world of objects, artefacts, and other actors, located in space and time, is no longer treated as an extraneous problem which the individual actor must contend, but rather is seen as the essential resource that makes knowledge possible and gives action its sense . . . [The second major change in her approach, as compared with others such as those in ergonomics, is] . . . a renewed commitment to grounding theories of action in empirical evidence: that is, to build generalizations inductively from records of particular, naturally occurring activities, and maintaining the theory's accountability to that evidence. Finally . . . this approach assumes that the coherence of action is not adequately explained either by preconceived cognitive schema or institutionalized social norms. Rather, the organization of situated action is an emergent property of moment-by-moment interactions between actors, and between actors and the environment of their actions.
>
> (Suchman 1988: 178–9)

Applying her approach to the analysis of secretaries undertaking photocopying, Suchman has constructed what she calls

> a descriptive foundation for the analysis of human-machine communication. A growing corpus of observations from the analysis of everyday human conversation provides a baseline from which to assess the state of interactivity between people and machines. First, the mutual intelligibility that we achieve in our everyday interactions – sometimes with

apparent effortlessness, sometimes with obvious travail – is always the product of *in situ*, collaborative work. Secondly, the general communicative practices that support work are designed to maximize sensitivity to particular participants, on particular occasions of interaction. Thirdly, face-to-face communication includes resources for detecting and remedying troubles in understanding as part of its fundamental organization. And fourthly, every occasion of human communication is embedded in, and makes use of, an unarticulated background of experiences and circumstances. Communication in this sense is not a symbolic process that happens to go on in real-world settings, but a real-world activity in which we make use of language to delineate the collective relevance of our shared environment.

(Suchman 1988: 180)

The particular project described in full by Suchman was that of designing expert help instructions to users of the photocopier. The machines that were used had complex functions and tended to provide complex instructions, often setting out steps in operation that did not follow the sequence in which the secretary operated. One interesting observation that Suchman made was that the more detailed the instruction, the more the secretary felt she had made an error when the machine malfunctioned. Complex instructions, in the sense of offering too many points of information that were not clearly focused on the problem in hand, not only presented a problem in themselves, but led to the machine itself being seen as expert and to the secretaries seeing themselves as lacking competence. Suchman recorded the secretaries in their use of the machines and persuaded the design engineers to use the secretaries' own descriptions of problems as the basis for offering advice when the machines malfunctioned. Her work led to a generation of photocopying machines being designed on the basis of providing clear and direct advice when particular functions had to be undertaken. The situated action perspective continues to lead to new developments in computer-based work, particularly when distributed tasks are involved. The situated action perspective could usefully have been applied to space flights and other such incredibly complex projects, rather than a route being followed that led to one level of complexity being added to another and so on, until no one group could comprehend the system in operation.

Gender and technology

Bodker and Suchman offer a perspective to human–machine interaction that enables not only the balance implied by that term to be maintained, and indeed exploited to the extent of full developments in exciting new products, but better account to be taken of the diversity of users and their needs. Too often, technology has been portrayed in such a way that women in particular have found it something with which they do not wish to engage.

The cultural association between masculinity and technology in Western societies is hard to exaggerate. It operates not only as a popular assumption – from which much sexist humour about women's 'technical incompetence' has been generated – but also as an academic 'truth'. Some analysts see it as biological in origin, others as social, but there are few who seek explicitly to challenge the idea that technology and masculinity go together. Even feminist writers, usually at the forefront of attacks on assumptions about gender, have mostly accepted the association, and, rather than challenging its existence, have sought to understand how and why this state of affairs has come about – and how it might be disrupted. Faulkner and Arnold, introducing a collection of articles on the subject, give voice to a common belief: 'To talk about women and technology in the same breath seems strange, even incongruous. Technology is powerful, remote, incomprehensible, inhuman, scientific, expensive and – above all – male. What does it have to do with women?' (Faulkner and Arnold 1985: 1).

While this quotation captures the tone of much feminist writing about technology, it is not the whole story. Interestingly, alongside the belief that technology is masculine, there exists in feminist writing a different argument – namely, a seemingly paradoxical appreciation that women are not entirely alienated from technology. Indeed, as feminist writers have argued, historically, women could be understood to have invented early technologies, and they continue to have relations with technology that are not characterized wholly by fear and anxiety. Some feminists see as a key task the 'recovery' of those female inventors and technologists who have been 'hidden from history' (Rothschild 1983). Women's contributions to technological innovation, overlooked by male historians of the subject, are 'rescued' and accorded the respect which is rightfully theirs.

> More fundamentally, feminist writers on technology have been concerned to interrogate the very nature of what counts as technical (Cockburn, 1992; Wacjman, 1991). They have shown that the technical has been defined in such a way as to exclude both those technologies which women invented and those which are primarily used by women. The link between technology and masculinity is thus an ideological one. Maureen McNeil (1987) warns that we should retain a 'healthy scepticism' about the assumption that men have, and women lack, technical knowledge.
>
> (Gill and Grint 1995: 3–4)

Social psychology makes a considerable contribution to the debates within feminism, just as feminism makes a considerable contribution to debates within social psychology (Williams 1984; Wilkinson 1986; Bhavnani 1993). These debates deserve, and are the subject of, books of their own. What is perhaps the central issue of concern here is that technology can be situated in such a way as to make both gender groups less than effective. It has taken no special effort to find that the most satisfying accounts of the development of technology have been authored by women. Both accounts offered benefits that accrue to broad sectors of the population. Perhaps, their most salient contribution comes from their several abilities to move the central assumptions of the debate towards people and away from an arena that added complexities one after and another.

Gender, technology and self-efficacy

It is easy to infer that the more unnecessarily complex a particular system is, the more it is likely to undermine people's own belief in their own ability. Uncertainty about a system is almost bound to affect people's belief in their own ability to control a situation. Bandura (1986, 1992) has put the sense of personal efficacy at the heart of his theory of self-efficacy.

> Efficacy in dealing with one's environment is not simply a matter of knowing what to do. Nor is it a fixed act that one does or does not have in one's behavioural repertoire, any more than one would construe linguistic efficacy in terms of a collection of words or a colony of fixed sentences in a verbal repertoire. Rather, efficacy involves a generative capability in which cognitive, social, and behavioural sub-skills must be organized into integrated courses of action to serve innumerable purposes. Success is often attained only after generating and testing alternative forms of behaviour and strategies, which requires perseverant effort. Self-doubters are quick to abort this generative process if their initial efforts prove deficient . . . Competent functioning requires both skills and self-beliefs of efficacy to use them effectively. Operative efficacy calls for continuously improvising multiple sub-skills to manage ever-changing circumstances, most of which contain ambiguous, unpredictable, and often stressful elements. Even routinized activities are rarely performed in exactly the same way. Initiation and regulation of transactions with the environment are, therefore, partly governed by judgements of operative capabilities – what people think they can do under given circumstances. Perceived self-efficacy is defined as people's judgements of their capabilities to organize and execute courses of action required to attain designated types of performances. It is concerned not with the skills one has but with judgements of what one can do with whatever skills one possesses . . . Perceived self-efficacy is a judgement of one's capability to accomplish a certain level of performance . . . Drivers who judge themselves inefficacious in navigating winding mountain roads will conjure up outcomes of wreckage and

bodily injury, whereas those who are fully confident of their driving capabilities will anticipate sweeping vistas rather than tangled wreckage. The social reactions people anticipate for asserting themselves depend on how adroitly they can do it. Tactless assertiveness will produce negative counter-reactions, whereas adept assertiveness can elicit accommodating reactions. In social, intellectual, and physical pursuits, those who judge themselves highly efficacious will expect favourable outcomes, self-doubters will expect mediocre performances of themselves and thus negative outcomes.

(Bandura 1986: 391)

Bandura mentions technology as a factor in environmental change at several points in his extensive book but does not have a study that links technological change to self-efficacy directly. He probably does not see technology as lending itself to rigorous experimental design. However, read together with the studies of technology that are available, his approach has clear implications for technological change. He sees self-efficacy as favouring a conception of interaction based on triarchic reciprocality, rather than environmental determinism or personal influences. What he refers to are behaviour, cognitive and other personal factors and environmental influences all operating as determinants of each other mutually. He uses the term factors, rather than stages, quite purposely. In his approach, many factors are necessary in order to obtain a particular effect. These factors interact in a particular blend to create a given effect and become associated on a probabilistic rather than a deterministic basis. Viewed in this way, technology and social systems achieve processual parity rather than fundamental opposition, and this has important consequences for understanding issues.

Self-efficacy and management

Bandura does report one study that cannot escape the attention of a book on social psychology and management. He, together with Wood (Wood and Bandura 1989) had executives manage a computer-simulated organization in which they had to match their supervisees to subfunctions based on their talents, and to learn and implement managerial rules to achieve organizational levels of performance that were difficult to fulfil. At periodic intervals, they measured the managers' perceived self-efficacy, the goals of group performance they sought to achieve, the adequacy of their analytic thinking for discovering managerial rules and the level of organizational performance they realized. They instilled different conceptions of ability and then examined their effects on the self-regulatory mechanisms governing the utilization of skills and performance accomplishments. Managers who viewed decision-making ability as reflecting basic cognitive aptitude were beset by increasing self-doubts about their managerial efficacy as they encountered problems. They became more and more erratic in their analytic thinking, they lowered their organizational aspirations and they achieved progressively less with the organization they were managing. In contrast, construal of ability as an acquirable skill fostered a highly resilient sense of personal efficacy. Under this belief system, the managers remained steadfast in their perceived managerial self-efficacy even when performance standards were difficult to fulfil, they continued to set themselves challenging organizational goals and they used analytic strategies in efficient ways that aided discovery of optimal managerial decision rules. Such a self-efficacious orientation paid off in high organizational attainments. Viewing ability as an inherent capacity similarly lowers perceived self-efficacy, retards physical skill development and diminishes interest in the activity (Jourden *et al.* 1991).

Another important belief system that affects how efficacy-relevant information is cognitively processed is concerned with people's beliefs about the extent to which their environment is influenceable or controllable. This aspect of the exercise of control represents the level of system constraints, the opportunity structures to exercise personal efficacy and the ease of access to those opportunity structures. Organizational simulation research underscores the strong impact of perceived controllability on the self-regulatory factors governing decision-making that can enhance or impede performance (Bandura and Wood 1989).

> People who managed the simulated organization under a cognitive set that organizations were not easily changeable quickly lost faith in their decision-making capabilities even when performance standards were within easy reach. They lowered their aspirations. Those who operated under a cognitive set that organizations are controllable displayed a strong sense of managerial efficacy. They set themselves increasingly challenging goals and used good analytic thinking for discovering effective managerial rules. They exhibited high resiliency of self-efficacy even in the face of numerous difficulties. The divergent changes in the self-regulatory factors are accompanied by large differences in organizational attainments.
>
> When initially faced with managing a complex unfamiliar environment, people relied heavily on their past performance in judging their efficacy and setting their personal goals. But as they began to form a a self-schema concerning their efficacy through further experience, the performance system is powered more strongly and intricately by self-perceptions of efficacy. Perceived self-efficacy influences performance both directly and through its strong effects on personal goal setting and proficient analytic thinking. Personal goals, in turn, enhance performance attainments through the mediation of analytic strategies.
>
> (Bandura 1992: 14–15)

Technology, gender and diversity

Bandura's study used a computer simulation of an organizational process based on self-efficacy factors, rather than being directly concerned with the technology itself. His experimental series with Wood enabled him to vary important factors adequately and without there being real-world consequences. The self-efficacy approach has some important considerations for gender and diversity in respect to technology. Carter and Kirkup (1990) estimated that, in 1986, only 4.6 per cent of professional engineers working in British industry were women. During the 1980s attempts were made to address the gender imbalances in science and engineering occupations. A survey of entrants into science and engineering degree courses suggested that the proportion of women had increased to 12 per cent in 1987/8. The figures may increase a little further as a result of continued campaigning, but the base level is very low and parity is a considerable way off. The psychological mechanisms underlying these large discrepancies may be explained in self-efficacy terms, but once more the evidence is largely not direct. Julia Evetts (1996) has completed a thorough sociological analysis of career development along gender lines in science and engineering, and her evidence indicates processes that could well have been predicted by Bandura at a psychological level. Looking at young people as they embarked on career discussions at school indicated that lack of encouragement to achieve in mathematics was one of the first factors taking women away from the academic route into science. This lack of encouragement was not always direct or based on external assessments of ability. Indeed, all recent studies indicate that there is no gender difference in mathematical ability. Few women on the maths and science teaching staff, male-dominated classes and abstract, rather than involving, lessons and exercises were oft reported factors in Evetts's cohort. In universities the balance of forces was similarly unfavourable, and even when women joined companies the social support for their position was not of the kind that could have led to high self-efficacy. One quote that parallels Bandura's approach illustrates this latter issue.

> For the women engineers at Airmax, their positions were especially difficult. They were as able as the men to develop their expertise and skills. But the continuous and single-minded dedication to the organization for long periods of time which was now required for career promotion to chief and head of function positions (company senior staff) constituted a significant hurdle. Only women and men with a single-minded focus on career were likely to climb to this level. In Airmax there were no women in senior company staff positions.
>
> (Evetts 1996: 150)

So, there was no direct determinism but a series of factors that interacted so as to produce a process of continuing imbalance. The system was presented as something that was difficult to change, and so might well have induced feelings of low self-efficacy.

Bandura notes that 'although the findings vary across tasks and age levels, the evidence generally shows that girls view themselves as less efficacious than boys at intellectual activities that have been stereotypically linked with males. These differences stem from a combination of developmental influences each of which fosters underestimation of the capabilities of girls' (Bandura 1986: 419–20). If technology is presented as being the provenance of men, then we might expect women not to see it as in their interests to become involved. However, once they do, their contributions change basic assumptions in fundamental ways that take technology forward in more wholly acceptable ways. Whether we begin from the perspective of disaster or of triumph, new ways have always to be found.

A culture of confidence

Beliefs, such as those creating self-efficacy, are an important part of the culture of an organization. The belief system is the result of collective responses to tasks and situations. The example of Airmax provided by Julia Evetts indicates the possibility that self-efficacy can still be denied even when an organization has entered a programme of structural change intended to improve the opportunities available to its women employees. Organizational culture is, I wish to propose, much more concerned with social psychological factors than has been explicitly acknowledged by writers on organization thus far. Culture is about the way in which organizations seek to motivate and reward people, about how people are encouraged to work together as individuals and as groups, how communication is distributed and maintained, and how beliefs about how things are done are sustained in the ongoing activities of organizational work. It is about leadership and its relation to groups and to culture. Technology is a crucial factor in creating an organizational culture, particularly when change is on the agenda. The research on accidents can be interpreted as indicating that technology can be viewed as dominating social organization. Yet the technology is fallible. It is quite possible that much technological change has been introduced so as to produce cultural change, even though cultural change issues seem to be rarely addressed as a priority. Social change produced as an after-thought is never likely to be fruitful. Alternatively, the contrasting positions of designers of technology identified in this chapter indicate that technological change can provide opportunities to create participative, integrative and supportive work, or it can create alienated and denatured work. There will be huge problems of identity and identification when technology is not used to enhance work. Above all, there are choices. It is the task of social psychology and its related disciplines to make these choices explicit. It is the task of managers to realize these choices. As Leonardo DaVinci said, 'Ne pas prevoir c'est deja gemir – to fail to anticipate is already to complain!' Social psychology has a special place in anticipation – it assists in the prediction of specifiable outcomes in particular situations.

7

The rise of networked organizations and boundaryless careers

Careers are probably the mechanism by which we identify and develop through work. Will the networked society enhance our development or eliminate work as we know it?

Writing in the early 1990s, Wally Mueller (1992) surveyed the impact that technology was having on organizations across the world at that time.

> Organizations which have adapted best to the changing circumstances are those which have, among other strategic measures, adopted new technology and implemented more flexible working and management practices (Curtain, 1988; Newton, 1989; Yamashita, 1989). Changes in technology and working practices have also been accompanied by radical organizational restructuring, resulting in leaner, flatter structures. The move towards responsive organizational structures sets the pace for constant change, now a reality of organizational life from the 1990s.
>
> Changes in labour market strategies and in technology have also placed another major stakeholder group, the unions, under increasing pressure. Union membership is declining rapidly, mainly because of stagnant employment growth in the blue collar section (e.g. manufacturing and mining), which was their traditional area of strength, and because of the inability of unions to attract new members in the growing information/service area. Furthermore, the unions have been struggling to provide adequate representation for the labour market segment that is experiencing the greatest rate of employment increase, namely, part-time or temporary work, which attracts predominantly females, young job-seekers or minority groups.
>
> (Mueller 1992: 314)

The processes that Mueller summarizes here have accelerated in the years that have followed. What began as an innovation has become a revolution: the technology of the computing industry itself; the growth of personal computing; the Internet as a means of transmitting information and marketing opportunities, including home shopping; telecommunications as a means of reducing geographic distance as an obstacle and as providing possibilities for entertainment and education; manufacturing technology, including the development of new tools and computer-aided design; defence technology, with multifaceted simulations and with 'smart weapons' such as minefields that tell each other what is going on; medicine, with image-guided therapy offering surgeons the ability to see into and through the patients' bodies, robotics that add critically to the precision with which operations can be conducted and advances in medical record administration; the financial world, with a new found ability to produce rapid returns and advanced calculations of turbulent activities; expert system development, with its capability of producing rule-like procedures for complex business operations; nano-technology, with the immense power to miniaturize. The list could be extended. All developments have put us on the verge of a networked world that has transformed work in all its forms (Emmott 1996; Hammond 1996).

What characterizes this wide range of technological revolutions is

> their pervasiveness, that is by their penetration of all human activities, not as an exogenous source of impact, but as the fabric in which the activity is woven. In other words, they are process-oriented, besides inducing new products. On the other hand, unlike any other revolution, the core of the transformation we are experiencing in the current revolution refers to technologies of information processing and communication. What characterizes the current technological revolution is not the centrality of knowledge and information, but the application of such knowledge and information to knowledge generation and information processing/communication devices, in a cumulative feedback loop between innovations and the uses of innovation . . . diffusion of technology endlessly amplifies the power of technology as it is appropriated and redefined by its users.
>
> (Castells 1997a: 147)

Networks

Castells goes on to describe and analyse the overall dynamics of society in the information technology age. It is one of networks. A network is a set of interconnected nodes. A node is a point at which a curve intersects itself. The actual form the network takes at an empirical level depends on the kind of activity in which it is engaged.

They are stock exchange markets, and their ancillary advanced services centres in the global network flows. They are the national councils of ministers and European Commissioners that govern the European Union. They are coca fields and poppy fields, clandestine laboratories, secret landing strips, street gangs, and money-laundering financial institutions, in the network of drug traffic that penetrates economies, societies and states throughout the world. They are television systems, entertainment studios, computer graphics milieux, news teams, and mobile devices generating, transmitting and receiving signals, in the global network of the news media at the roots of cultural expression and public opinion in the network age.

(Castells 1997a: 469–70)

It is the connections between points, or nodes, in the network that matters in Castells's analysis, rather than any necessary geographic or spatial relationship. He continues:

The inclusion/exclusion in networks, and the architecture of relationships between networks, enacted by light-speed operating information technologies, configurate dominant processes and functions in our societies. Networks are open structures, able to expand without limits, integrating new nodes as long as they are able to communicate within the network, namely as long as they share the same communication codes (for example, values or performance goals). A network-based social structure is a highly dynamic, open system, susceptible to innovating without threatening its balance. Networks are appropriate instruments for a capitalist economy based on innovation, globalization, and de-centralized concentration; for work, workers and firms based on flexibility, and adaptability; for a culture of endless deconstruction and reconstruction; for a polity geared towards the instant processing of new values and public moods; for a social organization aiming at the supersession of public space and the annihilation of time.

(Castells 1996: 469–70)

Castells tells us that capital and production remain global, while workers are largely local. Capital is invested, globally, in all sectors of activity: information industries, media business, advanced services, agricultural production, health, education, technology, old and new manufacturing, transportation, trade, tourism, culture, environmental management, real estate, war-making and peace-selling, religion, entertainment and sports. Some activities are more profitable than others, as they go through cycles, market upswings and downturns and segmental global competition. Yet whatever is extracted as profit is reverted to the meta-network of financial flows, where all capital is equalized in the commodified democracy of profit making.

In this electronically operated global casino specific capitals boom or bust, settling the fate of corporations, household savings, national currencies, and regional economies. The net result sums to zero: the losers pay for the winners. But who are the winners and losers changes by the year, the month, the day, the second, and permeates down to the world of firms, salaries, taxes, and public services . . . Financial capital needs, however, to rely for its operation and competition on knowledge and information generated and enhanced by information technology. This is the concrete meaning of the articulation between the capitalist mode of production and the informational mode of development. Thus, capital would remain purely speculative if submitted to excessive risk, and ultimately washed out by simple statistical probability in the random movements of the financial markets . . . So it depends on productivity, on competitiveness, and on adequate information on investment and long-term planning in every sector.

(Castells 1997a: 472)

Castells does not argue for the existence of a unified capitalist class that presides over these global processes. Rather, he says there is an integrated global capital network, whose movements and variable logic ultimately determine economies and influence societies. These processes are not driven by the forces of the market, with factors of supply and demand determining the outcome, they are determined by turbulence and non-calculable anticipations and unpredictable movements induced by psychology and society. His thesis reaches massive proportions and is carried by no less than three volumes of work. The first volume, cited at some length here, is set at a very high level of generality. Castells is no less sparing in the scale of his approach in the later volumes. We need some examples to illustrate the processes he analyses.

Networked businesses

There are both success and failures in the management of network business ventures. Hammond (1996) reports that virtual bookstores and computer sales companies using the Internet are doing very well. Hotel and tourism activities are being boosted by Web site booking agencies that can search for hotels by type, price and map location, downloading details and street maps for printout. Linking directly to major airline reservation centres, visitors to the Web site can check all airline schedules and book airline tickets direct using a credit card. All these ventures are utilizing the Internet in ways that exploit the technology and provide new services. Hammond also reports business failures, such as those of the Argos catalogue store, which left, complaining that after a year's effort it had sold only 22 items, the most expensive of which was a £22.95 'Wallace and Gromit' alarm clock. Hammond points out that the catalogue offered a linear print collection of goods in catalogue format rather than utilizing the super-vertical nature of the Net, with all its opportunities to browse intelligently. However, the use of the Internet for business and for other purposes is rising very significantly each year.

The Internet is just one way in which networking can be developed. There is also a convergence of computing and telecommunications technologies that has made it possible to link together widely separated computers and pass information between them with reliability, speed and accuracy. This convergence allows, for example, products to be sold in shops across the country and for sales figures to be sent to head office, design facilities and warehouses by the next morning, together with almost instantaneous replacement from suppliers of items sold. Engineering data can be exchanged instantly between design offices in different countries and so on.

Networked organizations

The Harvard Business School drew attention to the prospect of considering social organizations from the perspective of networks as long ago as 1992. Indeed, the notion of social networks overlaying organizational structures through the formation of friendships and cliques rather than formally prescribed roles set out in the form of a hierarchy can be seen in the work of Roethlisberger and Dickson (1939), and has a strong literature dating from at least that time. Nohria (1982) writes that:

> Typically, the term 'network' is used to describe the observed pattern of organization. Typically, the term 'network' is used normatively: to advocate what organizations must become if they are to be competitive in today's business environment . . . The concept of networking has . . . become a popular theme at the individual level of analysis: Individuals are alerted to the importance of their so called 'connections' in getting things done or moving ahead in life and therefore urged to network more – to build relationships that they can use to their advantage . . . the model of the New Competition (signified by the small but powerful new companies forming to develop computing and biotechnology in Silicon Valley, Prato and Modena) is a network, of lateral and horizontal inter-linkages within and among firms. They are trying to redefine their relationship with vendors, customers, and even competitors; instead of arm's length, competitive relations, they are seeking more collaborative relations that will bind them together in a network. Organizations are composed of ties of a myriad nature. Ties can differ according to whether they are based on friendship, advice, or work;

whether what flows through them is resources, information, or affection, whether they have strong or weak ties, unitary or multiplex ties, face-to-face or electronic ties; and so on.

(Nohria 1982: 1–14)

Generally, organizational theorists have used the network approach as a metaphor and this has led to a lack of specificity in analysing precisely what actions have been undertaken by managers. Ibarra (1992) draws our attention to the possibility that innovativeness and creativity are related to the extent to which members of an organization move outside the constraints of formal structures to communicate among themselves.

Innovative tasks require new knowledge, experimentation, flexibility of organizational structure, and often since it is necessary to be able to mobilize support for ideas quickly and efficiently – very different implementation strategies than do routine tasks . . . [here the concern is with] the extent to which the action or the task is central to the organization's livelihood and is associated with the degree of visibility and risk inherent in the action. One would expect different strategies to be efficacious for actions that have a critical bearing on the organization versus those having a more peripheral effect.

(Ibarra 1992: 169)

These dimensions relate to the ability of management to 'get things done' within the organization, and suggests a large element of skill in managing the interplay between the dimensions. Careful management of the balance of network strategies is seen as an important skill. Being able to circumvent inhibiting factors and mobilize facilitative activities must be a primary goal of management and will certainly demand all the leadership skills that can be applied.

The network approach indicates incredible fluidity in the fortune and the direction of particular configurations within organizations and beyond their structures. In my own contacts with the industries involved in network activities, it seems that nations vary in their capacities to deal with developments. For example, in one particular project we found that Brazil – which had just installed the latest connections technology – was able to participate, while Switzerland – which still worked with an earlier generation of connection – could not. At that point, Switzerland's technology had too narrow a bandwidth to carry our proposed development. Castells tells us that groups and communities will also vary in terms of the ability to access technologies. There will be groups that are intimately connected to central developments, groups that are connected to less central developments and groups that are not connected to developments at all. Power and influence will shift rapidly between and within groups in these circumstances. Today's dominant, powerful, majority influence will be tomorrow's minority.

Culture within the networked organization can appear unitary, with dissent being disencouraged and marginalized. The control of social processes may be in the hands of the owners of the network architecture rather than in the hands of governments. Entry to the debates on ideas and on policies may be by compliance rather than by discussion. It is a world in which today's included can be tomorrow's excluded. For individuals, skills and self-confidence at an individual level will be as important as the good fortune to be in the right place at the right time. It is, of course, a matter of balance and judgement of the managers of networked organizations as to how far the social processes of the networked society are allowed to go in any one direction, but it is a world in which the only yardsticks that are available are those that are relative.

Social psychology and networks of influence

Social psychological analysis supports a dynamic view of network influence. Social cognitive theory (Bandura 1986) distinguishes between two separable processes in the diffusion of innovation through networks: the acquisition of knowledge concerning the innovation and the adoption of that innovation in practice. Psycho-social factors include which adopter is held to have prestige and the status that can be accrued by adopting a particular change, and analysis of the cost-benefits involved in change and the extent to which the production of tangible benefits is possible following adoption, the role of the innovation within the general belief pattern and so on. So, the sheer number of linkages that a person is involved in is not the best guide to the strength of a network and its capacities for innovation: it is a question of to whom they talk and about what. To be successful, an innovation has to be able to tap the sources of prestige within it at general and localized level. Granovetter's (1985) analyses of the strength of structural relationships suggests that innovations may be diffused most extensively through weak social ties. People who have strong social ties tend to hold the same view and interact mainly with each other. In contrast, those who have weak ties are apt to travel in more diverse social circles where they can learn different things. Consultative programmes seldom take account of these observations. Wide sampling frameworks and sensitively designed questions are essential if the influence process is to be understood. The other side of the social cognition evidence on network technology is that the impact effect cannot be direct. The uptake of video on demand, home shopping and home banking will depend to a considerable extent on the way in which benefits and so on are perceived, how they impact on individuals and how those individuals beliefs in their own efficacy will be affected. Most importantly, the social psychological literature tells us that each node in the network is active in its own right. It would be a mistake to consider that linkages made in network activity were passive or acted in one direction alone. Such a mistake would lead managers to concentrate on marketing and not on product quality, and on network capacity rather than on content. By analogy, social psychology indicates important directions for the future of the networked society, at the level of the company.

Networked technologies and organizational change

Boddy and Gunson reinforce these points. They indicate the need to 'make significant changes to organizational structure and practice in order to support the new technology so that it makes a full contribution to business performance. It introduces the probability of major changes in the way organizations operate and are constructed; the organizational issues are in consequence far more complex than those created by earlier systems' (Boddy and Gunson 1996: 1).

Boddy and Gunson (1996) present a number of case studies of networked organizations, and analyses of the particular organizational changes that have been brought about as a result of technological changes. Organizational downsizing, the flattening of management hierarchies and the disappearance of middle management layers are facilitated by information technology systems. Introducing innovatory computing systems almost invariably leads to organizational change in terms of strategy, work organization in the short term and horizontal and vertical structural changes in the medium and long term. But these changes may not be effective or successful. Boddy and Gunson point to the low level of user acceptability as one of the major reasons for lack of success, and see this as a problem in the political, managerial and cultural arenas rather than due to the technology itself. They point to the fact that centralized control over compatibility, and maintaining links with customers and suppliers throughout the network, limits the prospect for user involvement in design, and presumably adds to the problems of changing culture too. Yet the commitment and support of operational users is essential. The system designers have to demonstrate an ability to design and develop systems that fit local circumstances. There does seem to be a remarkable lack of awareness of participative approaches in the network literature. Two of Boddy and Gunson's case study organizations had participative approaches to implementation. One of them used a prototyping approach similar to that outlined in Bodker's work, reported in the previous chapter. Lloyd (1996) has edited a series of papers that have been strongly promoted in Britain by government departments. The series addresses the issue of groupware. Just one jointly authored paper discusses design, and that does not carry to the word 'participation'. There is, in the series, an acknowledgement that various software approaches do not actually fit together, and, worse, that their producers do not seem to know that they should fit together. So managers of networked organizations in the second half of the last decade of the twentieth century are likely to face significant problems simply in managing the technology. Management of technology is greatly facilitated by an approach that has its foundation in a participative and psychologically based process.

Boddy and Gunşon report that organizations are seeing it as necessary to allow information technology representatives to take part in strategic decision-making and so see the introduction of the new networked systems as being organizational change issues rather than simply technological ones. They also indicate that integrated computing networks are likely to increase the interdependence of one part of the organization with another, and thus lead to tighter prescription over the manner and timing of data collection and entry. This in turn has implications for the numbers of clerical staff required to maintain these functions in the organization. Companies could either reduce their clerical staff or grow the function with the same number of people employed in these areas. The manual administration of products was similarly reduced in networked systems. Decision-making could be brought much closer to the point of activity, so the number of people involved at that level could be reduced. In the majority of cases, the tasks in which people were involved were made more complex by the networked technology, since it meant entering data often in the presence of the customer. In many cases, manual skills were replaced by intellective skills and tacit knowledge about the job was still required, particularly in being able to visualize the customers' requirements. The greatest change brought by the networked system was that it allowed greater understanding by people involved in service delivery of the process as a whole. Managers' jobs changed too. They frequently received far more data than could be useful to them without further analysis. The technology was used to transmit policy communications to staff, so the managers' communicative role was reduced and managers received very precise targets to achieve from the central control functions in the organizations. In some cases, the networked system made it possible for managers to be made directly accountable for the performance of their unit; in others, the decision-making role of local managers was reduced by the capability of the system to facilitate centralized decision-making.

Communication in networks

Early social psychological studies of computer-based networking indicated that the level of change at an interpersonal level could be profound. Siegel *et al.* (1986) have summarized the changes in interpersonal behaviour produced by computer-mediated communication. First, uninhibited behaviour may appear as a consequence of the relative absence of social context information. Second, there may be depersonalization of the situation and the behaviour as a result of lack of communication of the social context. Third, reduction of emotional aspects such as feeling of embarrassment, guilt and empathy for others may result. Finally, there may be a reduction of social comparison with others and of the fear of rejection. However, it is possible to compensate for these factors, and the reduction of cues may only be relevant in situations of interpersonal conflict or interpersonal exchange tasks (Short *et al.* 1976). The extent of the effects of the filtering out of social cues may be compensated for by knowledge of the person and/or knowledge of the organizational context in which he or she works. Mediated communication reinforces rather than substitutes for face-to-face communication. Eveland and Bikson (1987) found that people who had access to electronic mail interacted more frequently at a face-to-face level than those who only communicated in person. Task characteristics, functions to be fulfilled and the availability of alternative ways to communicate the filtered cues moderate any potential negative effects. One issue to note is that the simple number of communications increases dramatically once computer-based communication is available, whether as a result of direct management policy in seeking structural change or indirectly as a result of introducing technology.

Cooperative strategy in change

The management of change literature is concerned with issues of strategic alliance. This tells us that there seems to be little evidence to demonstrate the great effectiveness of strategic cooperation. The changes, whether structural or technological, must have a congruent, supporting framework and processes which support the chosen strategy. Piecemeal attempts at following a competitive strategy usually fail. It is difficult to single out particular innovations while the rest of the organization goes about its usual business. The entire organization has to be behind the new strategy in all of its respects. Wilson (1992) points out that the literature now enables the following synthesis.

Co-operative strategies have been said to have the following advantages and possibilities:

1 The ability to think and act on a larger scale than ever before. Organizations which collaborate enjoy economies of scale. For example, why limit the extent of service provision or product innovation to what the organization can do alone? The best alliance partners have what the organization has not (and vice versa). The result should be a strategic synergy between organizational partners as they learn from each other.

2 The facility to expand technological interdependence. Expansion in
the field of technology has been rapid. It has certainly outstripped the
rate of economic growth to which most individual organizations are
tied. In some areas (e.g. information technology) the pace of developments has often grown beyond the ability of the single organization
to use them. Co-operation could allow organizations in any alliance
to 'hybridize' and share the technological advantages between them.
3 Reduce the risks and costs of innovation and development. Large-
scale projects can be shared between partners in alliance. Again this
can be a process of expertise sharing. It can also be a factor in reducing overall administrative costs, since the alliance only requires one
administrative support function. Similarly, the financial structure of
project support can be immensely simplified by organizations in
alliance.
4 Making the best use of management talent and expertise. In situations where highly trained and expert managers are a scarce
resource, alliances between organizations can allow existing levels of
expertise to be shared around. It can also provide a forum for future
management development strategies beyond the limitations of current competence approaches.

(Wilson 1992: 114–45)

Wilson provides straightforward analysis of the benefits of networked
alliances. Making the transition to the changed structure is less easily con-
ceptualized in Wilson's careful review of the literatures of change. He, like
me, regards many of them as not advancing either the practice or the science
underpinning the prescriptive, and often questionable, models of change.
The problem that is faced is that technology, and for that matter organizational structure, can be effectively neutral. However, both structure and
technology will have political and social consequences. Marshalling evidence that assists an understanding of process is not easy, because any single
methodology will be inadequate at one or another level. There can be little
certainty in the interpretation of evidence such that the practitioner can be
guided. So, much of the change literature ignores fundamental psychological
process embedded in the ongoing situation to the varied extent that the
fundamental science demands and deserves. Instead, change itself has been
the focus and this is limiting both the science and the practice. The result is
that the paradigms offered in the majority of change texts have not developed significantly since Lewin's (1951) research on groups and attitudes,
and Blake and Mouton's (1964) managerial grid studies, which linked task
and social support factors. Much of the change literature still draws very
heavily on paradigms that follow from this early work with little variation,
although it is unfair to select particular examples for criticism on these lines.
Let me make the point directly. Social psychology and management needs to

consider carefully the range of organizational relationships framed by the network approach, particularly when the relationships depend upon technology as the focal point for social maintenance.

Technology management in networked organizations

There are many examples available in the general literatures of the science, rather than the specific literatures on change. For example, Bjorn-Anderson *et al.* (1986) presents empirical evidence showing that 'computers are associated with greater horizontal differentiation in organizations'. However, they warn against the explanation often given that this differentiation implied a support of bureaucratic organizational forms. Computers can also play a relevant role in cross-functional designs, as the 'matrix structure' that emphasizes 'lateral relations'. Networks emerge as the natural pattern of organization because

> the interdependencies between functional activities are made more visible through integrated control systems and shared data services, so the logic of teamworking and networking emerges rather than patterns of work and communication defined predominantly by Departmental boundaries ... information technology facilitates integration by making information readily accessible to different personnel and departments through joint terminals access to common files.
>
> (Child 1984: 147)

The technology offers the possibility of extending management control in several ways. First, remote supervision becomes possible through telematic services which make it possible to increase surveillance without depending on face-to-face supervision. Control automatically built into systems operations makes it possible to replace several supervisory activities. Greater access to subordinates' information in real time offers new possibilities for control of subordinate information processing and decision-making. Greater knowledge of operations, not only of their outcomes, makes it possible to obtain more accurate and comprehensive operations control. Unification of possibilities of previously segmented control systems permits a more comprehensive and global control (Peiro and Prieto 1994). These changes may have several organizational and individual consequences. At the organizational level, a reduction in management staff and, provided there is an increase in the span of control, an extension of organizational management efficiency and concentration of power may follow (Child 1984). At a personal level, closer and stronger control will probably limit employee risk-taking behaviour and attitudes, and there may be changes in perception of authority in the workplace (Peiro and Prieto 1994). The direct access of top managers to subordinates' information can alter the relationships between them. This easy accessibility can also produce an overload of information for top managers that may hamper their efficiency in decision-making and planning strategies (Zuboff 1982). Of course, there is choice and discretion in each of these possibilities. They are not directly determined by the technology, but become possible because of the facilities offered by it. Zuboff (1982) asks us to consider how management in the abstract world of the networked organization becomes possible. Indeed, it might be asked what an organization is if people do not have to come face-to-face in order to accomplish their work. What is clear is that organizations, and so managers, are in an increasingly turbulent environment in which the process of influence, as well as its source, can change swiftly.

If we take on board the points being made by Castells, the turbulence can be created externally as well as internally, as Boddy and Gunson's presentation of case studies indicates. Turbulence creates problems for management, in that social influence over events within organizations can be difficult to maintain, particularly when external events lead to situations in which the viability and credibility of decisions come under constant scrutiny. It seems worth looking at what social psychology has to say about the influence process. Maintaining consensus about how things might be done could prove to be a constant battle in turbulent conditions.

Social influence

The principle sources of social influence, according to social psychology, are pressures towards conformity. We have seen something of the dangers of conformity in an earlier chapter. The task of influence is to adapt the individual to the social system. The need is for social stability and equilibrium, with people adapting to pre-established social roles and norms. The French social psychologist Moscovici (1976) argues that conformity can be maladaptive, that times, situations and needs of groups change and that social norms must change to be adaptive to new conditions. If conformity were the only process of influence, then groups could not function effectively to meet these changes. Moscovici proposed a model which emphasized that growth and innovation are fundamental processes of social existence, that influence does not merely adapt people to a given social system, but continually produces and changes that system.

The conformity approach, Moscovici argues, implies unilateral influence from the top down and is therefore incompatible with the facts of social change. In the theory, influence is based on power, prestige, authority, material resources, information and so on. This influence is exerted unilaterally by those with resources – the leaders, the experts, the majority or their representatives – upon those who are dependent because they lack these things, those at the bottom of the social hierarchy – the marginals, deviants, low-status groups, the societal minorities. Minorities lack the things that make influence possible by the very terms of the theory. According to Moscovici, social change from the top is implausible and an inadequate description of historical realities. Social change from the bottom, from minorities, is a widely acknowledged fact. It is the 'have-nots', the outsiders, the oppressed, not the ruling elites, who change society. By their nature, then, theories of conformity are inadequate to explain social change by minorities. Individual perception of the physical world is socially mediated. It is culture that allows us to impart meaning to physical events. Moscovici sees the individual acting in conformity experiments to be a representative of a group. What counts as information is defined by social norms and values. One is not influenced by experts because they present valid information. One accepts their information as valid because they are defined by social institutions whose values one has internalized. It is not the reduction of cognitive uncertainty but social conflict that is at the heart of the influence process. Influence, in its three modalities of innovation, conformity and normalization, reflects the production, resolution and avoidance of conflict. Influence is fundamentally about creating, coping with and negotiating social conflicts. Moscovici takes as a basic assumption the fact that people do not like conflict and disagreement with others; it makes them uncertain and anxious. It is aversive and we seek to avoid it by normalizing and conforming, i.e. by reaching agreements through influence.

For Moscovici, the power of the minority emerges from this process. The minority can create conflict, refuse to compromise, create doubt and uncertainty, and produce a situation in which the only solution is for the majority to shift to another point of view. The minority can exploit the majority's dislike of conflict and its need for consensus. Influence is then not unilateral but reciprocal; every group member, irrespective of rank, both influences and is influenced; influence creates social change as well as control, is related to the production and resolution of conflict, follows shared norms of objectivity, preference and originality; and effective influence depends upon the behavioural style of the source, the way its behaviour is organized and patterned.

The key empirical fact in the way the minority creates conflict and has influence is its behavioural style, the 'rhetoric' of behaviour, including the self-presentation of the sender and the sequence of arguments. These and other oratorical devices are symbolic variables. The most important behavioural style is consistency, both intrapersonal consistency – that is, across time and situations (including the simple repetition of a message) – and the interpersonal – that is, across individuals, or consensus. Consistency is a sign of certainty and commitment to a coherent choice. It ranges from 'persevering repetition . . . through the avoidance of contradictory behaviour, to the elaboration of logical system of demonstration' (Moscovici and Faucheux 1972: 158). A consistent minority is distinctive and visible, creates conflict, doubt and uncertainty about established norms and signals that it will not compromise or budge, that it is confident, committed, certain and that it provides an alternative norm, a new way of looking at things, which will resolve the conflict if the majority will move. In Moscovici's view, for which he has experimental evidence in support, minorities can compromise to reduce the danger of social division and the exclusion of the minority people. Compromise takes place because influence represents a negotiation of reality, in which people work out their social differences and reduce conflict. To maintain this stance, the minority must remain cognitively distinctive and consistent but not appear to be socially divisive or rejecting. As Turner (1991) points out, it is unclear how these aspects of disagreement might be varied independently, as they must be if they are to be amenable to experimental investigation. However, it is possible to understand the behaviour of a political party that has just fought from being in opposition to a massive majority in government, i.e. managing internal dissent in a way that Moscovici must recognize as minority influence. Once again, social psychology articulates social processes. One would need quite detailed accounts of organizational management before the same analysis could apply at company level. It is also the case that the social influence process requires much more research before its experimental programme can fully support the general propositions put forward by Moscovici. The research seems urgently needed in this networked world in which we live. Moscovici tells us enough to appreciate the complexities of influence and of how consensus might be maintained. It is now for later researchers to tell us how influence can operate in a turbulent world without polarization and without conflict reaching unmanageable proportions.

It is not easy to see how the processes that Moscovici elaborates would translate into computer-based communications media. Some aspects of his approach might operate at a macro-level and involve mass media communication. Others aspects of his approach seem too subtle for anything less than face-to-face contact to operate. Moscovici, as is clear in his 1994 publication with Doise, is struggling with the fact that in any organized setting there is a plurality of groups and, additionally, although this is not something that he gives attention too, individuals will have membership of more than one group at any one time. Castells (1997b) sees the processes leading to a struggle for social identity as occurring in parallel with the forces developing a networked society. This book argues that managers and psychologists need to be aware of these processes in considering the utilization of the networked technologies.

Diversity is an all-pervasive issue. There is evidence that communication using computing and telecommunications media does not map directly on to the social processes taking place in groups which meet physically. Oravec (1996) indicates that there are distorting effects across most media and most context settings. McGrath and Hollingshead (1994), as we saw in Chapter 6, find that different media are able to function differently in terms of the social processes they focus on. McGrath and Hollingshead's TIP theory models what they regard as important dimensions of group behaviour. Media, in different and not always optimal ways, interplay with group processes. Groups themselves offer great diversity in their behaviours and strategies. So to provide a technological system that was completely compatible with every aspect would be difficult and possibly undesirable in itself. The task for social psychology is to make it clear what the processes are when the many forms of groups interact with the many forms of communications technology. The task for management is to make choices that best suit the circumstances in which they are operating. Above all, management needs to know that different technologies interact differently with tasks and with groups. McGrath's analysis greatly assists this understanding. It also identifies a range of issues that require further research in social psychology.

The networked society and work

It is possible to see the impact on work of the changes driven by technology in doomsday terms. Rifkin writes:

> While earlier industrial technologies replaced the physical power of human labour, substituting machines for body and brawn, the new computer-based technologies promise a replacement of the human mind itself, substituting thinking machines for human beings across the entire gamut of economic activity. The implications are profound and far reaching. To begin with, more than 75 percent of the labour force in most industrial nations engage in work that is little more than simple repetitive tasks. Automated machinery, robots and increasingly sophisticated computers can perform many if not most of these jobs. In the United States alone, this means that in the years ahead more than 90 million jobs in a labour force of 124 million are potentially vulnerable to replacement by machines. With current surveys showing that less than 5 percent of companies around the world have even begun to make the transition to the new machine culture, massive unemployment of a kind never before experienced seems all but inevitable in the coming decades . . . Peter Drucker, whose many books and articles over the years have helped facilitate the new economic reality, says quite bluntly that 'the disappearance of labour as a key factor of production' is going to emerge as the critical 'unfinished business of capitalist society' . . . We are entering a new market age of global markets and automated production. The road to a near-workless economy is within sight.
>
> (Rifkin 1995: 7–12, 292–3)

Castells (1997a), after reviewing a number of detailed economic simulation studies, takes a more balanced view.

In sum, it seems, as a general trend, that there is no systematic structural relationship between the diffusion of information technologies
and the employment levels in the economy as a whole. Jobs are being
displaced and new jobs are being created, but the quantitative relationship between the losses and the gains varies among firms, industries,
sectors, regions, and countries, depending upon competitiveness, firms'
strategies, government policies, institutional environments, and the
relative position of the global economy. The specific outcome of the
interaction between information technology and employment is largely
dependent upon the macroeconomic factors, economic strategies, and
socio-political contexts . . . However, these projections are highly sensitive to variations in the assumptions on which they are based (such as
migration and labour participation rates). This is precisely my argument. The evolution of the level of employment is not a given, which
would result from the combination of stable demographic data and a
projected rate of diffusion of information technology. It will largely
depend on socially determined decisions on the uses of technology, on
immigration policy, on the evolution of the family, on the institutional
distribution of working time in the lifecycle, and on the new system of
industrial relations. Thus, information technology *per se* does not cause
unemployment, even if it obviously reduces working time per unit of
output. But, under the informational paradigm, the kinds of jobs
change, in quantity, in quality, and in the nature of the work being performed. Thus a new production system requires a new labour force;
those individuals and groups unable to acquire informational skills
could be excluded from work or downgraded as workers. Also because
the informational economy is a global economy, widespread unemployment concentrated in some segments of the population (for
example, French youth) and in some regions (such as Asturias) could
indeed become a threat in the OECD area if global competition is unre-
stricted, and if the 'mode of regulation' of capital–labour relationships
is not transformed. The hardening of capitalist logic since the 1980s has
fostered social polarization in spite of occupational upgrading. This
tendency is not irreversible: it can be rectified by deliberate policies
aimed at rebalancing the social structure. But left to themselves, the
forces of unfettered competition in the informational paradigm will
push employment and social structure towards dualization.

(Castells 1996: 263–4)

Work is coming to mean quite different things to everyone as the effects
of technological and organizational change unfold. Castells quotes the
growth of self-employment in the UK and in Italy, where it was around 29
per cent of the workforce in 1990, while 38 per cent of people included in
the 1993 Labour Force Survey who were in employment were not employed

on a permanent full-time basis. Some 85 per cent of the group were women working part-time. Part-time work increased in practically all industrialized countries during the 1980s. New forms of work emerge as technological developments offer opportunities. An increasing number of people engage in telework – using computers, faxes, telephones and so on to provide a link to their central office. Outplacement has grown as an activity and will continue to grow, as radio and television work as well as journalism and design are moved out to people's homes. Again, technological developments provide enabling opportunities in these movements. Work is becoming increasingly project based and relatively short term. 'Overall,' as Castells says, 'the traditional form of work, based on full-time employment, clear-cut occupational assignments, and a career pattern over the lifecycle is being slowly but surely eroded away' (Castells 1996: 268).

Careers in a networked society

Writing in 1989, Rosabeth Moss Kanter observed that:

> For much of the recent past, the idea of a career in the business world meant to most people a series of almost-automatic promotions to bigger and better jobs inside a company – a career pattern like the civil service of the government bureaucracy. Such a bureaucratic career is defined by the logic of advancement. The bureaucratic career pattern involves a sequence of positions in a defined hierarchy of positions. 'Growth' is equated with promotion to a position of higher rank that brings with it greater benefits; 'progress' means advancement within the hierarchy. Thus, a 'career' consists of formal movement from job to job changing title, tasks, and often work groups in the process . . . The bureaucratic business career had its moments of historical dominance in the United States with the rise of the large twentieth century industrial corporation based on mass-production mechanical technologies favouring routinized jobs, and American economic hegemony, which allowed companies to get 'fat'.
>
> (Kanter 1989: 305–7)

Kanter's analysis leads her to contrast the bureaucratic career with a pattern she terms the entrepreneurial, defined by the creation of a new product or service of value, and with professional careers. The professional career is defined by craft and by valued knowledge, as well as the reputation of the individual. Kanter tells us that 'Careers shaped by professional and entrepreneurial principles better fit the needs of businesses struggling to compete effectively in the corporate Olympics . . . Like it or not, more and more people will find their careers shaped by how they develop and market their skills and ideas' (Kanter 1989: 318).

Restructuring and networking had scarcely begun in the period Kanter describes. The picture she painted then has become much more vivid in more recent years. Arnold (1997) construes careers in personal terms, as having a subjective element, as concerning sequences of employment-related experiences that: are not necessarily confined to employment itself; can include employment in different occupations; do not necessarily involve high-status occupations; and do not necessarily involve promotion (Arnold 1997: 17–18). He sees careers as involving various stakeholders, ranging, for example, from the individual to the line manager, who manage the processes involved. He quotes Jackson *et al.* (1996: 7),

> who stated: Whatever soothsayers about the future of careers may assert, individual men and women remain passionately interested in . . . their personal development through work experience over the course of their lifetime. People are more concerned about their skills, competencies, future roles and opportunities for self-determination than they are about most other areas of their work experience.

Arnold reviews the dominant forces affecting careers. He examines the organizational changes that have been reported in this chapter and notes that one major effect is the creation of redundancy for large numbers of people and increased workloads for many of those remaining in employment. He notes that organizational changes have also been geared towards more effective use of labour, including, as we saw in Chapter 3, project teams of people working on a wider range of skills. Arnold reviews outsourcing as another form of labour flexibility in which people are brought in to perform various functions for an organization, even though they are not employed by it on a long-term basis, or even at all. Both relatively low-status and portable work, such as cleaning and catering, and highly skilled specialist work, such as information technology consultancy, can be organized on this basis. Arnold also reviews short-term contracts and notes that this form of work seems not to have increased as a proportion in Britain and to varying extents around Europe, at least, over the past ten or so years. Even so, Arnold notes 'there is a clear trend towards senior managers being brought into organizations for only a few weeks or months to sort out specific problems. This represents a potentially interesting new element of careers for, among others, near-retirement executives, or those wanting intermittent not constant employment' (Arnold 1997: 23).

Arnold's analysis supports Castells's position; both tell us that careers have become more complex as the pace of technological change has demanded increasing retraining and updating. One interesting point for those reading the present book, which has a predominantly social psychological focus, is that while technological change may incline the knowledge requirements towards computing and telecommunications, there is an increasing demand for the development of social and personal skills – the very stuff of social psychology. Organizations now demand that staff are increasingly aware of customers' needs and of customer service. Supervisors are facilitators and supporters, as well as motivators; they are not just concerned with production and its mechanisms. Organizations are increasingly image conscious and require high-level public relations skills from a broad base of their workforce. Work has become much more flexible as technology has provided the opportunity for it to be so. Arnold cites the Labour Force Survey for 1994 as stating that about 3 per cent of people in UK employment work predominantly or entirely from home using telecommunications technology. Telecommunications are used as an alternative to travelling to a workplace. The corresponding figure was about 5 per cent of the US workforce in 1992, which represents a doubling in the period since 1988.

Volatile careers and mobile jobs

The overall picture for careers is one of tremendous volatility. Burgess (1997) argues that job insecurity is a rather nebulous term which he takes to mean fear of joblessness. He reports that:

> jobs can range from lasting just one day to an average of 12 years for women and 18 years for men. The averages hide a wide disparity: while 24 per cent of men's jobs ended in less than five years, more than 40 per cent lasted more than 20 years and 24 per cent more than 30 years. For women, the figures are 41 per cent, 18 per cent and 12 per cent respectively. These figures show clearly that a substantial share of workers is in short-term jobs at any particular moment. A common argument is that this fraction has increased a lot in the past 20 years or so, and the proportion in long-term jobs has fallen correspondingly. In fact, the data show that this is not the case. Elapsed job tenure was the same for women in the early 1990s as it was in 1975; for men it has fallen by about one year . . . Of course, these averages might conceal offsetting changes for different groups in the economy. Our recent analysis has shown that sub-dividing the data to study particular groups defined by age, education level, occupation, industry and region does not overturn the broad conclusion. There is a more obvious decline in job tenure for low-earning men, mirroring their poor showing in earnings growth comparisons . . . Why is there this discrepancy between the facts on job tenure and the widespread public concern over insecurity? One explanation is that media folk have, possibly justifiably, been feeling insecure and have transmitted that fear to the rest of us. Another possibility is that individuals on temporary contracts, or with less formal job protection, may feel insecure even if the contract is generally renewed, as the data suggest. Finally, individuals feeling worried about their jobs

may take action to offset the perceived threats. The insecurity may reveal itself in longer working hours, lower wage claims and the like, all of which may counteract the forces of 'trade and technology' to produce stable job tenure outcomes.

(Burgess 1997: 6)

The discrepancy between actual and perceived conditions is usually of potential interest to psychologists. The difference between attitudes and behaviour has been a formal area of study within social psychology over some years (LaPiere 1934; Wicker 1969; Eiser 1986), but does not appear to have considered the issues raised here. We have to turn elsewhere for appropriate links between psychological and economic explanation. The opening chapter of this book dealt with motivation and its link with expectancy theory, which also focuses upon perceptions rather than objective conditions (Lawler 1971). The issues raised in Burgess's explanation are perceptual or are reactions to perceptions. Yet the psychological mechanisms that might underlie the findings Burgess presents seem convincing only at the level of economic theory.

Guest (1990) has shown how difficult it is to draw conclusions from economic indices of workers' effort, and points out that subjective accounts of workers' responses to changes are much more likely to be useful. However, Guest was seeking to evaluate ways in which the government of the day's policies were impacting on working people. In comparison, the networking revolution has had vastly greater impact nationally and internationally than the particular government in question at the time. I make the point not to belittle the analysis that was undertaken, but to suggest that while expectancy is important as a mechanism, there may well be other psychological mechanisms being activated by the broad processes of restructuring. Indeed, there may be many processes, yet evidence of the impact on individuals is still relatively sparse. This is a point to which this chapter will have to return. Meanwhile, the careers of individuals are clearly affected by the processes to which Burgess draws our attention.

Boundaryless careers

The boundaryless career perspective suggests that people take responsibility for their own career futures. If they do they do so, 'cultivating networks' and gaining access to other people's knowledge and resources are fundamental steps (Hirsch, 1987). Arthur and Rousseau (1996) see boundaryless careers as having arisen for the reasons explored by Cassells, Canter and by Arnold. Arthur and Rousseau see careers as being both subjective and objective. All of these authors see boundaryless careers as being the opposite of those conceived as unfolding within a single employment setting. Meanwhile, individual networks develop into social networks at the level of the firm, and define interfirm dependencies and exchange relationships (Burt, 1992; Granovetter, 1985). As a result, network relations simultaneously serve the career interests of individual actors and the strategic interests of firms. Both sets of interests are affected by the flow of information and influence, as well as by the career movements, to employers situations (Nohria, 1982).

Networks also serve as learning systems (Powell and Brantley, 1992), again with consequences for both individuals and firms. Learning over the course of a career prospectively adds to a person's employment value, or human capital (Becker, 1962). Meanwhile learning through 'communities of practice' (Brown and Duguid, 1991) can have a two-way effect, as people draw learning from, and infuse learning into, the work groups they join. Also, learning becomes embedded in a firm's 'routines' (Nelson and Winter, 1982) which – like a Broadway play – can still be performed after an individual actor moves on (and takes the benefit of his or her experience to another setting).

A broader influence of learning occurs at the level of the industry region – first, in promoting 'a pool of skilled and specially trained personnel' through whom new business can be formed; and second, in creating regional advantages as 'the stock of knowledge and skill ... accumulates as firms imitate each other and personnel move among firms' (Porter, 1990). The associated career mobility can be prompted by both individuals and firms – by individuals, in that the more they learn, the more employable they are likely to be elsewhere (Drucker, 1993); and by firms, in that 'great jobs' – with high levels of learning – are by their nature, not guaranteed jobs (Kanter 1991).

(Arthur and Rousseau 1996: 11)

The boundaryless career approach sees an interdependency between individuals and firms, in which individual networking, learning and enterprise interact with the other activities of the firm. The career becomes the binding power in the processes. Given the overall turbulence in which these processes are taking place, there are bound to be some problems in measuring effects and in determining trends. The entire process cries out for a social psychological approach that links individuals and systems in a way that offers some prospect of coherence.

Once again, we find that Bandura has something to offer. His theory of self efficacy, which was outlined in the previous chapter, is applied to the mastery of occupational roles:

Job rotation, transfers, promotions, and geographic relocations require employees to develop whatever skills they lack to meet the new work demands (Dewhirst, 1991). Employees who have cultivated diverse talents can handle such occupational transitions better than those who are skilled in only a few things . . . The pace of technological change is so fast nowadays that knowledge and technical skills are quickly outmoded unless they are updated to fit the new technologies. Efficacious adaptability applies at the industry level as well as at the workforce level . . . Prolonged success strengthens executives' beliefs in the efficacy of the old ways of doing business; fosters disinterest in, and dismissal of, unfavourable information; and promotes adherence to the old ways despite major changes in the marketplaces that beget losses in operating profit. Those who are supremely self-assured have the tougher problem of forsaking what brought them success. Rapid cycles of change place increasing importance on the adaptive forethought and skills for managing the inertia of success . . . For the many reasons mentioned, people experience a high rate of change either within or across vocations over the full course of their working lives. Whatever the source of dislocation, they have to keep updating their knowledge and skills and learning new ones to keep up with technological developments. To do so, they must take charge of their own self-development. Any insecurities about their learning capabilities are reactivated when they have to learn new ways of thinking and doing things. A perceived sense of inefficacy is a contributor to occupational transition problems . . . Jobs vary in their degree of clarity about the role employees are expected to play and how their role performances are evaluated.

(Bandura 1997: 449–60)

Role ambiguity makes it difficult for personal qualities to develop and become effective. Bandura sees self-efficacy as a major factor in the way individuals respond, in that those with high self-efficacy will exhibit gains in performance, whereas those with low self-efficacy improve only slightly when roles and standards are clear. This places a responsibility on managers to ensure that the structures of their organizations as well as the procedures that support those structures are capable of producing clarity for roles and standards. Often the scale and pace of change seems to ensure the conditions under which the necessity for clarity is overlooked.

Enablement through training: adding value to boundaryless careers

It may appear that Bandura is proposing that the race is won by those who are self-efficacious and that what organizations should therefore do is to promote and select those who score high on self-efficacy measures. While self-efficacy remains the major moderating factor in the many situations that Bandura reviews, guided mastery is seen as an important technique that can lead those who need support in meeting the demands of change. First, Bandura reviews the nature of skills and the place of modelling.

> In the development of complex competencies, modeling involves the acquisition of knowledge and skills, not merely behavioural mimicry. One can distinguish between two broad classes of skills: fixed and generative. Fixed skills specify the optimal ways of performing and activity, with little or no allowance for variation. For example, driving an automobile requires a set pattern of activities without much leeway for deviation if one seeks to arrive at selected destinations unharmed. Fixed skills are adopted in essentially the same form as they are modeled. In many activities, on the other hand, skills must be improvised to suit changing circumstances. In generative skills, appropriate subskills are flexibly orchestrated to fit the demands of particular situations. In cultivating generative skills, modeling influences are structured so as to convey rules for generative and innovative behavior by modeling different ways of applying the same rule under varying circumstances. For example, a model may demonstrate how to manage negotiation situations that differ widely in content and conditions using the same guiding rules and strategies. Or a model may encounter different types of moral dilemmas in business transactions but resolve them by applying the same moral standard. In this form of abstract modeling, observers extract the rules governing the specific modeled judgments or actions. Once they learn the rules, they can use them to make decisions and to generate courses of action in new situations they encounter that go beyond what they have seen or heard. Generative skills provide the tools for adaptability and innovativeness.
>
> Mastery modeling is being applied with good results to develop intellectual, social, and behavioral competencies (Bandura, 1986). It is one of the most effective modes of human enablement. The method that produces the best results includes three major elements. First, the appropriate occupational skills are modeled to convey the basic rules and strategies. Second, the learners receive guided practice under simulated conditions so they can perfect the skills. Third, they are helped to apply their newly learned skills in work situations in ways that will bring them success.
>
> (Bandura 1997: 440–1)

The techniques of mastery modelling begin by breaking complex skills down into subskills so as to produce better learning than trying to teach everything at once. This allows general rules and strategies to be taught for dealing with different situations rather than specific responses or scripted routines. Trainees are helped to understand the rules and strategies by voice-over narration as they are being modelled. This summarizing facilitates the acquisition and retention of rules and enhances skill development and generalization.

After trainees understand the new skills, they need guidance about how to translate abstract rules into concrete courses of action, and opportunities to perfect their skills. Practice is then required in simulated situations, such as role rehearsal at both cognitive and behavioural levels. In cognitive rehearsal, people rehearse mentally how they will translate strategies into what they say and do to manage given situations. Informative feedback on progress is seen as essential, particularly during this rehearsal stage. The third stage is to put the newly acquired competencies into practice in the workplace. Here it is important that people experience sufficient success using what they have learned, so it is important to choose situations in which the problems trainees face are graded in terms of difficulty, and they continue to receive feedback and support. Bandura reviews a significant range of studies that have successfully used mastery modelling programmes. They range from supervisory training and sales training to the improvement of morale and productivity. He then demonstrates how mastery modelling can be applied to the socialization situation facing new employees as they first commence work. He sees this form of training as vital in the situation where restructuring is resulting in greater responsibility being placed on people in operational positions who have to make decisions without the direct availability of management. Again, the overall climate with respect to self-efficacy is important within the organization.

Managers who have low efficacy for enabling leadership are likely to create a disconcerting work life of illusory control, in which operators are held responsible for their performances but the managers continue to wield actual control by subtle means. Supportive managers who provide informative feedback and seek to guide and develop those working with them are likely to assist the generation of self-efficacy across their organizational unit. Managers then carry considerable responsibility not only for the success of their productive or service operations but also for the efficacy of those working with them. Bandura's self-efficacy framework seems to offer both a practical programme and an invaluable conceptual framework to managers who are the interface of the global forces and those who are working to survive in the networked world. Being responsible for one's own career in a turbulent networked world becomes a different prospect if self-efficacy is high on the individual and organizational agenda. Those of us seeking to develop our boundaryless careers do well to find managers who are high in self-efficacy – they are most likely to make empowerment a reality for us personally.

Careers and diversity in networked organizations

As we saw in Chapter 6, wide gender disparities exist in career aspirations. Evetts (1996) has shown us that few women choose scientific and technological careers and even when they do they often face difficulties. Ethnic minorities are severely underrepresented in these fields in particular, in both Britain and the United States. Ethnicity moulds values and behavioural standards through its customs and practices. In addition, it provides social networks that shape and regulate major aspects of social and economic experience. Cultural expressions help to promote a sense of collective identity and with it a sense of attitudinal affinity, which in turn supports self-efficacy.

According to Bandura,

> Minority students generally have a low sense of efficacy for scientific and technological careers requiring quantitative skills ... The combined influence of low academic expectations and downgrading of scientific aspirations in the students' schooling, deficient academic preparation, lack of occupational role models and support systems for pursuits in science and technological fields, and social barriers in opportunity structures will constrain perceived occupational efficacy in various minorities and non-minorities alike. Indeed, because the sociostructural barriers for women and ethnic minorities are similar, their patterns of perceived occupational efficacy are much the same.
>
> (Bandura 1997: 438)

Bandura's approach is to analyse the interaction between social structure, psychological mechanisms and occupational pursuits. He is not taking a deterministic, still less a fatalistic stance in relation to race or gender. Solutions require both individual and social remedies. Bandura points out that mastery control has a part to play in developing basic entry skills for diverse careers and persuading people that they possess the potentialities and learning capabilities to succeed. We have seen in earlier chapters that diversity has to be celebrated. If diversity is celebrated, it is then just a short step to high self-efficacy.

Supportive programmes within the organization, as well as preparatory training, successful cohorts within the organization, the easing of financial barriers and the overcoming of adverse effects of institutional biases in practice, need to be handled by the social dimension. The individual faced with the prospect of enhancing progress has to maintain a high level of efficacy in the performance of tasks as well as interact with the institution. If both move together towards self-efficacy development, the expectation is a favourable outcome. There is some evidence to support the encouraging view – but there is even greater evidence of the forces seeking to quench optimism. Our organizations are a long way from celebrating diversity.

Insofar as management is concerned, Martin (1994), writing about British local government employment, observes that:

> When black and white women entered management posts, 'race' and gender talk was produced around those women and all that they undertook: their difference and otherness from the institutionalized notion of

the norm was continually commented on. Focusing on them seemed to conceal that these notions were institutionalized in the organizational discourse, and to mask that the deep structures of management thought, language and day-to-day practices are racist and heterosexist, and that women have to take up positions in relation to those discourses and practices whether they want to or not in order to undertake management.

For example, women spoke of the credit for their appointment being ascribed to the positive equality policies of their organization, or to the enlightened approach of white and male senior managers. Since no mention was made of the women's skills, expertise or experience, her blackness, her femaleness, and her otherness from the supposed norm of manager were covertly highlighted. By implication, she was deskilled and depowered; the managerial skills of the white and male manager asserted; the power relations of gender and race confirmed; her place as the subject in discourse decentred. She became the object of (racist and sexist) knowledge. Her 'difference' was reaffirmed, and legitimated as the subject of open, racist and sexist attention.

(Martin 1994: 116)

Martin is drawing attention to the articulation and expression of values. Bandura saw values as being important in the factors influencing self-efficacy.

Davidson (1997) reports one of her many interviewees, a 28-year-old Afro-Caribbean graduate junior manager, as saying

My career is very important. I feel terrible now that I have left the company but the job took over my life. I could never switch off. It felt initially strange being the boss because the people who worked for me tended to be older and had been in the company longer. They resented me. What made matters worse was that although I was supposedly in a position of power, my male (white) superiors had ensured in reality, I had no real power. This obviously made my situation impossible and undermined my authority. Nothing was done to enhance my career and I wasn't even given adequate training. Having to deal with racism was also a problem, it wasn't just directed towards me but often towards ethnic minority groups generally . . . I felt totally alone and isolated with no one (especially another black woman) to turn to – particularly in regards to fighting continual racism – which became more and more directed towards me. As far as my performance went I felt that I shouldn't ask for help and advice, as it was made clear to me that black women were seen as inferior and lowering the management standards and I didn't want to reinforce this fallacy.

(Davidson 1997: 1–2)

In the management of networked organizations, diversity has to take some precedence. It has to be seen as residing not in other people but in all of us. The processes of self-efficacy have to be central and available to, and engaging, everyone within the network. Otherwise, the process losses are huge and result in exclusion from work but in all probability from broader social activities too. Davidson reports the work of Gilkes (1990), who:

> explored childhood, educational, occupational and cultural experiences of 25 UK women community workers from various ethnic minority backgrounds in a Northern city by in-depth interviews. She reported that these women frequently referred to their powerlessness, isolation and victimisation stemming from inequality and status degradation, fostered by negative images and stereotypes attached to black women's work.
>
> (Gilkes, cited in Davidson 1997: 3)

Davidson goes on to present the work of Mirza (1992) whose five-year longitudinal study of black and ethnic minority women in London once again highlighting the wasted potential of both the men and women who reported slim chances of finding employment that matched academic potential.

> Occupational segregation by gender still persists in all European labour markets. More than 50% of employed women are found in service or clerical jobs, compared with 20% of men. According to Rubery and Fagan (1993), the majority of the new jobs women moved into in the 1980s were in two occupational areas: professional jobs and clerical jobs. Therefore while an increasing number of women are entering the lower level service and clerical jobs which are already female dominated; some women are gaining access to highly skilled professional jobs, including management.
> Similar trends are recurring in Australasia and the USA. In Australia, 55% of female employees in 1992 were concentrated in two major occupational groups: clerks and sales persons. While 20% of Australian female employees were in professional and para-professional occupations, 22% were registered nurses . . . Even in the USA, with the strongest legislation affecting the employment of women, women are most frequently found in the helping professions, and sales and retail jobs. In 1992, US women held 98% of secretarial, typist and stenographer positions, 79% of administrative jobs, and 94% of registered nurse positions.
>
> (Davidson 1997: 7)

Davidson is able to report some advances in women entering traditional male-dominated jobs, and she is able to state that, in all European countries, women have increased their share of professional jobs. However, even in those areas in which women predominate they tend to have the less prestigious jobs. She provides the example that in the UK only three in ten secondary school head and deputy head teachers are women, even though half of secondary school teachers are female. There is a similar position in other occupational situations, such as nursing and social work. Chapter 5 in this book presents some other figures for the employment of women and for ethnic groups across the world.

The opportunity of gender and race in networked organizations

Gender and race are significant factors in career choice and development. In the world of networked organizations, these factors can be significant barriers unless the interfaces with systems and structures can be better managed. Guided mastery training and the generation of self-efficacy processes can add to the opportunities for change in a more inclusive direction. Beverley Alimo-Metcalfe (1994) sees the restructuring of organizations leading to opportunities in which women can exercise processes of major transformation in the situations in which they work. She cites the work of Judy Rosener (1990), who surveyed prominent female leaders in diverse organizations in the USA using members of the International Women's Forum as a sample, and a comparable sample of men. Her survey demonstrated that women are more likely than men to use transformational leadership: namely, motivating others by transforming their self-interests into goals of the organization. Women are also much more likely than men to use power based on charisma, track record and contacts (personal power), as opposed to power based on organizational position, title and the ability to reward and punish (structural power). She cites a second study conducted in the UK by Susan Vinnicombe (1987), who used an instrument which integrated Mintzberg's notion of the three major sets of managerial roles (interpersonal, informational and decisional) with the Myers–Briggs type indicator to create a taxonomy of management styles which were described as 'traditionalist', 'trouble shooter/negotiator', 'catalyst' and 'visionary'. The most marked difference was the lower number of 'traditionalists' among the female managers. Whereas 57 per cent of the male managers tended to be 'traditionalists', there was an average of only 26 per cent among the females. The study by Vinnicombe indicates that significantly more women managers were 'visionaries' and 'catalysts', and notes that catalysts are excellent in public relations and shine as organizational spokespersons, since they work well with all types of people. They can sell the organization to its customers and can make employers feel good about themselves and the organization. They are excellent in the top positions if given free reign to manage, but they may rebel and become disloyal if they perceive themselves as having too many constraints. Women, on this view, tend to define power differently: that is, as the ability to use their own talents and to control their own lives. In working with people, they are much more collaborative and cooperative, and far less hierarchical and authoritative than men. So, says Alimo-Metcalfe, perhaps it is not surprising that men who may have a preference for the 'traditionalist' style feel uncomfortable when faced by women who are 'visionaries' or 'catalysts'. Networked organizations need visionaries and catalysts. Networked organizations need transformational leaders.

Perhaps some of the reaction of men in the kinds of interactions that could follow that pattern express themselves in ways that are interpreted by their female colleagues as being sexist or racist. Whichever way the situation is looked at, the future favours positive and active involvement in the dynamics of diversity. A further reading of the situation, which may be seen by some to push the available evidence beyond readily available proof, is that in networked organizations diversity favours adaptation and visionaries and catalysts will soon have a value beyond price. Organizations ignore these possibilities at a probable cost, and are likely to be constantly challenged. Social networks will be employed as a means of stimulating change. As two successful senior executives who took part in Davidson's study tell us

You need to try and access black women's networks but also management networks within the organization. Even though these are predominantly white, you have to take and get what you can from them.

Get a lot of relevant training and find mentors. These should be people who are sympathetic towards you and do not have the power to fire you. You need support to challenge organizations. Go for it. You need good support networks but always always remember to keep your own identity.

(Davidson 1997: 103)

However, while the diversity battle is being fought on one front, a step change is facing organizations on another front.

Virtual organizations

Digital systems include those technologies which permit the encoding of previously physical products and information media into an electronic format . . . Digital systems are therefore playing a key role in our transition of achievement focus from ingenuity to imagination. Indeed, in future it will in part be digital systems which empower the realization of almost any dream. As more and more products and services 'go virtual', so there will be fewer and fewer limits upon what we can afford to create.

Digital systems my also be used to automate the manufacturing of items – such as food, furniture, cars and clothing – which must continue to be produced in the physical world. As a consequence, digital systems have become integral to all forms of programmable productive plant . . . Today, many manufacturers can change what they produce by altering a computer program. In the past, they would have had to physically retool the line . . . Looking further ahead, digital systems will soon allow many processes to be integrated or 'internetworked' across organizations. This will permit the most rapid response to market events . . . Digital systems may be able to add value and flexibility in almost every stage of product or service design, creation, administration and distribution.

(Adams 1996: 225–6)

The career implications of these technological movements are 'portfolio lives', to use Adams's own terminology (the term 'careers' is not much in his vocabulary!). This means that for some people there is an acceptance that no job will be for life and that sooner or later they will have to move from their organizational home. However, for others, portfolio lives involve new freelance, free agent working relationships with flexible and shifting organizational ties. This brings a change in both the psychological and the physical nature of the employment contract. Flexible firms and numerically flexible labour forces are necessary. People may themselves wish to have a more flexible life, so that those with school-age children may prefer to work only during the middle part of the day. Older workers may relish the prospect of being able to work from home for large parts of their days. Those with the appropriate skills become advanced virtual 'teleworkers'. As digital work proliferates, those possessing portfolio lives become increasingly concerned with the ability to sell intellectual energies and skills electronically to an increasingly wide range of internetworked organizations. Groupware allows groups of individuals (remote or otherwise) to work together smarter, faster and in more productive ways and has become a pressure on organizations to become 'virtual'. 'Even "lowly" groupware tools like electronic mail may decimate formal hierarchies . . . Temporary interdepartmental project teams usually also spawn far more easily, and operate more effectively, within companies which operate electronic mail networks . . . Already electronic mail and access to the sprawling datasphere of the worldwide web are more commonplace. And, of course, there is also far more groupware today than just electronic mail' (Adams 1996: 227–9).

The greatest impact on organizational forms comes from the globally networked economic activity that becomes possible.

As organizations interconnect into the global hardware platform of modern business, so many barriers of time and space are becoming transparent. As Don Tapscott puts it in *The Digital Economy*, 'technology is eliminating the "place" in workplace'. Home may be where the heart is, but increasingly the office is anywhere the head can be connected . . . Indeed, the popularity of expanding global networks such as the Internet continues to prove that borders between nations have only ever been artificial. As digital systems and advanced groupware proliferate, so any economy choosing survival will be unable to exist within meaningful economic boundaries. Indeed, so many kinds of work may be shifted electronically around the globe, no economy can afford to erect economic barriers which may significantly impede trade into and out of its sphere . . . To the alarm of many governments, electronic business knows no national boundaries nor tax regimes.

(Adams 1996: 232)

This is clearly not a scenario which favours those who are 'conservative', or organizations that favour bureaucracy, or economies that favour inflexibility.

Adams makes an informed speculative assessment that the organizational form that seems most likely to adapt to the global networked economy may be characterized by a shifting cluster of loosely structured individuals held together by task and process demands, rather than by a bureaucratic structure – no matter how lean and slim. Members of the cluster may be dispersed geographically and even organizationally. Digital systems and advanced groupware will permit each cluster to function cohesively, and there must be some common members to serve as links between clusters. One set of links has to be concerned primarily with innovation and the generation of new ideas, as well as with the raising of resources. There has to be a setting of the strategic direction as well as a group of enablers and facilitators who translate strategic detail into action. Adams characterizes the virtual organization as being comprised of 'thinkers', 'connectors' and 'doers'. These are characteristics that we saw as being close to the styles of thought that were favoured by women. He also sees the possibility that many, initially independent, networked organizations will seek integration so as to find an extended funding base. This indicates even further turbulence.

Managers of careers

It may seem that financial inducements are all that are required if careers are to be lived 'portfolio' style. In a sense, careers may become self-managing, just as work in the pre-industrial era was largely self-managing. The classic paper on career resilience tells us that management thinkers have now shifted their attention from employment to employability (Waterman *et al.* 1994). In this, it may at first seem that careers are managed by individuals themselves. However, if the employees that are to be attracted are themselves highly educated and skills-oriented, it seems likely that their job search behaviours will be geared to skills and experience advancement. Opportunities to develop will be highly sought after in the networked society, and this needs to be taken into account by particular organizations. While employees may be being discouraged from thinking of their employment in career progression terms, opportunities to expand the skills portfolio will be foremost in the evaluatory calculations of individual employees. Managers will have a responsibility to maximize development opportunities for those who work with them. Waterman *et al.* (1994) tell us that they see the career resilient workforce as a group of employees who not only are dedicated to the idea of continuous learning but also stand ready to reinvent themselves to keep pace with change; who take responsibility for their own career management and who are committed to the company's success. Competitiveness is seen as keeping close to customers, staying on top of technology and market trends and attempting to be flexible. The demand is that management must maintain a continuous dialogue about the business direction of the company and about what is happening in the markets. Waterman *et al.* tell us that

> Managers have an obligation to give employees as much time as possible to prepare for the future . . . A company must help people explore job opportunities, facilitate lifelong learning and job movement. The best companies set up a 'career center' which helps employees find new jobs inside or outside the organization but also enables them to benchmark their skills . . . Companies and individuals often fail to realize that benchmarking without self-assessment may cause an employee to make the wrong choices.
>
> (Waterman *et al.* 1994: 90–2)

Of course, in the networked society, careers centres and self-assessment of skills are often accomplished using computer-based inventories and guidance tools. Companies that do not manage the risks involved in the career processes leave themselves open to unwelcome and difficult problems of recruitment and labour turnover. Guest and Mackenzie-Davey (1996) found a range of practices in career development in British companies. They argue that the traditional career is not dead, but that there are considerable changes.

In management in particular, the flattening of structures that has accompanied the move towards networking has made the steps in career development extremely steep. Perhaps because the networked career is now so project-based, succession planning is a particularly difficult problem for management.

The management of the careers of others is going to be a matter of balance, taking care that the level of expectation of the personal development of employees matches the chances created by the operation of the company.

None of this is easy, but we are beginning to find examples of good management careers despite the turbulence of the environment.

Careers at Microsoft

In the broader literatures on the networked organization, Microsoft gets little mention. Castells's first volume devotes just three lines to Bill Gates as having founded the company but otherwise does not mention the company. Nohria's edited work makes no reference to either the company or its founder. There may be no good reason why these foremost authorities on networks do not provide at least an illustration of the company at the heart of the revolution. It might indicate that even in the minds of the most eminent, social and technological considerations are analytically separated. It could be that, on a more prosaic basis, the shelves of our management libraries have only recently become attractive to those who leave the company and wish to write. There are some examples available now, and they provide at least anecdotal evidence of the likely career paths in the most successful networked organizations. It seems worth concluding a chapter on careers in networked organizations with a brief description of Microsoft, as a company, since it is at the heart of the network revolution. Microsoft has a structure that comes close to being virtual yet has a career framework, and marks the most financially successful career in the world – that of its founder.

My understanding of the structure of Microsoft is that employees do not have formal offices, the feature that characterizes bureaucracies everywhere; they have 'nests'. They move on to whichever terminal is available at the time they need to work and produce from there. It is not clear to what extent the managers of Microsoft are schooled in social psychology, but their approach to structure might well have come from the writings of Bavelas (1951) and Leavitt (1951), who demonstrated that the position that one held within a social structure was important in terms of the pattern and nature of communication. If the object is to have employees become committed to the tasks of production, then a viable social life outside the office and a minimal concern with position in it seems an optimal proposition.

Microsoft was founded in 1975 on the simple philosophy that software applications had to be accessible to the average person if computing was to become an integral part of commercial organization, as well as a central feature of our home lives. Ichbiah (1993) sees the site of the Microsoft headquarters at Redmond, Washington state, as looking like a university campus.

Two programmers juggle; just a short distance away, an Asian woman taps delicately with thin sticks on an Oriental harplike instrument that is lying flat on a polished stand. She is accompanied by a bearded guitarist straight out of the 1960s. Squirrels dart playfully to and fro, and ducks bask on the lawn, unfazed by the occasional joggers, unicycle riders, and other activities around them.

These rare moments of relaxation complement the intense activity that result from the high level of devotion to the company. The lifestyle of a programmer looks laid-back from the outside. Work hours are flexible; some programmers arrive at 9 p.m. and leave at 5 a.m. Their offices are decorated with stuffed animals, aquariums, bows and arrows, and other assorted collector's items. They dress however they want and go barefoot. One member of the company says that whenever he goes to lunch in town, the friends he meets ask him why he isn't working. They can't believe he can go to work dressed as casually as he does.

'Writing software is a very intensive activity, and we try to make it as pleasant as possible', Jon Shirey explains. One day, a visitor asked Charles Simonyi why the programmers were so casual. Simonyi simply replied, 'Because its good for business.'

He is right. The external appearance of relaxation on the Redmond campus masks the unrelenting productivity. Gates, himself a programmer, knows that programmers need a working environment with as few constraints as possible.

(Ichbiah 1993: 223–4)

Ichbiah describes how much concern there is to enable Microsoft employees to play an active part in the community around them, as well as the world beyond that. He is keen to indicate how international the Redmond campus is.

The company believes in choosing the best, hardest-working people and turning them loose to prove themselves . . . It is not uncommon for Microsoft to hire people with no professional programming experience or formal training. After all, neither of its two founders obtained college degrees . . . The company spends large sums seeking out and then attracting the best people possible. Even when a candidate has impressive diplomas and recommendations, he has to answer a series of questions designed to test his knowledge and analytical skills.

(Ichbiah 1993: 225)

Each year Microsoft employees undergo a review and, if satisfactory, are rewarded with a salary increase or a stock issue or a bonus. Gates's own personal style of working hard and demanding excellence is transmitted through the work culture to each employee. Small, often very small, teams work directly with single products or on defined products. Cusamano and Selby describe how Microsoft have developed career tracks.

The typical career path within a functional speciality is to move from being a new hire to being a mentor, team lead, and then manager of the functional area for an entire product unit (such as the group program manager, development manager, or test manager for Excel). Above these managers are special positions that cut across production units. These include the directors for the functional areas, or positions in the Office product unit, which oversees the Excel and Word product groups and builds common features used in the different Office applications.

(Cusamano and Selby 1997: 115–16)

There is a comparable grading structure, with levels that reflect experience in the company as well as performance and skill. The salaries have a low base and a high incentive compensation. There are, according to Cusamano and Selby, around 3,000 of Microsoft's 17,800 employees who are millionaires because of the stocks they own. The management of Microsoft encourages mobility across the product groups, and does not prevent qualified people from moving to different product groups. Programme managers have loosely defined roles and broadly defined responsibilities, but increasingly work in coordination functions. Developers are usually recruited directly to that position and look after a team, as well as fulfilling the demands of a work schedule designed on a footing that is equal to a team member. Employees seem to be moved according to the extent to which they need new challenges, but a careful watch is taken to ensure that sufficient expertise, skill balance and knowledge of the product is still available within the team. Cusamano and Selby conclude by saying that:

In general, Microsoft seems to manage its people well, especially for a company that has grown so much so fast, with little 'professional' management on the way. In a 1991 survey in the applications division, most employees felt Microsoft was one of the best places to work in the industry . . . There were complaints about inadequate training for new employees and some lack of cooperation among the divisions, problems that Gates and other managers are working to rectify. There was also some grousing about low salaries (but not total compensation) and a conflict between demands for 'quality' versus 'quantity' in work. But the survey suggests that Microsoft provides a very good, if imperfect, atmosphere in which to work. There are capable and accessible managers, little internal politics or bureaucracy, interesting and varied assignments, a strong teamwork culture, and plenty of opportunities to learn and make decisions as well as a few mistakes.

(Cusamano and Selby 1997: 126)

Motivation, teamwork, diversity, technology and networks have been the central contexts addressed in this book. Microsoft, as a place at which to work, seems to bring these themes together. In doing so in practice, it has become the world's single most powerful company in any industry. Indeed, as my long time friend and colleague Geoffrey Stephenson said to me when we discussed Microsoft, 'It seems to me that this is where social psychology has come home.'

Bibliography

Abbot, A. (1988) *The System of Professionals*. London: University of Chicago Press.

Acker, J. (1990) Hierarchies, jobs, bodies: a theory of gendered organizations. *Gender and Society*, 4, 139–58.

Adair, J. (1986) *Effective Teambuilding*. London: Pan.

Adams, D. (1977) 'Global hero' creative technology. Cited in C. Barnatt (1997) *Challenging Reality – in Search of the Future Organization*. Chichester: Wiley.

Adams, D. (1996) Global hero. *Creative Technology*, 31, 225–6.

Adams, J.S. (1965) Inequity in social change, in L. Berkowitz (ed.) *Advances in Experimental Social Psychology, Vol. 2*. London: Academic Press.

Adorno, T.W., Frenkel-Brunswick, E., Levinson, D.J. and Sandford, R.N. (1950) *The Authoritarian Personality*. New York: Harper and Row.

Alimo-Metcalfe, B. (1994) Waiting for fish to grow feet! Removing organizational barriers to women's entry into leadership positions, in M. Tanton (ed.) *Women in Management – a Developing Presence*. London: Routledge.

Allport, F. (1924) *Social Psychology*. New York: Houghton Mifflin.

Allport, G. (1954) *The Nature of Prejudice*. Cambridge, MA: Addison-Wesley.

Antal, A.B. and Kresbach-Gnath, C. (1987) Women in management: Unused resources in the Federal Republic of Germany. *International Studies of Management and Organization*, 16, 133–51.

Argyle, M. (1972) *The Social Psychology of Work*. London: Allen Lane, The Penguin Press.

Argyris, C. (1982) *Reasoning, Learning, Action: Individual and Organizational*. San Francisco: Jossey-Bass.

Argyris, C. (1992) *On Organizational Learning*. Oxford: Blackwell.

Argyris, C. and Schon, D. (1974) *Theory in Practice*. San Francisco: Jossey-Bass.

Arnold, J. (1997) *Managing Careers into the 21st Century*. London: Paul Chapman.

Arnold, J., Robertson, I.T. and Cooper, C.L. (1991) *Work Psychology – Understanding Human Behaviour in the Workplace*. London: Pitman.

Arthur, M.B. and Rousseau, D.M. (1996) *The Boundaryless Career*. New York and Oxford: Oxford Psychology Press.

Bainbridge, L. (1987) The ironies of automation, in J. Rassmussen, K. Duncan and J. Leplat (eds) *New Technology and Human Error*. London: Wiley.

Baltes, P.B. and Schaie, K.W. (1976) On the plasticity of intelligence in adulthood and old age: where Horn and Donaldson fail. *American Psychologist*, 31, 720–5.

Bandura, A. (1986) *Social Foundations of Thought and Action: a Social Cognitive Theory*. Englewood Cliffs, NJ: Prentice Hall.

Bandura, A. (1992) Exercise of personal agency through the self-efficacy mechanism, in R. Schwarzer (ed.) *Self-efficacy: through Control of Action*. Washington, DC: Hemisphere.

Bandura, A. (1997) *Self-Efficacy: the Exercise of Control*. New York: W.H. Freeman.

Bandura, A. and Wood, R.E. (1989) Effect of perceived controllability and performance standards on self-regulation of complex decision-making. *Journal of Personality and Social Psychology*, 56, 805–14.

Barnatt, C. (1997) *Challenging Reality: in Search of the Future Organization*. Chichester: Wiley.

Baron, R.S., Kerr, N.L. and Miller, N. (1992) *Group Process, Group Decision, Group Action*. Buckingham: Open University Press.

Bass, B.M. (1981) *Stogdill's Handbook of Leadership: a Survey of Theory and Research*. New York: Free Press.

Bass, B.M. (1990) *Bass and Stodgill's Handbook of Leadership Research*, 3rd edn. New York: Free Press.

Bavelas, A. (1951) Communication patterns in task-oriented groups, in D. Lerner and H.D. Lasswell (eds) *The Policy Sciences: Recent Developments in Scope and Method*. Stanford, CA: Stanford University Press.

Becker, G. (1962) Investment in human capital: a theoretical analysis. *Journal of Political Economy*, 70, 9–44.

Beer, M., Spector, B., Lawrence, P.R., Quinn Mills, D. and Walton, R.E. (1984) *Managing Human Assets: the Ground-breaking Harvard Business School Program*. New York: Macmillan.

Berkowitz, L. (1962) *Aggression: a Social Psychological Analysis*. New York: McGraw-Hill.

Bernard, L.L. (1926) *An Introduction to Social Psychology*. New York: Holt.

Berrgren, C. (1992) *Von Ford zu Volvo: Automobiherstellung in Schweden*. Berlin: Springer.

Betancourt, H. and Lopez, S.R. (1993) The study of culture, ethnicity, and race in American Psychology. *American Psychologist*, 48, 629–37.

Bhavnani, K.-K. (1993) Talking racism and the editing of women's studies, in D. Richardson and V. Robinson (eds) *Thinking Feminist: Key Concepts in Women's Studies*. New York: Guilford.

Billig, M. (1985) Prejudice, categorisation and particularisation: from a perceptual to a rhetorical approach. *European Journal of Social Psychology*, 7(4), 393–432.

Binet, A. and Simon, T. (1908) Le developpement de l'intelligence chez les enfants. *L'Anee Psychologique*, 14, 1–94.

Birnbaum, M.H. (1983) Perceived equity of salary policies. *Journal of Applied Psychology*, 68, 49–59.

Bjorn-Anderson, N., Eason, K. and Robey, D. (1986) *Managing Computer Impact. An International Study of Management and Organizations*. Norwood, NJ: Ablex.

Blackler, F. (1988) Information technologies press and organizations: lessons from the 1980s and issues for the 1990s. *Journal of Occupational Psychology*, 23, 40–5.

Blackler, F. and Shimmin, S. (1984) *Applying Psychology in Organizations*. London: Methuen.

Blake, R.R. and Mouton, J.S. (1964) *The Managerial Grid*. Houston, TX: Gulf.

Blauner, R. (1964) *Alienation and Freedom: the Factory Worker and His Industry*. Chicago: University of Chicago Press.

Boddy, D. and Gunson, N. (1996) *Organizations in the Network Age*. London: Routledge.

Bodker, S. (1990) *Through the Interface: a Human Activity Approach to User Interface Design*. Hillsdale, NJ: Lawrence Erlbaum Associates.

Bodker, S. (1991) Design in action: from prototyping by demonstration to co-operative prototyping, in J. Greenbaum and M. Kyng (eds) *Design at Work: Cooperative Design of Computer Systems*. Hillsdale, NJ: Lawrence Erlbaum Associates.

Bower, T. (1988) *Maxwell: the Outsider*. New York: Viking.

Bower, T. (1995) *Maxwell: the Final Verdict*. London: HarperCollins.

Breakwell, G.M. (1979) Women: group and identity? *Women's Studies International Quarterly*, 2, 9–17.

Brotherton, C. (1988) Technological change and innovation – setting the agenda for occupational psychology. *Journal of Occupational Psychology*, 61, 1–5.

Brotherton, C. (1991) *New Developments in Research on Adult Cognition*. Nottingham: Adult Education Occasional Paper, University of Nottingham.

Brown, J.A.C. (1954) *The Social Psychology of Industry*. Harmondsworth: Penguin.

Brown, J.A. and Duguid, P. (1991) Organizational learning and communities of practice: Toward a unified view of working, learning, and innovation. *Organizational Science*, 2, 40–56.

Brown, R.J., Condor, S., Mathews, A., Wade, G. and Williams, J.A. (1986) Explaining intergroup differentiation in an industrial organization. *Journal of Occupational Psychology*, 59, 273–86.

Burgess, S. (1997) Jobs for life aren't dead yet. *Independent on Sunday*, 14 December.

Burt, R. (1992) The social structure of competition, in N. Nohria and R.G. Eccles (eds) *Networks and Organizations*. Boston: Harvard Business School Press.

Carter, A. and Kirkup, C. (1990) *Women in Engineering*. Basingstoke: Macmillan.

Carver, C.S. (1979) A cybernetic model of self attention processes. *Journal of Personality and Social Psychology*, 37, 1251–71.

Castells, M. (1997a) *The Information Age: Economy, Society and Culture.Volume 1, The Rise of the Network Society*. Oxford: Blackwell.

Castells, M. (1997b) *The Information Age: Economy, Society and Culture. Volume 2, The Power of Identity*. Oxford: Blackwell.

Castells, M. (1998) *The Information Age: Economy, Society and Culture. Volume 3, End of the Millennium*. Oxford: Blackwell.

Child, J. (1984) *Organisation: a Guide to Problems and Practice*, 2nd edn. London: Harper and Row.

Clegg, S.R., Hardy, C. and Nord, W.R. (1996) *Handbook of Organization Studies*. London: Sage.

Coch, L. and French, J.R.P. (1948) Overcoming resistance to change. *Human Relations*, 1, 512–32.

Cockburn, C. (1992) The circuit of technology: gender, identity and power, in R. Silverstone and E. Hirsch (eds) *Consuming Technologies: Media and Information in Domestic Spaces*. London: Routledge.

Collins, R. (1979) *The Credential Society: an Historical Sociology of Education and Stratification*. New York: Academic Press.

Collinson, D., Knights, D. and Collinson, M. (1990) *Managing to Discriminate*. London: Routledge.

Condor, S. (1988) Race stereotypes and racist discourse. *Text*, 8(1–2), 68–9.

Cornfield, D.B. (ed.) (1987) *Workers, Managers and Technological Change: Emerging Patterns of Labor Relations*. New York and London: Plenum.

Cornfield, D.B., Phipps, P., Bates, D.P., Carter, D.K., Coker, T.W., Kitzmuller, K.E. and Wood, P.B. (1987) Office automation, clerical workers, and labor relations in the insurance industry, in D.B. Cornfield (ed.) *Workers, Managers and Technological Change: Emerging Patterns of Labor Relations*. New York and London: Plenum.

Couch, A.A. and Carter, L.F. (1953) A factorial study of the rated behavior of group members. *American Psychologist*, 8, 333.

Cox, T. (1993) *Cultural Diversity in Organizations. Theory, Research and Practice*. San Francisco: Berrett-Koehler.

Craft, J., Doctors, S.I., Shkop, Y.M. and Benecki, T.J. (1979) Simulated management perceptions, hiring decisions and age. *Aging and Work*, 95–102.

Culler, J. (1976) *Saussure*. Glasgow: Fontana.

Curtain, R. (1988) Skill formation in manufacturing: obstacles and opportunities. *Human Resource Management Australia*, November, 7–21.

Cusamano, M.A. and Selby, R.A. (1997) *Microsoft Secrets: How the World's Most Powerful Software Company Creates Technology, Shapes Markets, and Manages People*. London: HarperCollins.

Daft, R.L. and Lengel, R.H. (1986) Organizational information requirements, media richness and structural design. *Management Science*, 32, 554–71.

Daniel, W.W. (1987) *Workplace Industrial Relations and Technical Change*. London: Frances Pinter.

Davidson, M. (1997) *The Black and Ethnic Minority Woman Manager: Cracking the Concrete Ceiling*. London: Paul Chapman.

Davies, C. (1995) *Gender and the Professional Predicament in Nursing*. Buckingham: Open University Press.

Decker, W.H. (1983) Stereotypes of middle-aged and elderly professionals. *Psychology: a Quarterly Journal of Human Behaviour*, 20(3), 60–7.

Deutsch, M. (1949) A theory of cooperation and competition. *Human Relations*, 2, 129–52.

Deutsch, M. (1975) Equity and need: what determines which values will be used as the basis for distributive justice. *Journal of Social Issues*, 31, 137–50.

Dewhirst, H.D. (1991) Career patterns: Mobility specialization, and related career issues, in R.F. Morrison and J. Adams (eds) *Contemporary Career Development Issues*, pp. 73–107. Hillsdale, NJ: Erlbaum.

Doise, W. (1982) *Levels of Explanation in Social Psychology*. Cambridge: Cambridge University Press.

Drucker, P.F. (1955) *The Practice of Management*. London: Butterworth-Heinemann.

Drucker, P.F. (1961) *The Practice of Management*. Oxford: Butterworth-Heinemann.

Drucker, P.F. (1993) *Post Capitalist Society*. New York: Free Press.

Dunnette, M.D. (ed.) (1976) *Handbook of Industrial and Organizational Psychology*. Chicago: Rand-McNally.

Eason, K. (1988) *Information Technology and Organisational Change*. London: Taylor and Francis.

Ehn, P. and Kyng, M. (1984) Cardboard computers: mocking-it-up or hands-on the future. In *Design at Work: Cooperative Design of Computer Systems*. Hillsdale, NJ: Lawrence Erlbaum Associates.

Eiser, J.R. (1986) *Social Psychology: Attitudes, Cognition and Social Behaviour*. Cambridge: Cambridge University Press.

Emery, F.E. (1978) *The Emergence of the New Paradigm of Work*. Canberra: Centre for Continuing Education.

Emmott, B. (1996) *Going Digital: How New Technology Is Changing Our Lives*. London: The Economist/Profile Books.

Engestrom, Y. (1990) *Learning, Working and Imagining: Twelve Studies in Activity Theory*. Helsinki: Orienta-Konsultit-oy.

Eveland, J.D. and Bikson, T.K. (1987) Evolving electronic communications networks: an empirical assessment. *Office Technology and People*, 3(2), 103–28.

Evetts, J. (1996) *Gender and Career in Science and Engineering*. London: Taylor and Francis.

Faulkner, W. and Arnold, E. (eds) (1985) *Smothered by Invention*. London: Pinto.

Ferdman, B. (1990) Literacy and cultural identity. *Harvard Educational Review*, 60, 181–204.

Ferdman, B. (1995) Cultural identity and diversity in organizations: bridging the gap between group differences and individual uniqueness, in M. Chivers, S. Oskamp and M.A. Costanzo (eds) *Diversity in Organizations*. Thousand Oaks, CA: Sage.

Ferdman, B. and Cortes, A. (1992) Culture and identity among Hispanic managers in an Anglo business, in S.B. Knouse, P. Rosenfield and A. Cuthbertson (eds) *Hispanics in the Workplace*. Newbury Park, CA: Sage.

Festinger, L. (1954) A theory of social comparison processes. *Human Relations*, 7, 117–40.

Fiedler, F.E. (1978) Recent developments in research on the contingency model, in L. Berkowitz (ed.) *Group Processes*. New York: Academic Press.

Fierman, J. (1990) Why women still don't hit the top. *Fortune*, 40–62.

Fleishman, E.A. (1953) The measurement of leadership attitudes in industry. *Journal of Applied Psychology*, 37, 153–8.

Fleishman, E.A. and Harris, E.F. (1962) Patterns of leadership behavior related to employee grievances and turnover. *Personnel Psychology*, 15, 43–56.

Flood, R.L. and Romm, N.A. (1996) *Diversity Management: Triple Loop Learning*. Chichester: Wiley.

Ford, M.E. (1992) *Motivating Humans, Goals, Emotions and Personal Agency Beliefs*. Newbury Park, CA: Sage.

Friedson, E. (1970) *The Profession of Medicine*. New York: Dodd, Mead and Co.

Gale, A. (1994) Futures for applied psychology, in P. Spurgeon, R. Davies and T. Chapman (eds) *Elements of Applied Psychology*. Chur, Switzerland: Harwood Academic Publishers.

Garran, P. and Stewart, P. (1992) *The Nissan Enigma: Flexibility at Work in a Local Economy*. London: Mansell.

Giles, H. (1978) Linguistic differentiation in ethnic groups, in H. Tajfel (ed.) *Differentiation Between Social Groups*. London: Academic Press.

Giles, H. and Johnson, P. (1981) The role of language in ethnic group relations, in J.C. Turner and H. Giles (eds) *Intergroup Behaviour*. Oxford: Blackwell.

Gill, R. and Grint, K. (1995) *The Gender–Technology Relation: Contemporary Theory and Research*. London: Taylor and Francis.

Goffman, E. (1976) Replies and responses. *Language in Society*, 5, 257–313.

Gortz, A. (1980) *Farewell to the Working Class*. London: Pluto.

Gortz, A. (1985) *Paths to Paradise: on the Liberation from Work*. London: Pluto.

Gortz, A. (1988) *Critique of Economic Reason*. New York: Verso.

Granovetter, M. (1985) Economic action, social structure, and embeddedness! *American Journal of Sociology*, 91, 481–510.

Greenbaum, J. and Kyng, M. (1991) *Design at Work: Cooperative Design of Computer Systems*. Hillsdale, NJ: Lawrence Erlbaum Associates.

Greenberg, J. (1986) Determinants of perceived fairness of performance evaluations. *Journal of Applied Psychology*, 71, 340–2.

Greenberg, J. (1988) Equity and workplace status: a field experiment. *Journal of Experimental Psychology*, 73, 606–13.

Grint, K. (1995) *Management: a Sociological Introduction*. Cambridge: Polity Press.

Guest, D. (1987) Human resources management and industrial relations. *Journal of Management Studies*, 24(5), 503–21.

Guest, D. (1990) Have British workers been working harder in Thatcher's Britain? A re-consideration of the concept of effort. *British Journal of Industrial Relations*, 28(3), 293–312.

Guest, D. (1991) Personnel management: the end of orthodoxy? *British Journal of Industrial Relations*, 29(2), 149–75.

Guest, D. (1992) Right enough to be dangerously wrong: an analysis of the In Search of Excellence phenomenon, in G. Salaman (ed.) *Human Resource Strategies*. London: Sage.

Guest, D. and Mackenzie-Davey, K. (1996) Don't write off the traditional career. *People Management*, 22 February, 22–5.

Gutman, H.G. (1977) *Work, Culture and Society in Industrializing America*. Oxford: Oxford University Press.

Hackman, J.R. (1990) *Groups that Work (and Those that Don't). Creating Conditions for Effective Teamwork*. San Francisco: Jossey-Bass.

Hackman, J.R. and Oldham, G.R. (1975) Development of the job diagnostic survey. *Journal of Applied Psychology*, 60, 159–70.

Haldeman, H.R. (1978) *The Ends of Power*. London: Sidgwick & Jackson.

Hales, A. (1986) What do managers do? A critical review of the evidence. *Journal of Management Studies*, 23(1), 88–115.

Halpin, A.W. and Winer, B.J. (1957) A factoral study of the leader behaviour description, in R.M. Stogdill and A.E. Coons (eds) *Leader Behavior: Its Description and Measurement*. Columbus OH: Bureau of Business Research, Ohio State University.

Hammond, R. (1996) *Digital Business: Surviving and Thriving in the On-line World*. London: Hodder and Stoughton.

Handy, C.B. (1985) *Understanding Organizations*. New York: Facts on File.

Handy, H. (1984) *The Future of Work*. Oxford: Blackwell.

Harding, S. (1993) *The Racial Economy of Science*. Bloomington, IN: Indiana University Press.

Hartley, J. and Lord, A. (1997) Organizational commitment and job insecurity in a public service organization. Paper presented to Occupational Psychology Conference, Blackpool.

Harvey-Jones, J. (1993) *Managing to Survive: a Guide to Management through the 1990s*. London: Heinemann.

Heider, F. (1958) *The Psychology of Interpersonal Relations*. New York: Wiley.

Hemphill, J.K. and Coons, A.E. (1957) Development of the leader behaviour description questionnaire, in R.M. Stogdill and A.E. Coons (eds) *Leader Behavior: Its Description and Measurement*. Columbus, OH: Bureau of Business Research, Ohio State University.

Henwood, K.L. (1994) Resisting racism and sexism in academic psychology: a personal/political view, in K.-K. Bhavnani and A. Pheonix (eds) *Shifting Identities, Shifting Racisms*. London: Sage.

Heppenheimer, T.A. (1997) *A History of Space Flight: Countdown*. New York: Wiley.

Hertzberg, F., Mausner, B. and Snyderman, B. (1959) *The Motivation to Work*. New York: Wiley.

Hertzberg, F. (1966) *Work and the Nature of Man*. Cleveland: World.

Hewstone, M. (1989) *Causal Attribution: from Cognitive Processes to Collective Beliefs*. Oxford: Blackwell.

Hill, S. (1981) *Competition and Control at Work*. London: Heinemann.

Hill, S. (1991) Why quality circles failed but total quality management might succeed. *British Journal of Industrial Relations*, 29(4), 541–68.

Hirsch, P.M. (1987) *Pack Your Own Parachute*. Reading, MA: Addison-Wesley.

Hobsbawm, E.J. (1964) *Labouring Men*. London.

Hoffman, L.R. and Maier, R.F. (1964) Valence in the adoption of solutions by problem-solving groups: concept, method and results. *Journal of Abnormal and Social Psychology*, 69, 264–71.

Hofstede, G. (1980) *Culture's Consequences: International Differences in Work Related Values*. Beverley Hills, CA: Sage.

Hogg, M.A. and Abrahms, D. (1988) *Social Identifications*. London: Routledge.

Hollenbeck, J.R. and Klien, H.J. (1987) Goal commitment and goal-setting process: problems, prospects and proposals for future research. *Journal of Applied Psychology*, 72, 212–20.

Hollway, W. (1991) *Work Psychology and Organizational Behaviour*. London: Sage.

Homans, G.C. (1961) *Social Behaviour: Its Elementary Forms*. London: Routledge and Kegan Paul.

Horn, J. (1982) The ageing of human abilities, in B. Wolman (ed.) *Handbook of Developmental Psychology*. Englewood Cliffs, NJ: Prentice Hall.

Horn, J. and Donaldson, G. (1976) On the myth of intellectual decline in adulthood. *American Psychologist*, 31, 701–19.

Hosking, D.M. (1981) A critical review of Fielder's contingency theory, in G.M. Stephenson and J.H. Davis (eds) *Progress in Applied Social Psychology, Volume 1*. Chichester: Wiley.

Hosking, D.M. and Morley, I.E. (1991) *A Social Psychology of Organizing: People, Processes and Contexts*. Hemel Hempstead: Harvester Wheatsheaf.

Huczynski, A. (1996) *Management Gurus: What Makes Them and How to Become One*. London: Routledge.

Hunt, J.G., Sekran, U. and Schreishien, C.A. (1982) Beyond establishment views of leadership: an introduction, in J.G. Hunt, U. Sekran and C.A. Schrieshein (eds) *Leadership: Beyond Establishment Views*. Carbondale, IL: Southern Illinois University Press.

Hurtado, A., Rodriguez, P., Gurin, P. and Beals, J. (1993) The impact of Mexican descendants' social identity on the ethnic socialization of children, in M.E. Berbal and G.P. Knights (eds) *Ethnic Identity: Formation and Transmission among Hispanics and Other Minorities*. Albany: State University of New York Press.

Ibarra, H. (1992) Structural alignments, individual strategies, and managerial actions: elements toward a network theory of getting things done, in N. Nohria and R.G. Eccles (eds) *Networks and Organizations*. Boston: Harvard Business School Press.

Ichbiah, D. (1993) *The Making of Microsoft: How Bill Gates and His Team Created the World's Most Successful Software Company*. Rocklin, CA: Prima.

Jackson, C., Arnold, J., Nicholson, N. and Watts, A.G. (1996) *Managing Careers in 2000 and Beyond*. IES Report 304. Brighton: Institute for Employment Studies.

Jackson, S.E. and Ruderman, M.N. (1995) *Diversity in Work Teams*. Washington, DC: American Psychological Association.

Jacques, E. (1961) *Equitable Payment. A General Theory of Work. Differential Payment and Individual Progress*. London: Heinemann.

Jacques, E. (1967) *Equitable Payment*. Harmondsworth: Penguin.

Janis, I.L. (1982) *Victims of Groupthink*. Boston: Houghton Mifflin.

Jenkins, W.O. (1947) A review of leadership studies with reference to military problems. *Psychological Bulletin*, 44, 54–79.

Johnson, D. (1968) Factory time, in R. Fraser (ed.) *Work: Twenty Personal Accounts*. Harmondsworth: Penguin.

Johnson, P. and Gill, J. (1993) *Management Control and Organizational Behaviour*. London: Paul Chapman.

Johnson, W. (1991) Global work force 2000: the new world labour market. *Harvard Business Review*, 69, 114–27.

Johnston, W.B. and Packer, A.H. (1987) *Workforce 2000: Work and Workers for the Twenty-first Century*. Indianapolis, IN: Hudson Institute.

Jones, E. (1986) Black managers: the dream deferred. *Harvard Business Review*, 64, 84–93.

Jourden, F.J., Bandura, A. and Banfield, J.T. (1991) The impact of conceptions of ability on self-regulatory factors and motor skill acquisition. *Journal of Sport and Exercise Psychology*, 8, 213–26.

Kahn, H. (1987) New technology and job satisfaction: a case study of travel agents, in H.M. Bullinger and B. Shackel (eds) *Human Computer Interaction: Interact 87*. Amsterdam: Elsevier.

Kalleberg, A.L., Wallace, M., Loscocco, K.A., Leicht, K.T. and Ehm, H.H. (1987) The eclipse of craft: the changing face of labor in the newspaper industry, in D.B. Cornfield (ed.) *Workers, Managers and Technological Change: Emerging Patterns of Labor Relations*. New York and London: Plenum.

Kandola, B. and Fullerton, J. (1994) *Managing the Mosaic: Diversity in Action*. London: Institute of Personnel Development.

Kanter, R.M. (1984) *The Change Masters*. London: George Allen and Unwin.

Kanter, R.M. (1989) *When Giants Learn to Dance: Mastering the Challenges of Strategy, Management, and Careers in the 1990s*. London: Unwin Hyman.

Kanter, R.M. (1991) Globalism/localism: A new human resources agenda. *Harvard Business Review*, March/April, 9–10.

Kast, F. E. and Rosenweig, K. (1985) *Organization and Management*. New York: McGraw-Hill.

Katz, D. and Kahn, R. (1966) *The Social Psychology of Management*. New York: Wiley.

Keegan, W.J. (1989) *Global Marketing Management*. Englewood Cliffs, NJ: Prentice Hall.

Kelley, H.H. and Thibaut, J.W. (1969) Group problem solving, in G. Lindzey and E. Aronson (eds) *The Handbook of Social Psychology*, 2nd edn, vol 4. Reading, MS: Addison-Wesley.

Kelley, H.H. and Thibaut, J.W. (1978) *Interpersonal Relations: a Theory of Interdependence*. New York: Wiley.

Kelly, J. and Kelly, C. (1991) 'Them and us': social psychology and 'the new industrial relations'. *British Journal of Industrial Relations*, 29(1), 25–48.

Kerr, N.S. and Baum, S.E. (1983) Dispensability of member effort and group motivation losses: free-rider effects. *Journal of Personality and Social Psychology*, 44, 78–94.

Kirkpatrick, I. and Martinez Lucio, M. (1995) *The Politics of Quality in the Public Sector*. London: Routledge.

Kondriev, W. (1925) The major economic changes. *Voprosy Konjunktury*, 1, 28–79.

Labobouvie-Vief, G. (1982) Growing and ageing in life-span perspective. *Human Development*, 25, 161–91.

LaPiere, R.J. (1934) Attitudes vs. actions. *Social Forces*, 13, 230–7.

Larson, M.S. (1977) *The Rise of Professionalism: a Sociological Analysis*. London: University of Chicago Press.

Lathan, G.P., Erez, M. and Locke, E.A. (1988) Resolving scientific disputes by the joint design of crucial experiments by the antagonists' participation in goal-setting. *Journal of Applied Psychology*, 73, 753–72.

Latour, B. (1996) *Aramis or the Love of Technology*. Cambridge, MA: Harvard University Press.

Latour, B. and Woolgar, S. (1979) *Laboratory Life: the Construction of Scientific Facts*. Princeton, NJ: Princeton University Press.

Laukkanen, M. (1994) Comparative cause mapping of organizational cognitions. *Cognition Within and Between Organizations*. Thousand Oaks, CA: Sage.

Lawler, E.E. (1971) *Pay and Organizational Effectiveness: a Psychological Review*. New York: McGraw-Hill.

Lawler, E.E. (1975) Using pay to motivate job performance, in R.M. Steers and L.M. Porter (eds) *Motivation and Work Behavior*. New York: McGraw-Hill.

Leavitt, H.J. (1951) Some effects of certain communication patterns on group performance. *Journal of Abnormal and Social Psychology*, 46, 38–50.

Leavitt, H.J. and Mueller, R.A.H. (1951) Some effects of feedback on communication. *Human Relations*, 4, 401–10.

Leeson, N. (1996) *Rogue Trader: His Own Amazing Story*. London: Little, Brown & Co.

Legge, K. (1978) *Power, Innovation and Problem-solving in Personnel Management.* London: McGraw-Hill.

Legge, K. (1995) *Human Resource Management: Rhetorics and Realities.* London: Macmillan.

Leventhal, G.S. (1980) What should be done with equity theory?, in K.J. Gergen, M.S. Greenberg and R.H. Willis (eds) *Social Exchange: Advances in Theory and Research.* New York: Plenum.

Lewin, K. (1951) *Field Theory in Social Science.* New York: Harper and Row.

Likert, R. (1961) *New Patterns of Management.* New York: McGraw-Hill.

Lloyd, P. (1996) *Groupware in the 21st Century: Computer Supported Cooperative Working toward the Millennium.* London: Adamantine Press.

Locke, E.A., Shaw, K.N., Saari, L.M. and Latham, G.P. (1981) Goal setting and task performance 1969–1980. *Psychological Bulletin,* 90, 125–52.

Lord, R.G. and Maher, K.J. (1990) Perceptions of leadership and their implications in organizations, in J.S. Carroll (ed.) *Applied Social Psychology and Organizational Settings.* Hillsdale, NJ: Lawrence Erlbaum Associates.

Mabey, C. and Salaman, G. (1995) *Strategic Human Resource Management.* Oxford: Blackwell.

Maccoby, E.E. and Jacklin, C.N. (1974) *The Psychology of Sex Differences: Volume 1 (text), Volume 2 (Annotated Bibliography).* Stanford, CA: Stanford University Press.

McEvoy, G.M. and Cascio, W.F. (1989) Cumulative evidence of the relationship between employee age and job performance. *Journal of Applied Psychology,* 74, 11–17.

McGrath, J.E. (1990) Time matters in groups, in J. Galegher, R. Krant and C. Egido (eds) *Intellectual Teamwork: Social and Technological Foundations of Cooperative Work.* Hillsdale, NJ: Lawrence Erlbaum.

McGrath, J.E. and Hollingshead, A.B. (1994) *Groups Interacting with Technology.* Thousand Oaks, CA: Sage.

McGregor, D. (1960) *The Human Side of the Enterprise.* New York: McGraw-Hill.

McHugh, M.L. (1996) Competitive pressure, employee well being and the healthy organisation. DPhil thesis, University of Ulster.

McNeil, M. (1987) It's a man's world, in M. McNeil (ed.) *Gender and Expertise.* London: Free Association Books.

Makin, P., Cooper, C. and Cox, C. (1996) *The Psychological Contract.* Leicester: British Psychological Society.

Mant, A. (1976) *The Rise and Fall of the British Manager.* London: Macmillan.

Marchington, M. (1992) *Managing the Team.* Oxford: Blackwell.

Martin, J. (1993) Inequality, distributive injustice, and organizational illegitimacy, in J.K. Murnighan (ed.) *Social Psychology in Organizatons.* Englewood Cliffs, NJ: Prentice-Hall.

Martin, L. (1994) Power, continuity and change: decoding black and white women managers experience in local government, in M. Tanton (ed.) *Women in Management.* London: Routledge.

Maslow, A.H. (1943) A theory of human motivation. *Psychological Review,* 50(4), 370–96.

Maslow, A.H. (1970) *Motivation and Personality,* 2nd edn. New York: Harper and Row.

Meindl, J.R. (1990) On leadership: an alternative to conventional wisdom, in B. Straw (ed.) *Research in Organizational Behavior Volume 12*. New York: JAI Press.

Melone, N.P. (1994) Reasoning in the executive suite: the influence of role/experience-based expertise on decision processes of corporate executives, in J.R. Meindl, C. Stubbart and J. Porac (eds) *Cognition Within and Between Organizations*. London: Sage.

Milgram, S. (1974) *Obedience to Authority*. London: Tavistock.

Millar, G.A. (1969) Psychology as a means of promoting human welfare. *American Psychologist*, 24, 1063–75.

Millerson, G. (1964) *The Qualifying Associations*. London: Routledge and Kegan Paul.

Mills, A.J. and Murgatroyd, S.J. (1991) *Organizational Rules: a Framework for Understanding Organizational Action*. Milton Keynes: Open University Press.

Mintzberg, H. (1980) *The Nature of Managerial Work*. Englewood Cliffs, NJ: Prentice Hall.

Mirza, H.S. (1992) *Young, Female and Black*. London: Routledge.

Mitchell, T.R. (1974) Expecting models of job satisfaction, occupational preference and effort: a theoretical, methodological and empirical appraisal. *Psychological Bulletin*, 81, 1053–77.

Mitchell, T.R. (1979) Organizational behavior. *Annual Review of Psychology*, 30, 243–81.

Morgan, G. (1986) *Images of Organization*. Beverly Hills, CA: Sage.

Morrison, A.M. and vol Glinow, M.A. (1990) Women and minorities in management. *American Psychologist*, 45(2), 200–8.

Moscovici, S. (1976) *Social Influence and Social Change*. London: Academic Press.

Moscovici, S. and Doise, W. (1994) *Conflict and Consensus: a General Theory of Collective Decisions*. London: Sage.

Moscovici, S. and Faucheux, C. (1972) Social influence, conformity bias and the study of active minorities, in L. Berkowitz (ed.) *Advances in Experimental Social Psychology 6*. New York: Academic Press.

Mueller, W. (1992) Flexible working and new technology, in J.F. Hartley and G.M. Stephenson (eds) *Employment Relations*. Oxford: Blackwell.

Mumford, E. (1983) *Designing Human Systems*. Manchester: Manchester Business School.

Nelson, R. and Winter, S. (1982) *An Evolutionary Theory of Economic Change*. Cambridge, MA: Harvard University Press.

Nemeth, C.J. (1985) Dissent, group process, and creativity. *Advances in Group Processes*, 2, 57–75.

Nemeth, C.J. and Wacher, J. (1983) Creative problem solving as a result of majority versus minority influence. *European Journal of Social Psychology*, 13, 45–55.

Newton, K. (1989) Technological and organizational change in Canada. *New Technology, Work and Employment*, 4(1), 42–7.

Nohria, N. (1982) Is a network perspective a useful way of studying organizations?, in N. Nohria and R.G. Eccles (eds) *Networks and Organizations*. Boston: Harvard Business School Press.

Northcott, J. and Rogers, P. (1985) *Microelectronics in Industry: What's Happening in Britain*. London: Policy Studies Institute.

Nutt, P. (1993) *The Formulation Processes and Tactics Used in Organizational Decision Making*. London: Sage.

Opsahl, R.H. and Dunnette, M.D. (1966) The role of financial compensation in industrial motivation. *Psychological Bulletin*, 66, 94–118.

Oravec, J.A. (1996) *Virtual Individuals, Virtual Groups*. Cambridge: Cambridge University Press.

Orne, M.T. (1962) On the social psychology of the psychological experiment: with particular reference to demand characteristics and their implications. *American Psychologist*, 17, 776–83.

Parker, I. (1989) *Discourse Dynamics*. London: Routledge.

Parker, I. and Shotter, J. (1990) *Deconstructing Social Psychology*. London: Routledge.

Pascale, R. (1985) The paradox of 'corporate culture': reconciling ourselves to socialization. *California Management Review*, 27(2), 26–41.

Pascale, R.T. (1991) *Managing on the Edge*. Harmondsworth: Penguin.

Peiro, J.-M. and Prieto, F. (1994) Telematics and organizational structure and processes: an overview, in J.H.E. Andriessen and R. Roe (eds) *Telematics and Work*. Hove: Lawrence Erlbaum Associates.

Perrow, C. (1984) *Normal Accidents: Living with High-risk Technologies*. New York: Basic Books.

Peters, T. and Waterman, R.H. (1982) *In Search of Excellence: Lessons from America's Best Run Companies*. London: Harper and Row.

Peterson, P. (1987) Computerized instruction, information systems and school teachers: labor relations in education, in D. Cornfield (ed.) *Workers, Managers and Technological Change: Emerging Patterns of Labor Relations*. New York and London: Plenum.

Phinney, J.S. (1989) Stages of ethnic identity development in minority group adolescents. *Journal of Early Adolescence*, 91(1–2), 34–9.

Pollard, H. (1971) *The Idea of Progress*. Harmondsworth: Penguin.

Porter, M.E. (1990) *The Competitive Advantage of Nations*. New York: Free Press.

Potter, J. and Weatherall, M. (1987) *Discourse and Social Psychology*. London: Sage.

Powell, W.W. and Brantley, P. (1992) Competitive cooperation in biotechnology: learning through networks?, in N. Nohria and R.G. Eccles (eds) *Networks and Organizations*. Boston: Harvard Business School Press.

Rahim, A. (1981) Organizational behaviour course for graduate students in business administration: Views from the tower and battlefield. *Psychological Reports*, 49, 583–92.

Rassmussen, J. (1988) *Interdisciplinary Workshops to Develop a Multidisciplinary Research Program Based on a Holistic System Approach to Safety and Management of Risk in Large Scale Technological Operations*. Washington, DC: World Bank.

Rauschenberger, J., Schmitt, N. and Hunter, J.E. (1980) A test of the need hierarchy concept by a Markov model of change in need strength. *Administrative Science Quarterly*, 25, 654–70.

Reason, J. (1990) *Human Error*. Cambridge: Cambridge University Press.

Redding, S.G. (1982) Cultural effects on the marketing process in South East Asia. *Journal of Market Research Society*, 24(19), 98–114.

Reicher, S. (1986) Contact, action and racialization: some British evidence, in M.

Hewstone and T. Brown (eds) *Contact and Conflict in Intergroup Encounters.* Oxford: Blackwell.

Resnick, L.B. (1991) Shared cognition: thinking as social practice, in L.B. Resnick, J.M. Levine and S.D. Teasley (eds) *Perspectives on Socially Shared Cognition.* Washington, DC: American Psychological Association.

Rice, A.K. (1958) *Productivity and Social Organizations: the Ahemedabad Experiment.* London: Tavistock Publications.

Rice, R.W. (1978) Construct validity of the least preferred co-worker score. *Psychological Bulletin,* 85, 1199–237.

Rifkin, J. (1995) *The End of Work: the Decline of the Global Labor Force and the Dawn of the Post-market Era.* New York: Putnam.

Robinson, S.L. and Rousseau, D.M. (1994) Violating the psychological contract: not the exception but the norm. *Journal of Organizational Behaviour,* 15, 245–59.

Rodriguez-Scheel, J. (1980) An investigation of the components of social identity for a Detroit sample. Cited in M.M. Chemers, S. Oskamp and M.A. Coztanzo (1995) *Diversity in Organizations.* Thousand Oaks, CA: Sage.

Roethlisberger, F.J. and Dickson, W. (1939) *Management and the Worker.* Cambridge, MA: Harvard University Press.

Rohner, R.P. (1984) Toward a conception of culture for cross-cultural psychology. *Journal of Cross-cultural Psychology,* 15, 111–38.

Rommetveit, R. (1988) On literacy and the myth of literal meaning, in R. Saljo (ed.) *The Written Word: Studies in Literate Thought and Action.* Berlin: Springer-Verlag.

Rose, E.J.B. and associates (1969) *Colour and Citizenship. A Report on British Race Relations.* London: Institute of Race Relations.

Rose, M. (1975) *Industrial Behaviour: Theoretical Development since Taylor.* Harmondsworth: Penguin.

Rosen, B. and Jerdee, T.H. (1976) The nature of job related age stereotypes. *Journal of Applied Psychology,* 61, 180–3.

Rosenbaum, M.E., Moore, D.L., Cotton, J.L., Cook, M.S., Heiser, R.A., Shovar, M.N. and Gray, M.J. (1980) Group productivity and process: Pure and mixed reward structures and task interdependence. *Journal of Personality and Social Psychology,* 39, 626–42.

Rosener, J.B. (1990) Ways women lead. *Harvard Business Review,* 68(6), 119–25.

Rothschild, J. (ed.) (1983) *Machina ex Dea: Feminist Perspectives on Technology.* New York: Pergamon.

Rothwell, S. (1995) Human resource planning, in J. Storey (ed.) *Human Resource Management: a Critical Text.* London: Routledge.

Rubery, J. (1992) Pay, gender and the social dimension to Europe. *British Journal of Industrial Relations,* 30(4), 607–21.

Rubery, J. and Fagan, C. (1993) *Bulletin on Women and Employment in the European Commission.* Brussels: European Commission.

Rybash, J.M., Hoyer, J. and Roodin, P.A. (1986) *Adult Cognition and Aging.* New York: Pergamon Press.

Salthouse, T.A. (1991) *Theoretical Perspectives on Cognitive Aging.* Hillsdale, NJ: Lawrence Erlbaum Associates.

Sanders, G.S., Baron, R.S. and Moore, D.L. (1978) Distraction and social comparison as mediators of social facilitation and social loafing. *Journal of Experimental and Social Psychology,* 46(14), 291–303.

Schein, E.H. (1972) *Professional Education: Some New Directions*. New York: McGraw-Hill.

Schein, E.H. (1980) *Organizational Psychology*. Englewood Cliffs, NJ: Prentice Hall.

Schein, E.H. (1985) *Organizational Culture and Leadership*. San Francisco: Jossey-Bass.

Schon, D. (1983) *The Reflective Practitioner*. London: Temple Smith.

Schwab, D.P., Olian-Gottlieb, J.D. and Heneman, H.G. (1979) Between-subjects expectancy theory research: A statistical review of studies predicting effort and performance. *Psychological Bulletin*, 86, 139–47.

Shaw, M.E. (1932) A comparison of individuals and small groups in the rational solution of complex problems. *American Journal of Psychology*, 44, 491–504.

Sherif, M. (1966) *Group Conflict and Cooperation*. London: Routledge and Kegan Paul.

Shimmin, S. and Wallis, D. (1994) *Fifty Years of Occupational Psychology in Britain*. Leicester: The Division and Section of Occupational Psychology of the British Psychological Society.

Short, J., Williams, E. and Christie, B. (1976) *The Social Psychology of Tele-communications*. London: Wiley.

Siegel, J., Dubrovsky, V., Keisler, S. and McGuire, R. (1986) Group processes in computer-mediated communication. *Organizational Behaviour and Human Processes*, 37, 157–87.

Skevington, S.M. (1980) Intergroup relations and social change within a nursing context. *British Journal of Social and Clinical Psychology*, 19, 201–13.

Skevington, S.M. (1981) Intergroup relations in nursing. *European Journal of Social Psychology*, 11, 43–59.

Skevington, S.M. and Baker, D. (1989) *Introduction to the Social Identity of Women*. London: Sage.

Slater, R. and Kingsley, S. (1976) Predicting age-prejudiced employers, a British pilot study. *Industrial Gerontology*, 3(2), 121–8.

Sorge, A. (1984) *Technological Change, Employment Qualifications and Training*. Berlin: CEDEFOP.

South Australian Department of Labour (1992) *Guidelines for Skill Identification*. Adelaide: South Australian Department of Labour.

Sparrow, P.R. and Hiltrop, J.-M. (1994) *European Human Resource Management in Transition*. Hemel Hempstead: Prentice Hall.

Sparrow, P.R. (1994) Organizational competencies: creating a strategic framework for selection and assessment, in N. Anderson and P. Heriot (eds) *Handbook of Assessment and Appraisal*. Chichester: Wiley.

Starkey, K. (ed.) (1996) *How Organizations Learn*. London: Thompson.

Steiner, I.D. (1972) *Group Process and Productivity*. New York: Academic Press.

Steiner, I.D. (1976) Task-performing groups, in J.W. Thibaut, J.T. Spence and R.C. Carson (eds) *Contemporary Topics in Social Psychology*. Morristown, NJ: General Learning Press.

Steinhoff, P. and Tanaka, K. (1987) Women managers in Japan. *International Studies of Management and Organization*, 16, 108–32.

Stephenson, G.M. (1981) Intergroup bargaining and negotiation, in J.C. Turner and H. Giles (eds) *Intergroup Behaviour*. Oxford: Blackwell.

Stephenson, G.M. and Brotherton, C.J. (1973) The first-line supervisor in the British coal industry: a preliminary enquiry. *Industrial Relations Journal*, 4(3), 27–36.

Stephenson, G.M. and Brotherton, C.J. (1975) Social progression and polarization: a study of discussion and negotiation in groups of mining supervisors. *British Journal of Social and Clinical Psychology*, 14, 241–52.

Stephenson, G.M., Brotherton, C.J., Delafield, G.M. and Skinner, M. (1983) Size of organization and attitudes at work. *Industrial Relations Journal*, 14(2), 28–40.

Stephenson, G.M., Skinner, M. and Brotherton, C.J. (1975) Group participation and intergroup relations: an experimental study of negotiation groups. *European Journal of Social Psychology*, 6, 51–70.

Stewart, R. (1967) *Managers and their Jobs*. Maidenhead: McGraw-Hill.

Stewart, R.M. (1976) *The Reality of Management*. London: Pan.

Stodgill, R.M. (1948) Personal factors associated with leadership. *Journal of Psychology*, 25, 35–71.

Stodgill, R.M. (1974) *Handbook of Leadership*. New York: Free Press.

Storey, J. (1983) *Managerial Prerogative and Questions of Control*. London: Routledge and Kegan Paul.

Storey, J. (1989) *New Perspectives on Human Resource Management*. London: Routledge.

Storey, J. (1992) *Developments in the Management of Human Resources*. Oxford: Blackwell.

Storey, J. (ed.) (1995) *Human Resource Management: a Critical Text*. London: Routledge.

Suchman, L. (1987) *Plans and Situated Actions: the Problem of Human Machine Communication*. Cambridge: Cambridge University Press.

Suchman, L. (1988) Representing practice in cognitive science. *Human Studies*, 11, 305–25.

Tajfel, H. (1972) Experiments in a vacuum, in J. Israel and H. Tajfel (eds) *The Context of Social Psychology: a Critical Assessment*. London: Academic Press.

Tajfel, H. (1978) *Differentiation between Social Groups: Studies in the Social Psychology of Intergroup Relations*. London: Academic Press.

Tajfel, H. (1979) Individuals and groups in social psychology. *British Journal of Social and Clinical Psychology*, 18, 183–90.

Tajfel, H. (ed.) (1981) *The Social Dimension: European Developments in Social Psychology*. Cambridge: Cambridge University Press.

Tajfel, H. (1982) *Social Identity and Intergroup Relations*. Cambridge: Cambridge University Press.

Tajfel, H. and Turner, J.C. (1979) An integrative theory of social conflict, in W. Austin and S. Worschel (eds) *The Social Psychology of Intergroup Relations*. San Francisco: Brooks/Cole.

Taylor, P.E. and Walker, A. (1994) The ageing workforce: employers' attitudes towards older people. *Work, Employment and Society*, 8(4), 569–91.

Thayer, L. (1988) Leadership/communication: A critical review and a modest proposal!, in G.M. Godhaber and G.A. Barnett (eds) *Handbook of Organizational Communication*. Norwood, NJ: Ablex.

Thibaut, J. and Walker, L (1975) *Procedural Justice: a Psychological Analysis*. Hillsdale, NJ: Erlbaum.

Thomas, A.B. (1993) *Controversies in Management*. London: Routledge.

Thomas, D.A. (1990a) The impact on race on managers' experiences of developmental relationships: an intraorganizational study. *Journal of Organizational Behaviour*, 11(6), 479–92.

Thomas, R.J. (1987) Microchips and macroharvests: labor–management relations in agriculture, in D. Cornfield (ed.) *Workers, Managers and Technological Change: Emerging Patterns of Labor Relations*. New York and London: Plenum.

Thomas, R.R. Jr (1990b) From affirmative action to affirming diversity. *Harvard Business Review*, 68(2), 107–17.

Tjsvold, D. (1991) *Team Organization: an Enduring Competitive Advantage*. Chichester: Wiley.

Toffler, A. (1970) *Future Shock*. London: Bodley Head.

Torrington, D. and Hall, L. (1987) *Personnel Management: a New Approach*. Englewood Cliffs, NJ: Prentice Hall.

Torrington, D. and Hall, L. (1995) *Personnel Management: HRM in Action*. Englewood Cliffs, NJ: Prentice Hall.

Towers, B. (1996) *The Handbook of Human Resource Management*. Oxford: Blackwell.

Townley, B. (1994) *Reframing Human Resource Management: Power, Ethics and the Subject at Work*. London: Sage.

Triandis, H. (1994) *Culture and Social Behavior*. New York: McGraw-Hill.

Triplett, N. (1898) The dynamogenic factors in pacemaking and competition. *American Journal of Psychology*, 9, 507–33.

Trist, E.L. and Bamforth, K.W. (1951) Some social and psychological consequences of the long-walk method of coal-getting. *Human Relations*, 4, 3–38.

Turner, B. and Pidgeon, N. (1997) *Man-made Disasters*, 2nd edn. London: Butterworth-Heinemann.

Turner, J.C. (1991) *Social Influence*. Milton Keynes: Open University.

Turner, J.C. (1982) Towards a cognitive redefinition of the social group, in H. Tajfel (ed.) *Social Identity and Intergroup Relations*. Cambridge: Cambridge University Press.

Turner, J.C., Hogg, M.A., Oakes, P.J., Reicher, S.D. and Wetherall, M. (1984) *Rediscovering the Social Group: a Self-categorization Theory*. Oxford: Blackwell.

van Dijk, T. (1984) *Communicating Racism: Ethnic Prejudice in Thought and Talk*. London: Sage.

Vaughan, D. (1996) *The Challenger Launch Decision: Risky Technology, Culture and Deviance at NASA*. Chicago: University of Chicago Press.

Vechio, R.P. (1983) Assessing the validity of Fiedler's contingency model of leadership effectiveness: a closer look at Strube and Garcia. *Psychological Bulletin*, 93, 404–8.

Vinnicombe, S. (1987) What exactly are the differences in male and female working styles? *Women in Management Review*, 3(1), 13–21.

Vroom, V.H. (1964) *Work and Motivation*. New York: Wiley.

Wacjman, J. (1991) *Feminism Confronts Technology*. Cambridge: Polity Press.

Warner, M. (1986) Human-resource implications of new technology. *Human Systems Management*, 6(4), 279–87.

Warr, P.B. (1976) Theories of motivation, in P. Warr (ed.) *Personal Goals and Work Design*. London: Wiley.

Warr, P.B. (ed.) (1996) *Psychology at Work*, 4th edn. Harmondsworth: Penguin.

Warr, P.B. and Pennington, J. (1993) Views about age discrimination and older workers, in *Age and Employment: Policies, Attitudes and Practices*. London: Institute of Personnel Management.

Warr, P.B. and Pennington, J. (1994) Occupational age-grading: jobs for older and younger non-managerial employees. *Journal of Vocational Behavior*, 45, 328–46.

Waterman, R.H., Waterman, J.A. and Collard, B.A. (1994) Toward a career resilient workforce. *Harvard Business Review*, 72(4), 87–95.

Watson, T.J. (1996) *Management, Organization and Employment Strategy*. London: Routledge.

Weber, M. (1946) The characteristics of bureaucracy, in H.H. Gerth and C.W. Mills (trans.) *From Max Weber: Essays in Sociology*. Oxford: Oxford University Press.

Weick, K. (1995) *Sensemaking in Organizations*. Thousand Oaks, CA: Sage.

Wertsch, J. (1991) *Voices of the Mind: a Sociocultural Approach to Mediated Action*. Hemel Hempstead: Harvester Wheatsheaf.

West, M.A. (1994) *Effective Teamwork*. Leicester: British Psychological Society.

West, M. (ed.) (1996) *Handbook of Work Group Psychology*. Chichester: Wiley.

Wicker, A.W. (1969) Attitudes versus actions: the relationships of overt and behavioural responses to attitudes to objects. *Journal of Social Issues*, 25, 41–78.

Wikstrom, S. and Normann, R. (1994) *Knowledge and Value*. London: Routledge.

Wilkinson, S. (ed.) (1986) *Feminist Social Psychology: Developing Theory and Practice*. Milton Keynes: Open University Press.

Williams, J. (1984) Gender and intergroup behaviour: towards an integration. *British Journal of Social Psychology*, 23, 311–16.

Williams, J. and Giles, H. (1978) The changing status of women in society: an intergroup perspective, in H. Tajfel (ed.) *Differentiation between Social Groups*. London: Academic Press.

Willis, S.L. and Baltes, P.B. (1980) Intelligence in adulthood and aging: contemporary issues, in L.W. Poon (ed.) *Aging in the 80s: Psychological Issues*. Washington, DC: American Psychological Association.

Wilpert, B. (1982) Various paths beyond establishment views, in J.G. Hunt, U. Sekran and C. Schreishien (eds) *Leadership: Beyond Establishment Views*. Carbondale, IL: Southern Illinois University Press.

Wilson, D.C. (1992) *A Strategy of Change Concepts and Controversies in the Management of Change*. London: Routledge.

Wood, R.E. and Bandura, A. (1989) Social cognitive theory of organizational management. *Academy of Management Review*, 14, 361–84.

Wright, P.L. (1968) *The Coloured Worker in British Industry*. London: Oxford University Press.

Yamashita, T. (1989) Training and development in Japan. *Asia Pacific Human Resource Management*, 40–7.

Zajonc, R.B. (1965) Social facilitation. *Science*, 149, 269–74.

Zimbardo, P. (1970) The human choice: individuation, reason and order versus deindividuation, impulse and chaos, in W.J. Arnold and D. Levine (eds) *Nebraska Symposium 1969*. Lincoln: University of Nebraska Press.

Zuboff, S. (1982) *In the Age of the Smart Machine: the Future of Work and Power*. Oxford: Heinemann.

Index